FOR MEMBERS ONLY

A History and Guide to Chicago's Oldest Private Clubs

by

LISA HOLTON

LAKE CLAREMONT PRESS

www.lakeclaremont.com

Chicago

To my sister,
Lea Holton

For Members Only: A History and Guide to Chicago's Oldest Private Clubs

Lisa Holton

Published June 2008 by:

P.O. Box 711
Chicago, IL 60690
lcp@lakeclaremont.com

www.lakeclaremont.com

Publisher's Cataloging-In-Publication Data

(Prepared by The Donohue Group, Inc.)

Holton, Lisa.
  For members only : a history and guide to Chicago's oldest private clubs / by Lisa Holton. — 1st ed.

    p. : ill. ; cm.

  Includes bibliographical references and index.
  ISBN-13: 978-1-893121-28-7
  ISBN-10: 1-893121-28-3

  1. Clubs—Illinois—Chicago—History. 2. Societies—Illinois—Chicago—History.
  3. Businesspeople—Illinois—Chicago—Societies, etc. 4. Socialites—Illinois—Chicago—Societies, etc. 5. Clubs—Illinois—Chicago—Directories. I. Title.

HS2725.C4 A3 2007
367/.9773/11
2006925493

11 10 09 08   10 9 8 7 6 5 4 3 2 1

TABLE OF CONTENTS

INTRODUCTION

.

———————◆———————

*"To associate with other like-minded people in small,
purposeful groups is for the great majority of men and women
a source of profound psychological satisfaction. Exclusiveness
will add to the pleasure of being several, but as one;
and secrecy will intensify it almost to ecstasy."*
—Aldous Huxley

Have you ever walked down Michigan Avenue and stopped briefly under the awning of 626 North, wondering what that beautiful Parisian-style building actually was? Or have you wandered past that ruddy, stately building at 81 E. Van Buren? And in Streeterville, have you ever run across that strange little ebony building that looks a bit like a turtle at Delaware and Mies van der Rohe? If so, you've passed the Woman's Athletic Club of Chicago, the Chicago Club, and The Casino—names that may not mean much to most Chicagoans but that mean a great deal to the city's history. These clubs have been oases for the rich and privileged, playgrounds for the social set, private watering holes for the city's movers and shakers. Places that, certainly at their inception, most of us couldn't get in due to birthright, race, wealth, where we worked, or where we went to school.

It's tempting to write these exclusive clubs off the way that so many of these institutions wrote off large parts of Chicago's population at their inception. Yet virtually every major political, business, or civic milestone in Chicago—both good and bad—can be traced back to the members and activities of many of these invitation-only city clubs. Sometimes they led, sometimes they followed, albeit reluctantly—but Chicago's private clubs were always a part of the changing landscape and culture of the city.

Without the members of these organizations, essentially Chicago's most powerful people, there might not a Burnham Plan. The World's Columbian Exposition might not be in our history books. Al Capone might have lived out his days with a comfortable grasp on Chicago's crime rackets. Much later, the 2000 moratorium on the death penalty in Illinois might not have had the support it did, and Millennium Park might still be merely a grand idea instead of the showpiece it is today.

The members of Chicago's private clubs—businessmen, politicians, artists, writers, architects, and assorted gadflies—were part of all these landmark events. These were the "clubbable" men— and yes, for the majority of this book, we will be talking about men—who gravitated toward individuals and clubhouses of like minds, ideas, and typically great wealth. They did important things and frivolous things and reveled in both. That so many of these organizations that began in the late 1860s to the Depression era remain open today—despite many near-death experiences—is something of a wonder.

That's not to assert that the agendas at Chicago's private clubs were all altruistic and based in good fellowship. For more than a century, many of these clubs that were dominated by white males helped sustain bigotry and barriers toward women, minorities, Jews, and Catholics.

However, for the longest time, there was one category of individual barred from membership that virtually all these groups could agree on: women. The ban against women members at Chicago's private male clubs was literally the last major one to fall, and this ban didn't fall easily or for good until the late 1980s. Only after 15 years of lawsuits and the irreversible movement of women into the white-collar workforce did old-line members finally relent and allow women to join as full members.

With nearly two decades of hindsight, many observers say the admission of women actually helped *sustain* the clubs. Why? Because women's money turned out to be as green as anyone else's.

Regarding women and clubs, some of Chicago's oldest city and literary clubs were founded, run, and populated by women. Ironically, the oldest women's clubs remain the only truly segregated clubs today—not by race, but largely by gender. And to this date they remain the most secretive. In fact, while courteous to this author, the oldest and most society-steeped women's clubs in the city—Woman's Athletic Club, The Fortnightly, and The Casino— a co-ed club founded by women—all declined participation in this book.

Exclusion and exclusivity weren't the province only of Protestant-led, whites-only clubs. This book will also focus on how the excluded groups—particularly Jews and African-Americans— went on to form clubs that initially excluded others who shared their race, religion, and culture. They did so based on a variety of specific reasons ranging from which group arrived in Chicago first, to the way they practiced their religion, and even their skin tone. All that in addition to wealth and power.

If you look at a particular club and delve into its membership over time, you can see patterns of acceptance and alienation, higher purpose and rabid ambition—all among people who, at least from all appearances, really do seem to look, walk, and talk alike. Private clubs resemble family in so many ways—united under fire, divided behind closed doors, and accepting of change only under duress. Don't let the fine paneling, priceless art, and comfortable chairs fool you. Not much sleepy contemplation really goes on in private clubs. At least not in the historic private clubs of Chicago.

WHY SO MANY CLUBS?

As you read this book, you'll find yourself asking a number of questions. Why were there so many clubs? Why did everyone feel they had to join? Where did they get the money to build all the clubs anyway? For starters, clubs were a sensible solution for business gatherings and entertainment in the 1800s—an era with very little in-home entertainment, very few safe and elegant restaurants or hotels, and no quiet places to conduct business. In their true heyday—which ended in the most traditional sense more than a quarter-century ago—people joined clubs because of their critical mix of personalities and connections, good food and surroundings, which simply couldn't be found anywhere else. In fact, since 1980, Chicago's emerging reputation as a world-class restaurant city has put more pressure on the city's historic clubs. More places to eat, more places to meet.

Clubs and the exclusivity they offered were somehow more necessary to the business and social environment back then. Industries were local, and they bore distinct identities that gave rise to clubs in their image. If you weren't at the club, how did everyone know you were part of the establishment?

The golden era of club building ended right about 1930. The Gilded Age and the Roaring Twenties changed the city's skyline, and a number of the notable buildings that shot up in those eras were actually private clubhouses, as you'll see. But 1930 was the demarcation line. Before that decade, clubs were eager to buy and build on their own real estate, and many clubs mortgaged themselves to the hilt to do so, leading to more than a few failures. Afterward, clubs tended to become tenants—often in opulent skyscraper surroundings, but tenants nonetheless. The cachet of the private, member-owned clubhouse from that point on was left to those who were wise enough to pay off their debts before the Great Depression and keep borrowing to a minimum during the downturn.

NO CLUB FITS ALL

This book started out as a study of Chicago's historic *business* clubs. That was the assignment, anyway. But as research began, it soon became clear that many of the same people kept starting up clubs to extend their connections in various directions critical to the growth of the city. Commerce was only one part of the puzzle. For example, if you belonged to a particular business-oriented club, you also had to belong to clubs that had a connection to the same people in the arts or athletics. Clubs were *the* strategic means to stay connected in Chicago society.

The earliest clubs, formed in thirteenth-century Europe, were definitely focused on business—they needed to be. In a developing city, it was natural for power, money, and like ways of thinking to consolidate. That's what humans do. Clubs got the job done fast. It really is no wonder why two of the city's most powerful clubs—the Chicago Club and the Standard Club—are approaching their 140th birthdays. The first built by Protestant businessmen, the other by Jewish businessmen, both used their exclusivity to build centers of power that endure today.

But the strength of the city's private clubs went far beyond money. Their members—and their wives, who started clubs of their own—built the city culturally and intellectually, two elements fiercely needed in Chicago's early days. The memberships that built the business-focused clubs in the early days also went on to create the Art Institute, the Lyric Opera, the Chicago Public Library, and many other cultural institutions that were also necessary to the city's world reputation.

Business networking today is not so easily categorized, in Chicago or elsewhere. These elite groups continue, but the business world functions with wider acceptance of gender, race, and social class. There really is no single set of local destinations to establish contact with business partners. Business relationships can truly take place anywhere in this day and age.

Entrepreneurs have always met in public spaces and restaurants, but today you're just as likely to see a CEO and a prospect talking business in a Starbucks as in a boardroom. The Armours, Swifts, Blairs, and McCormicks of the Gilded Age could never have foreseen the era of the online community and the soy latte!

Bob Reed, former editor of *Crain's Chicago Business* and now a writer for *Chicago* magazine and *Business Week*, thinks the way business works today has many of the traditional private clubs "fighting for relevance" in a networking environment that tends to be much more democratic.

I think the real power clubs in the city are now the Economic Club [Chapter 15] and the Executives' Club [Chapter 16], which are invitation-only clubs, but they aren't the traditional private clubs that were built 100 years ago. These are the sort of ad hoc clubs where people from different leadership positions in the community get together every now and then to discuss issues and policy. They tend to be more visible.

And Seth Godin, a marketing expert, speaker, and author who spends a lot of time watching how people interact, particularly on the Internet, shares this perspective:

I think that the old clubs offer something that [Internet communities] Meetup and Friendster and LinkedIn do not, which is the stability of membership, You know that the person you're dealing with will be there next week, too, so the expectations of the exchange are very different.

The debate continues.

HOW THIS BOOK IS STRUCTURED

The organizations you'll see profiled in this book range from clubs that are thriving to those struggling to stay afloat. The private club is definitely under siege. Since this book began production in 2005, two major clubs had announced closure and a third was considering a merger. The Chicago Association closed its doors in August 2007 to make way for a hotel development; the Mid-Day Club was scheduled for closure at the year end 2007 in the Chase Towers; and the Tavern Club, located in the historic penthouse space landmark in 333 N. Michigan Ave. building, was losing its lease and weighing a merger with the Cliff Dwellers. The 11th-hour rescue attempts that have kept so many clubs alive during their history are fewer and far between today.

This book is divided into four parts: the historical environment these clubs were created in, stories of individual clubs and the events that shaped them, today's club environment, and an appendix featuring a guide to many current private clubs (including a listing of their features, space, and services; and a glossary of club terms). Not all the clubs written about in this book participated in the guidebook section, but I have attempted to include as many as possible.

I've also purposely elected not to cover country clubs or fraternal organizations in this book. Though some mention of fraternal organizations was relevant—particularly because they were so prevalent in Chicago's African-American community—these are organizations that have a broad and extensive local history worthy of their own separate study.

Also, because this book is directed toward clubs with unique missions and longtime histories, I've minimized the coverage of post–World War II dining clubs to the listings in the back of the book. Why? Because these clubs were primarily created by real estate developers who wanted exclusive dining and meeting space in their new generation of skyscrapers after 1945. While many have now existed for decades and have very interesting programs and events, they're primarily places to eat and meet. That's not a value judgment on their members or their services, and indeed, some of their members share memberships in many of the historic clubs that are written about in more detail here. Dining clubs are simply a different beast.

Was it easy getting all these clubs to open their doors? For the most part, yes. The only exceptions I met were from The Fortnightly, the Woman's Athletic Club, the Racquet Club, The Casino, and the Arts Club of Chicago. These particular clubs refused my requests for staff and officer interviews and onsite visits, but they were entirely gracious and made sure I was aware of all the research material available on them, including their own published histories.

The bottom line—some private clubs just want to remain private.

A point about sourcing. I conducted many interviews for this book and referred to news clippings and archival materials in local libraries and inside the clubs. With regard to minority clubs, I regret I have only scratched the surface. I hope to learn more for future editions of this book.

In the end, the most enjoyable moments took place inside the clubs, looking at the facilities and meeting members and staff.

Some of these clubs have taken a more journalistic view of their past, and for that, they should be applauded. However, I tried never to lose sight of the point that many of the clubs produced remembrances rather than real histories. These are private clubs, not public entities, and because of poor archiving, loss of institutional memory, or simply a desire not to tell all, there will probably be gaps in the individual club histories told in this book.

Lastly, this book is not really finished. Why? Because so much club history exists in the memories of its members. If you are reading this book and have access to club history you don't see here, please contact me at Lisa@TheLisaCompany.com.

Sources:
Godin, Seth. E-mail response to author's questions. 31 May 2005.
Reed, Bob. Interview by author. 14 June 2005.

PART I

THE PAST

Chicago's Historic Private Clubs—
Founding Chronology

Chicago Club	1869*
Standard Club	1869**
The Fortnightly of Chicago	1873
Chicago Literary Club	1874
Chicago Woman's Club	1876
Commercial Club of Chicago	1877
Union League Club of Chicago	1879
Chicago Architectural Club	1885
Friday Club	1887
University Club of Chicago	1887
Chicago Athletic Association	1890
Caxton Club	1895
Woman's Athletic Club	1898
City Club of Chicago	1903
Mid-Day Club	1903
The Cliff Dwellers	1907
Woman's City Club of Chicago	1910
Executives' Club of Chicago	1911
Adventurers Club	1911
The Casino	1914
Original Forty Club	1915
Arts Club of Chicago	1916
Racquet Club of Chicago	1924
Economic Club of Chicago	1927
Tavern Club	1927
Mid-America Club	1958
Metropolitan Club	1974

*The Chicago Club was founded in January 1869 and opened the first formal clubhouse in May.
**The Standard Club was founded on July 7, 1869.

I

THE
FAMILIES
THAT
BUILT CHICAGO
. . . AND THE
CLUBS

———

Wisdom is like electricity. There is no permanently wise man, but men capable of wisdom, who, being put into certain company, or other favorable conditions, become wise for a short time, as glasses rubbed acquire electric power for a while.
— Ralph Waldo Emerson

From the 1700s through the early 1800s, Chicago was a swampy patch of land with two major advantages. The first was Lake Michigan, the body of water that would link its commercial fortunes to the rest of the country. The second was rich farmland to the North, West, and South that would eventually help feed the nation. At the start, the city was crawling with trappers, Frenchmen, Native Americans, and more than a few early con artists who graduated into the nascent city's political arena.

They did fine. But they weren't the real money that built Chicago. That came from out east.

Perhaps the most familiar name in East Coast aristocracy—Rockefeller—fed a local lineage of wealth that included names like

Prentice and McCormick. As Emmett Dedmon writes in his book *Fabulous Chicago: A Great City's History and People*, "of the first 32 mayors (of Chicago), twenty came from New England. The first was William Butler Ogden, who came west to check out some property his brother-in-law bought sight unseen. He never left."

For a city as ethnically, religiously, and financially diverse as Chicago, no one made it into early Chicago society without being Protestant and from the East Coast. Definitely no Jews, Catholics, or people of color were allowed—at least not for the better part of a century.

And at that time, nobody was calling Chicago and its neighboring cities and towns the Midwest. To these settlers, anything that wasn't from the East was from the West. Period.

THE EARLIEST BOLDFACE NAMES

A young merchant named Potter Palmer from New York made his fortune here in dry goods and then sold out to Marshall Field, a young merchant from Pittsfield, Massachusetts. Philip D. Armour, a New Yorker who tried his luck in the California gold rush before going into the meat business in Milwaukee, eventually ended up in Chicago, lured by its Great Lakes transportation system and growing rail network. Cyrus Hall McCormick, son of a prosperous Virginia farmer, tinkered with a harvesting machine that would

Cyrus Hall McCormick, head of the McCormick Reaper Co., predecessor to the International Harvester Corp. (From History of Chicago, *Vol. 2, by A.T. Andreas.)*

start a farm implements giant in Chicago. Joseph T. Ryerson, an agent for a Pittsburgh iron manufacturer, opened his own store selling boilers and other iron products and built it into one of the nation's biggest processors and wholesalers of steel.

These names and dozens of others not only built significant business empires in Chicago—a few remain today—but they transferred the East Coast model of social and business civility into completely uncivilized territory. Whether these early Chicago millionaires were actually all that blue-blooded themselves is open to question, but in Chicago, amassed wealth and power have historically been a good substitute for breeding. And wealth and power were typically good enough to gain access to the world of private clubs.

As Cleveland Amory explained in his 1960 bestseller, *Who Killed Society?*:

> The History of American clubdom is actually a story of Social Security—with capital "S's." From the very beginning, clubs were formed not primarily to get people in, but rather to keep people out. . . . The American city clubs were patterned originally on the English idea of a gentlemen's club. Although they never carried this pattern to the extreme of the English club, where in the old days members wore their hats everywhere in the club except the dining room, the American gentleman found, like the Englishman, that his club, and not his home, was his real castle.
>
> Here he had the best of his well-bred friends, the most comfortable of his well-stuffed chairs, the best of food, drink and cigars from his well-stocked larders and cellars, the least irritating of reading material from a well-censored library and the best of games from well-mannered losers. Here he could do what he pleased when he pleased where he pleased and with whom he pleased; here, and only here, did he find sanctuary and his four freedoms: freedom of speech against democracy, freedom of worship of aristocracy, freedom from want from tipping, and, above all, freedom from fear of women.

JOIN ONE, JOIN ALL

One of the most fascinating patterns that emerge in the study of various club histories is how many wealthy men—and their wives—belonged to the same clubs, to the point where if they devoted themselves to using all the memberships they had, they'd never have time for anything else. It was not unusual, for example, for leading businessmen to have in excess of five to ten memberships, depending on the status and stature of the club. Of course, then as today, clubs sought out big-name members (and often gave them a break on initiation fees and dues if they agreed to come aboard).

How did they justify it? Admittedly, the ultrarich have never had to worry much about affording dues and meal expenses, particularly when the economy was booming. That's always been true. And unlike today, the taxman didn't really get all that involved in the deductibility—or even the tracking of—such duplicative business expenses.

Chicago in the mid-1800s was still a town with few of the creature comforts that were common on the East Coast. Therefore, not only were Chicago's clubs a sanctuary for the city's rich, but they were a calling card and an enticement to draw more out-of-town money and development to the city. They were a sign that Chicago planned to crown itself the dominant city of the West.

Consider, for a moment, a Chicago that had no restaurants of any particular quality, no modern communication, no means by which people of a certain class, ambition, and thinking could easily connect with one another. It then becomes easier to understand why dozens of clubs with any number of themes sprang up around the then-small confines of the city, why the same people were part of so many of them, and why money flowed so freely toward them. Clubs were the networking organization, the industry association, the TV, the movies, the local watering hole for people with money and power—or for those with their eyes trained on it. Clubs were the center of a social and commercial universe.

Today, it's a smaller universe. But the alchemy still exists.

The earliest clubs, with their elaborate décor, competitive art collections, and savory food, were a sign to the outside world that Chicago aimed for more than commerce—it aimed for sophistication and permanent status on the world stage. Its members would make it so.

SPOTLIGHT

ᕙ— THE ORIGIN OF THE BLACKBALL —ᕗ

The blackball was, as might be obvious, a process involving, literally, a little black ball that could knock a person out of contention for a valuable membership in a club. It was used in elections to memberships of gentlemen's clubs as far back as the sixteenth century in England. It was a factor in some German clubs, too.

The term is derived from the traditional practice of members voting anonymously on admitting new members, using either a white marble (acceptance) or a black marble (denial). In most cases, acceptance would have to be unanimous; therefore, one black marble in the ballot box could be enough to keep the applicant out of the organization. Ballot boxes were designed so others couldn't see the color of the marble being dropped in.

The term is now applied generally to efforts—especially unreasonable or vengeful actions—to keep people out of organizations they wish to join or jobs they wish to have or keep them from achieving a goal they wish for but cannot attain.

Blackballing survives, but the marbles are optional.

CLUB NOTES

✐ WHAT'S *THE SOCIAL REGISTER* ✐ & HOW DO I GET IN?

Let's start with the last question first. If you've successfully found a copy of *The Social Register* and failed to find your name in it, we have three words for you: Give. Up. Now. It's probably not going to happen.

Founded in 1886 as an early directory of New York City society, *The Social Register* is right up there with the Trilateral Commission in its appreciation for secrecy and safeguarding whatever magic formula it uses to allow the right people in and keep the rest of the riffraff out. In a recently introduced Web page, however, *The Social Register* does disclose that anyone may apply but that they need to "furnish letters of recommendation from several families already listed."

Who runs *The Social Register?* Steve Forbes, actually. His *Forbes* magazine publishing empire bought it a few years ago.

What's ironic is that today's *Social Register* is actually an elective listing with full names, addresses, and, welcome to the Internet Age, even e-mail addresses. That's right. You have the nation's richest people actual-

In Kevin Callahan's book about The Casino (Chapter 19), he provides an amusing wrap-up of the top clubs and the people who belong. His observations are worth keeping in mind for the chapters ahead:

By the time The Casino was founded in 1914, many different clubs had emerged in Chicago. There were the men's clubs, like the Standard Club and the Chicago Club, both founded in 1869, the latter being the first club of its kind in the middle west. Its entrance policy stated, "No dogs, Democrats, Women or Reporters." [The Casino, a bit less selective in this regard, stated in the Club rules, "There will be no dogs

ly wanting to put all their private contact information in a hardbound book that anyone can read at their nearest public library.

But according to several sources, including Amory's book, the people who make it into *The Social Register* have to pass a litmus test of the right bloodline, schooling, marriages, and finally, private club memberships. All those factors tend to support the others.

Like the human listees, the private clubs listed in *The Social Register* are ones with status and staying power. In the 2006 edition of *The Social Register* in the stacks of the Winnetka Public Library— one of the few Chicago-area libraries that carries the latest

volume published twice a year— the following bricks-and-mortar Chicago-area clubs (both city, country, and yacht clubs) made the list:

- Bath & Tennis Club (Lake Bluff)
- Chicago Club (Chicago)
- The Casino (Chicago)
- Chicago Yacht Club (Chicago)
- The Contemporary Club (A club housed at The Fortnightly, Chicago)
- Indian Hill Club (Winnetka)
- Onwentsia Club (Lake Forest)
- Racquet Club (Chicago)
- Saddle & Cycle Club (Chicago)
- Shoreacres Country Club (Lake Bluff)
- Woman's Athletic Club (Chicago)

allowed in the clubhouse." As for Democrats and reporters, well, they could take their chances.]

The Chicago Club was described as "neat but not gaudy" and a place that preserved its pioneer integrity. The University Club, "No longer just Harvard or Yale anymore," had a great library, but its defects were "lack of youth, little eccentricity, little abnormality, no home for lost causes or impossible beliefs." The Union League was described as "dignified, even civic," with members who were "solid citizens, more Oak Park than Lake Forest."

Men's clubs were often segregated along business lines: bankers got together at the Mid-Day; brokers at the Attic; manufacturing and department store heads at The Chicago Club; authors and architects at The Tavern Club; and doctors at the University Club.

Jonathan McCabe, general manager of the Union League Club of Chicago, believes clubs continue today even with smaller numbers because human beings, even with all the technology out there, are still hardwired to make a face-to-face connection with people of like minds. He explains:

> When I talk to people about joining us, I have a silly little line that I use. When we were kids, our folks would get a new refrigerator or a new TV or a new washing machine, and we'd get a great big cardboard box. And we'd take that cardboard box out in our back yard, and we'd use our crayons, and we'd color on it, and we'd call it our clubhouse. And we would invite our pals to come to our clubhouse. And we didn't invite everybody. We only invited our pals.
>
> This is the same thing. Bricks and mortar are a little bit more expensive, and the crayons have been replaced with a Monet. But it's still a clubhouse where people who like each other, who have a common bond, and who want to do things together come together. And it doesn't come across as exclusive in terms of keeping people out. It's inclusive in terms of bringing people who share those values together. That's not being snobby. That's what all people do.

In the following chapters, you'll meet these clubs in depth.

Sources:
Amory, Cleveland. *Who Killed Society?* New York: Harper, 1960.
Andreas, A. T. *History of Chicago*, Vol. 2. Chicago: A. T. Andreas, 1885.
Callahan, Kevin M. *Oasis in the City: A History of The Casino.* Chicago: The Casino, 1997.
Dedmon, Emmett. *Fabulous Chicago.* New York: Athenaeum, 1981.
McCabe, Jonathan. Interview by author. 9 June 2005.
The Social Register Association. *The Social Register.* Spring 2005, www.socialregisteronline.com.

II

THE
GREAT FIRE,
THE
COLUMBIAN EXPOSITION,
AND THE
CLUBS

———

There's only sketchy information on Chicago's earliest private clubs, most of it in the archives of clubs that exist today. By the early 1870s, The Dearborn Club and other early city clubs were already on their way out. The Chicago Club, still considered the most elite of the city's business-social clubs today, was hopping around various locales without a permanent space.

Members of The Standard—the club formed by some of the city's earliest German-Jewish entrepreneurs found unwelcome at the Chicago Club—built their first clubhouse in 1869 at Michigan Avenue and 13th Street, well south of the center of downtown. The Commercial Club, the Union League, the University Club, the City Club, and dozens of clubs that came afterward were not yet formed.

And then there was the Great Fire.

Everyone knows the devastation brought by the Great Fire of October 8–10, 1871, but even today the numbers are still staggering. At least 300 died, 18,000 structures were destroyed, hundreds of businesses were lost, and more than 300,000 people were displaced in less than four square miles of space. The tragedy was enormous for a city so young and, for better or worse, is second only to Al Capone in the lingering image that most outsiders still carry about Chicago.

Yet the Great Fire created something that we've only seen a few times in America, most recently with Hurricane Katrina: A chance for a city to start over.

The Great Fire of 1871 and the World's Columbian Exposition of 1893 proved how necessary the clubs were to the city's early development. These young organizations were critical not only in helping the city come back from devastation but in securing key events that helped solidify Chicago's place as a world-class city.

THE GREAT FIRE AND THE CLUBS

The Chicago Club's history details an almost whimsical reaction from members to the blaze that took out their clubhouse—perhaps that reaction was more than a bit apocryphal as well. The men, with drinks in hand, watched the fire approach. When it got too close for comfort, they grabbed some chairs—plus as much whiskey and cigars as they could carry—and then fled for safer ground to offer toasts while they watched their clubhouse burn. Upon returning the next morning to find the building still standing, they scrounged up champagne and breakfast.

The results weren't that amusing. Of all the clubs operating at the time, only the Standard Club's clubhouse escaped the fire because it was located on the Near South Side. Meanwhile, many of the members' homes went up in the blaze, displacing the exact people needed to direct the rebuilding of the city.

As the city began to rebuild, it faced another major obstacle—the Panic of 1873. In September of that year Philadelphia banking firm Jay Cooke and Co. closed its doors and declared bankruptcy, leading to a domino effect among major banks and a ten-day shut-

There are plenty of theories on how the Great Chicago Fire started—a cow knocking over a lantern in a barn, a meteor shower, and a thief accidentally setting fire to a barn while trying to steal some milk. What is known is that the fire started around 9 P.M. *Sunday, October 8, 1971, and by the time it was contained, it moved from downtown to circle Lincoln Park. (From* History of Chicago, *Vol. 2, by A.T. Andreas.)*

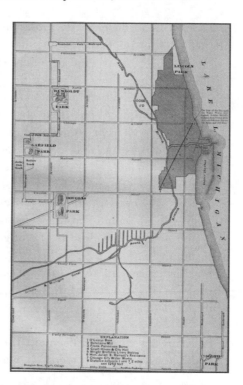

down of the New York Stock Exchange. Many early Chicago industrialists lost fortunes, and the clubs would struggle for the remainder of the decade.

But by the 1880s Chicago was a boomtown, already becoming the nation's second-largest population center after New York. The clubs were the center of talent for virtually every aspect of the city's recovery after the Great Fire. Bankers, lawyers, merchants—all were members, as were the architects who made history after the city burned, particularly William Le Baron Jenney, Dankmar Adler, William Holabird, Martin Roche, Louis Sullivan, John Wellborn Root, Charles Atwood, and Henry Hobson Richardson. The First Chicago School, as the group was known, created many of the greatest landmarks in the city: the Rookery, the Auditorium Theater, the Home Insurance Building, the Art Institute of Chicago, and many other historic structures.

In A.T. Andreas's *History of Chicago*, he notes in his chapter entitled "Social Progress" the "great transformation in the society and social life of the city" that followed the fire. He wrote that club life became, for the first time, "a distinguishing feature of the period" and "one of more than ordinary significance."

Indeed, club members of the time saw themselves as instrumental to the city's salvation and, of course, the building—and in some cases, the rebuilding—of their own fortunes. The fire created a clean slate to construct homes, factories, businesses, and eventually, untold fortunes. People needed networks to accomplish things and needed them fast. As new clubs formed and old ones were rebuilt, they were a sanctuary, the natural place, for the right people, the best people, to create a pattern for a new city. Clubs provided civilized, comfortable surroundings to do this important work, no matter how close to the edge of lawlessness some of that work might be.

The fire was actually a springboard for some of the best PR Chicago ever got. Edward T. Blair's early history of the Chicago Club put it this way:

Few foresaw the advertisement the fire was to be to the city, and the great improvements it was to make in the business

Only five of Chicago's historic private clubhouse structures have landmark status. The vast majority of clubs don't want it. Because all have some form of not-for-profit status, they wouldn't get a tax break, and many don't welcome the restrictions that go with landmark status either. The first four clubs are listed on the National Register of Historic Places; the last is a designated Chicago landmark—the year listed by their name is the year they received landmark status.

The Chicago Club (2005; See Ch. 8)
The Germania Club (1976; See Ch. 7)
The Bryan Lathrop House (1974;
  Home to The Fortnightly; See Ch. 12)
The Swedish Club of Chicago (1258 N. LaSalle St.)
The Steuben Club (2006; 188 W. Randolph)

and residence districts would more than compensate for the losses it had caused to individuals. The moving south of the Board of Trade and the Grand Pacific Hotel, and the establishment of a new wholesale district on Market Street considerably enlarged the business center and changed its character. Before the fire, Lake Street and the neighboring east and west streets had been the important business streets; now State Street, Clark Street and later Wabash Avenue and Dearborn Street began to grow in favor. Most of the residents of the Lake Front moved south on Michigan Avenue and Prairie and Indiana Avenues to the neighborhood of Eighteenth Street.

Despite the economic hardships that followed, Chicago had become a city of architects and builders and would go on to become a city like no other in the United States. The frenzy to rebuild would affect the clubs as well.

THE PROMISE OF THE WORLD'S COLUMBIAN EXPOSITION

Throughout history, city fathers have seen the benefit of what the Roman poet Juvenal called "bread and circuses"—big events staged to placate the masses, to take the public's eye off of larger problems.

The city desperately needed a huge public distraction after the Great Fire, the Panic of 1873, and what was to come in 1886. On May Day, thousands of socialists, union organizers, reformers, and anarchists marched on Chicago to create the center of a national movement for the eight-hour workday. Records show that between 30,000 and 35,000 workers walked off the job on that day—a Saturday—alone. Events only got worse in the next four days as crowds traveled from company to company urging those still on the job to strike. At Cyrus McCormick's reaper plant, police fired on two strikers, killing them. This set the stage for the May 4 Haymarket Riot, in which eight policemen were killed and an undetermined number of people died in the crowd after a bomb was thrown at police.

The Court of Honor at the World's Columbian Exposition, 1893. *(From* Plan of Chicago *by Daniel Burnham.)*

The undesired publicity would haunt the city's political and business leaders well into 1887 as the widely publicized Haymarket trials began. It was time to do something to burnish the city's image. Though the phrase "the whole world is watching" wouldn't become popular until the violent Democratic Convention of 1968, Chicago's leaders must have felt similar pressure as the 1890s approached.

The answer was the national sweepstakes to win the right to stage a fair celebrating the 400th anniversary of Columbus's landing in America. How big were the stakes? Think in terms of the Olympics coming to Chicago today—and then multiply that level of competition by ten.

By 1893 there were many more clubs in operation, in particular the Commercial Club, Chicago Woman's Club, Union League Club, University Club, and Chicago Athletic Association. Chicago's millionaires joined forces to best millionaires in other U.S. cities for the bragging rights and the one-time-only chance for urban redemption that the exposition would bring.

Bread and circuses meant not only big money but big spin for a city's image. The first world's fair, the Crystal Palace Exhibition (hosted in London in 1851), went a long way toward dissolving class unrest in England with a show of British might and ingenuity. As 1890 approached, St. Louis (which would later narrowly win the 1904 Olympic Games from Chicago), Washington, D.C., and New York started a heated battle to win the exposition.

New York's financial triumvirate, J.P. Morgan, Cornelius Vanderbilt, and William Waldorf Astor, pledged $15 million to underwrite the fair if Congress awarded it to New York City. Chicago's first string fired back. Streetcar magnate and much-hated robber baron Charles T. Yerkes made strange bedfellows with Marshall Field (whom he had actually swindled in a business deal years earlier), Philip Armour, Gustavus Swift, and Cyrus McCormick to match the New York offer. The Chicago team also presented additional financial support from the city and state as well as more than $5 million in stock subscriptions from people from every walk of life. The sweepstakes went down to the wire, and Chicago got the fair after banker Lyman Gage successfully raised several million additional dollars in a 24-hour period to best New York's final offer.

The design and creation of the White City, as the Columbian Exposition was known, was headed by Daniel Burnham, a member of most of the city's elite clubs. But as Burnham supervised the planning for the massive 1893 fair, he started thinking even bigger. He began speaking to all the other clubs and interested groups in the city about the benefits Chicago would reap from wider streets, museums, civic centers, parks, and forest pre-

The unbuilt Chicago Civic Center featured in Burnham's Plan of Chicago, sponsored by members of the combined Merchants and Commercial Club of Chicago. (From Plan of Chicago *by Daniel Burnham.)*

serves. The Merchants Club embraced Burnham's ideas and then merged with the Commercial Club to develop and implement his work in creating the visionary *Plan of Chicago* published in 1909, which established Chicago's street grid and safeguarded its lakefront for perpetuity.

The other, lesser-known genius in what became known as "the Burnham Plan," was Edward H. Bennett, who did the nuts-and-bolts of the project; he directed the planning and preparation of the drawings. Burnham, a self-taught architect and talented salesman, was the closer; he did the lion's share of getting private industry behind it. Though the Commercial Club published less than 1,500 copies of the original *Plan of Chicago*, a few original donated copies sit dusty on library shelves in the Chicago area. No Chicagoan should miss the chance to look through it—it's an inspiring book, beautifully illustrating a vision of a Chicago much like Paris with wide streets, jaw-dropping gardens, and majestic buildings.

The Columbian Exposition would bring 20 million people to Chicago. Furthermore, it set the stage for the Century of Progress Exposition in 1933—another event organized in the wake of national crisis.

BEYOND THE EXPOSITION

The early clubs continued with an aggressive public agenda. The Commercial Club's reaction to the Haymarket Riot went beyond the Columbian Exposition. It joined with the Merchants Club to organize a private purchase of land just south of Lake Forest and build the Great Lakes Naval Training Station. They believed peace would reign in Chicago with an armed militia nearby. And the Union League Club was a key participant in the Secret Six, a group of lawyers and businessmen who helped bring down Al Capone. Those events will be covered in more detail in Chapter 9.

Sources:

Andreas, A. T. *History of Chicago*, Vol. 2. Chicago: A. T.
    Andreas, 1885.
Blair, Edward T. *An Early History of The Chicago Club*.
    Chicago: The Chicago Club, 1898.

III

PROHIBITION,
DEPRESSION,
AND
RECOVERY

———

For the richest of the rich, economic downturns typically aren't that devastating—at least from the perspective of the lower classes. But the Great Depression left more than a mark on the rich, the intelligentsia, the professionals, and the borderline upper classes that made up the vast majority of Chicago's private club membership at the brink of the Depression years.

The 1920s were notable not only for the arrival of the 18th Amendment (January 16, 1920) and the ugly reality of Black Tuesday, but also for the last days of the great club-building boom, which hasn't been equaled since. Many clubs that footed the bill for this expansion were left in near-bankruptcy by the time they got their doors open.

Membership at all the clubs, even the white-stocking Chicago Club, took a dip between 1930 and 1935, with 1933–34 considered the worst year by consensus. By that time the City Club finally sold its clubhouse (today it is occupied by the John Marshall Law School), and virtually every club made cuts straight to the bone to keep the lights on and the rent paid.

But add dry times to hard times? That was adding insult to injury, particularly in places where people paid handsomely for a nightly drink with their friends when it was actually legal.

Meals became plainer, dues collection got more, well, innovative, and waiting lists for membership in virtually every club all but disappeared. But somehow most of the major clubs survived, and none of the wet clubs went dry, thanks to years of strategic planning, ingenious hoarding, and more than a few enlightened relationships with local law enforcement. And a few members with some money left in a mattress helped, too.

At the Cliff Dwellers' January 1919 annual meeting—exactly one year before the Volstead Amendment would take effect—a motion was passed authorizing the appointment of a committee to secure and store an adequate supply of "alcoholic beverages to provide for as many years as may be against the arid season which faces us." The Volstead Amendment, 18th Amendment to the Constitution, came courtesy of Minnesota Republican Congressman Andrew Volstead. It was passed on October 28, 1919, and repealed by the 21st Amendment on December 5, 1933.

But when membership began to erode during the perfect storm of a national alcohol ban and a worldwide economic collapse, architect Thomas Tallmadge, 1933–34 president of the Cliff Dwellers, put it this way:

> Don't give up on the Cliff Dwellers. If you find it impossible to pay the dues—a misfortune like a hole in one's sock, possible in the life of any gentleman these days, the club, the good old club, will moratorium you until easier days—but don't resign. Use the club to its fullest extent—I have been a member for 21 years and never has the food been as savory, the prices as pre-war, nor the companionship more delightful.

STAYING ALIVE

During the Depression the clubs worst hit were the ones that were fairly new and heavily mortgaged. As mentioned, the downtown building boom of the teens and 1920s created some of the most beautiful buildings still on the skyline. Within a few short years of opening, the landmark 333 N. Michigan Avenue building, home to the tony new Tavern Club, was already in bankruptcy, setting the stage for the Wirtz family's purchase of the skyscraper it still owns.

At the Racquet Club, many members quit because they still had the Chicago Club, and there was a run on the Racquet Club's shares. Members at that time held certificates of interest in the Racquet Club valued at $1,000 each, and the board had to issue a statement saying that it couldn't buy back certificates...so members couldn't resign. In 1932 the club allowed members to incur dues and assessment indebtedness up to $900 and either pay or surrender their certificates of interest. The Racquet Club's own mortgage was called that year, but fortunately investments in other buildings kept it narrowly afloat.

The Depression sunk the closest competitor of the Woman's Athletic Club—the Illinois Women's Athletic Club—but that didn't help the WAC for long.

According to the WAC's history, there were a few delinquencies during 1930, but the real slide started in 1931.

For many, it was no longer possible to belong to every or even any club in town. From a high of 1,770, the membership count began a precipitous slide across all categories. At the board meeting in September 1931, it was noted with concern that this was the first meeting in many years where no application for membership was presented. Instead, resignations were piling in, eight or nine at a clip, then escalating to 20, 30, or 40 or more a month. Sixty-eight members resigned during June 1932.

Most of the women on that long waiting list did not accept election after all, and eventually the list disappeared completely. A Life Membership was sold back to the club for the disappointing price of $1,000, and the next woman requesting same was offered only $500. Another member asked that all the silver she had presented to the club be returned to her.

LIFE WITHOUT BOOZE — SUPPOSEDLY

A trip to the Chicago Club's billiard room yields a wonderful dis-covery—rich, dark oak walls with square panels that, when pushed, swing back to reveal a nifty hiding place for one's precious single malt.

The Tavern Club had created a secret locker room for liquor in time for the opening of the club on June 28, 1927.

And at the Racquet Club, those left behind weren't hurting, even for a club that opened in the middle of Prohibition. They had an open channel to Canada for beer and the hard stuff. The club's his-tory reports that one of the members had a plane that he flew in with loads of whiskey from Canada. The club manager "used to have a police paddy wagon load up booze off the plane. Gin and Scotch—ten and fifteen dollars a bottle—good stuff. He'd have all the bellhops down at the back door ready." With the right payoff to a watch commander, the shipment arrived intact. The staff appar-ently also used to make beer in their closet, which was available chilled to anyone walking off the racquets court.

CLUBS THAT MADE IT — AND THOSE THAT DIDN'T

The City Club survived the Depression but permanently lost its clubhouse. The club vacated its space in 1933 and John Marshall Law School has occupied the space ever since. While it was reor-ganizing, the club reconstituted itself as the Plymouth Club and not long after renamed itself the Civic Club until May 5, 1934. At this time it became the City Club again and moved into office and meeting space in the Sherman House, then on the north side of Randolph Street between Clark and LaSalle, for free.

Two major athletic clubs that opened glittering skyscraper club-houses also shuttered their doors before the nation recovered. The Illinois Women's Athletic Club, which built the structure now known as Lewis Towers at Loyola University, fell into financial ruin in the early years of the Depression despite a membership that exceeded that of its closest competitor, the Woman's Athletic Club. And the Medinah Athletic Club, which is now the site of the InterContinental Chicago hotel at 505 N. Michigan Avenue, had shuttered its doors by 1930, setting the stage for a series of hotel tenants.

So much of the financial strain on clubs—particularly the clubs built in the teens and 1920s—was not because of a loss of membership. It was the result of the crushing debt from new construction. The huge building boom that preceded the Depression was shared in by many clubs whose members desired showplaces and were willing to leverage their investment.

In James L. Merriner's book on the City Club, he pointed to a 1955 letter from the estate of a former club member who had died in retirement in Florida inquiring about the value of his old City Club bonds that had helped pay for the construction of the clubhouse. Club officers wrote back, responding that the bonds were, unfortunately, worthless.

Sources:

Dedmon, Emmett. *A History of The Chicago Club*. Chicago: The Chicago Club, 1960.

Hilliard, Celia. *The Woman's Athletic Club of Chicago, 1898–1998: A History. Chicago:* The Woman's Athletic Club, 1998.

Maiken, Peter T. *The Racquet Club of Chicago: A History.* Chicago: The Racquet Club, 1994.

Merriner, James L. *The City Club of Chicago: A Centennial History.* Chicago: The City Club of Chicago, 2003.

Regnery, Henry. *The Cliff Dwellers: The History of a Chicago Cultural Institution.* Chicago: Chicago Historical Bookworks, 1990.

IV

RACE
AND THE
CLUBS

———————

If you were African-American, Hispanic, or Asian, you never had a problem getting into the city's best private clubs—as long as that's where you picked up your paycheck. That didn't change for good until the 1960s, when the city's largest clubs started the painful process of reversing decades of racism and finally started formally admitting nonwhites to their membership. In two tumultuous decades—from 1970 to 1990—America's advances in racial and gender equality had to be made painfully obvious before Chicago's private clubs would truly open their doors to everyone.

In fact, the color line was broken long before the gender line. At various points the Jewish clubs—the Standard Club and the Covenant Club—were believed to have admitted black members as

early as the late 1950s, though the Standard won't confirm and the
Covenant (now defunct) can't confirm. Other social clubs, such as
the Cliff Dwellers and the Metropolitan Club, say that, going back
to their inception, they've never had racial restrictions.

Trying to put a bead on discrimination based on color, religion,
and gender in the club world is like trying to hit a moving target.
At various points in history the city's private clubs changed their
minds about women, blacks, and Jews and then changed back
again. During certain time frames those groups could wander
freely—or almost freely—in the clubhouses. At other points they
were banned.

For Appendix A of this book, each club was asked the question
of composition of women and nonwhites and when they broke the
color and gender line. Several clubs had to be asked multiple times
before they answered the question, and most didn't want to answer
at all.

Why is that? Who can really say, except the clubs themselves.

The Union League Club of Chicago (ULCC) has made a singular
effort to air its past mistakes in cooperating with author James D.
Nowlan in his book *Glory, Darkness, Light: A History of the Union
League Club of Chicago*. The ULCC's past exclusionary tactics—
barring blacks from full membership until 1969 and being the last
of the four major clubs to drop its gender restriction, in 1987—
made it a notable offender, not because it was alone but because it
was so large and held on to such racist and sexist practices as long
as it did.

The ULCC's story is detailed here not because it is the worst
offender, but because it made a very specific effort to air its past
racial and gender practices in painstaking detail in Nowlan's 2004
book.

In the chapter entitled "Old Crow and Jim Crow," Nowlan
recalls the story of Taylor Hay, a Kentuckian and former manager
of the ULCC who ran the club with an iron fist. One of his pro-
nouncements was to change "longstanding policy in 1940; as of
that year, African Americans were no longer to darken the front
door of the Union League Club of Chicago." Prior to that time
black men were allowed in the clubs as guests, particularly to
attend board meetings with their white colleagues. The policy

change went out quietly by letter; some club members protested, but apparently not enough to reach critical mass. In 1951 Hay barred noted scientist and medical researcher Dr. Percy L. Julian from attending a meeting held at the club with fellow scientists. But Julian, having had his new home in Oak Park firebombed earlier in the year, didn't take it lying down. He went to the newspapers after the ULCC slight, making the following comments to the *Chicago Tribune* on July 19, 1951:

> It appears to me that organizations like the Union League Club are as deeply responsible as any other agency for such un-American incidents as the bombing of my home in Oak Park and the Cicero riot [July 10, 1951].
>
> When individuals supposedly in high places behave as the Union League club has behaved, ordinary citizens of lesser intelligence follow suit.

According to Nowlan, "Two months later, a Club spokesman issued a statement, reported in Chicago newspapers: 'Negroes will not be barred from club functions in the future when they are invited by club members.'"

Nowlan's book also recalls that in 1961, President John F. Kennedy nominated James B. Parsons to become a Chicago federal judge—the first African-American to be appointed to the federal bench. The ULCC's policy was always to extend privileges to federal judges without charge. However, the club immediately withdrew that consideration when Parsons was named. Bad blood swirled for years afterward until 1968, when, for the first time, an African-American businessman stood for nomination to membership. (It was mentioned quietly in the club's newsletter.) He was Frederick C. Ford, an accountant with the real estate firm Draper & Kramer.

Rancorous debate ensued, ending in a membership vote that rejected Ford's membership. However, the board went ahead and made an end run, electing him to membership on January 21, 1969. There followed a challenge to toss out the board and its Nominating Committee, but that failed, too.

By 1974 Taylor Hay was forced to resign several years earlier than planned, according to Nowlan.

*James B. Parsons.
(Courtesy of the
U.S. District Court,
Northern District of
Illinois.)*

In 1985 Ford was elected the club's first African-American president.

THE CITY CLUB'S EXPERIENCE

One club that approved African-American membership at a very early date was the City Club.

According to James L. Merriner's history of the club, published in 2003, the club actually opened membership to African-Americans as early as 1915. He wrote:

> In 1912, a member asked about Negroes as members or guests. Club officers replied that there was no rule and he could bring "any guest he might choose." Three years later, "the sense of the directors that character and point of view should be the tests of fitness for membership in this Club and not business or race" was adopted unanimously.

The Chicago Urban League, after its founding in 1915 by African-American Chicagoans, used the City Club's quarters on Plymouth Court, and the Chicago branch of the National Association for the Advancement of Colored People asked for and got permission to use the City Club's mailing list.

Ironically, though, the City Club never was that welcoming to its female counterpart, the Woman's City Club, founded in 1910. The City Club charged them $10 a month to use the clubhouse for meetings.

Sources:

Merriner, James L. *The City Club of Chicago: A Centennial History*. Chicago: The City Club of Chicago, 2003.

Nowlan, James D. *Glory, Darkness, Light: A History of the Union League Club of Chicago*. Evanston: Northwestern University Press, 2004.

V

THE
AFRICAN-AMERICAN
CLUBS

———

Segregation might have kept Chicago's minorities out of the club-houses in the Loop, but throughout Chicago's history there have always been exclusive private clubs—some with clubhouses, most without—that served the African-American community. Some very prominent ones in the African-American community exist today, albeit with fairly thin histories.

But in the earliest years there were clubs that catered to what were known as the Old Settlers in the African-American communi-ty, meaning the blacks who had created Chicago's first African-American community in the 1840s and their immediate descen-dents. In Chicago's black community as it was in the white Protestant, Catholic, and Jewish communities, those who arrived first got to the top.

The Appomattox Club, one of the few African-American private clubs with a noted clubhouse. When the white owners of this building sold to the Appomattox, a firebomb was thrown at the house. (Courtesy of the Vivian G. Harsh Research Collection of Afro-American History and Literature.)

The following are several notable historic clubs in Chicago's African-American community that had their roots in the early days of the city. Their dates of operation are approximate:

+ **The Appomattox Club** (1900), now defunct, is notable for having been one of the few clubhouse organizations based in the black community (at 3632 Grand Avenue) serving wealthy black business owners, attorneys, and professionals. Allan H. Spear's *Black Chicago: The Making of a Negro Ghetto* 1890–1920 describes the club this way: "By the 1920s, a Negro editor could state that 'every man in Chicago who holds any kind of responsible position or occupies a big place politically, belongs to the Appomattox Club.'"

  The Appomattox Club didn't operate without incident. In fact, the O'Brien family—who sold their residence to the club for its clubhouse—saw a bomb explode in their front yard before they moved out.

+ **The Old Settlers** (1904), now defunct, was one of the first black social clubs to embrace the ancestors of the city's black aristocracy. According to John H. Taitt's *Souvenir of Negro Progress, Chicago, 1779–1925,* the Old Settlers Club was

Ida McIntosh Dempsey, founder of the Chicago Old Settlers Club, an organization centered around the first African-Americans to arrive in Chicago prior to 1880. (Courtesy of the Vivian G. Harsh Research Collection of Afro-American History and Literature.)

formed "to keep the old settlers in touch with each other, and to cherish and keep fresh those memories of early colored life in Chicago."

According to T*he Negro in Chicago* (1779–1929, VI), the Old Settlers had designated "white friends" of the club. Among them were Julius Rosenwald, president of Sears, Roebuck and Co. and supporter of many black causes, and lawyer Clarence Darrow.

‡ **The Original Forty Club** (1920–present) is a club for affluent black males over the age of 40.

‡ **The Boule** (1904–present, Sigma Pi Phi Fraternity, Beta Chapter), a "council of noblemen" serving men with graduate and postgraduate degrees, was founded in Philadelphia by six black professionals: a pharmacist, a dentist, and four physicians. Chicago's chapter of the Boule was its second. It now holds its meetings at the once-restricted Union League Club.

Chicago is home to many other male black clubs as well, most more recent than those just described. Their names include:

+ The Royal Coterie of Snakes
+ The Druids
+ The Saints
+ 100 Black Men of Chicago
+ The Frogs
+ The Chicago Assembly
+ The Lunch Bunch
+ The New Committee
+ The Chicago–DC Connection
+ The Chicagoan

Dr. Everett White, a physician and a member of the Boule, is in the process of creating an umbrella group to channel these local organizations into more social action. It will be called COAL (the Coalition of African-American Leaders). In an interview, White explained, "Coal is black and coal starts a fire. Our primary target for now will be education. We want to be a sounding board." But White and former Illinois state treasurer Roland Burris stressed that the group was not political, but a way to zero in on educational and economic issues within Chicago's African-American community.

Chicago cultural historian Tim Samuelson says that the African-American clubs developed a structure similar to that of the white majority clubs in the city—the same highly educated men, leaders in their own professions and immediate neighborhoods, tended to belong to most of the clubs that were out there. As the post–World War I migration of African-Americans to Chicago intensified, these clubs also had the purpose of establishing who the true leaders in the community really were. In many cases, the southern migrants who came in what is now known as "the second wave" of black migration didn't need apply to these groups formed by the old settlers.

THE ORIGINAL FORTY CLUB

Roland Burris, president of the Original Forty Club in 2005, has long been a member of this organization. He credits it with providing a strict mentorship to younger black professionals and a sense of tradition and history as Chicago's African-American community has evolved. "When you consider the members of this club [the late Johnson Publishing founder] John [H.] Johnson, Dempsey Travis, and so many others, you realize how important it is to be a part of this history. All the older members are teachers to the younger ones," explains Burris. Meetings, he explained, will often include a presentation for a business or social idea, and when the floor opens up, the picking-apart can be quite strenuous. "But the presenter has the benefit of the best minds in the city and in his community," Burris added.

According to the Original Forty Club's 75th anniversary book, the group started to coalesce between 1913 and 1914:

A group of about six young friends began to meet periodically informally and unscheduled to unbeknowingly form the formative roots of the "Forty Club." As the meetings continued, and the circle of fellowship expanded, the idea of a more lasting organization began to take form. And around 1915, the Club was more formally organized, and the limit of membership was fixed at forty. This limitation was later relaxed to accommodate the demand in our history for as many as between 80–90 members.

There was a bloodline requirement, according to the history:

The common nature of these first of a kind rare breed of Black males is that they were usually the first or second generation of the freed ex-slaves, and had to carve a way for their evolving kind in a white hostile society setting up barriers and obstacles constantly as the occasion arises to deter or prevent their progress.

THE WOMEN'S CLUBS

Michael Flug, chief librarian of the Vivian G. Harsh Research Collection of Afro-American History and Literature at the Chicago Public Library's Carter G. Woodson Regional Library, points out that African-American Chicago women created their own network of society clubs that served the aristocracy, but there were also literary societies formed to educate and develop black women in the middle and upper classes. These literary societies mirrored those in white society.

Elizabeth Lindsay Davis, in her 1997 book *The Story of the Illinois Federation of Colored Women's Clubs*, pointed to a group of women's clubs called the Magic Seven back in 1899:

1. Ida B. Wells Club
2. Civic League
3. Progressive Circle of King's Daughters
4. Ideal Women's Club
5. G.O.P. Elephant's Club
6. Julia Gaston Club
7. Phyllis Wheatley Club

Flug points to two particular clubs that were the equal in Chicago's black community to The Casino or The Fortnightly. "The Girl Friends and the Links were two women's clubs that were national organizations, but very upper crust, and they still exist today."

⁂ **The Links** is shown by the book *Celebrating 50 Years of Friendship and Service: The Chicago Chapter of the Links Inc.* 1950–2000 (at the Harsh Library) to be a club that held debutante balls as well as regular discussions on the progress of civil rights. The book describes the group this way:

> Back in 1966, Links women who were employed were teachers. By 1978, they reported that the typical Link was married, but they were not only teachers, principals and homemakers but lawyers, judges, morticians, editors, beauty consultants, independent business entrepreneurs and professionals in health related fields.

Many members of the Links graduated from sororities at the nation's leading black colleges. For a woman to qualify for membership in the Links, the vote had to be unanimous.

A photograph of the Chicago Chapter of the Links, May 21, 1950.
(From the Chicago Public Library's Harsh Research Collection.)

The Links were founded in Philadelphia in 1946 by Lillian
Hudson Wall, a black college woman who picked the name
because "it best described how these friends linked themselves together into a formal organization," according to
Celebrating 50 *Years of Friendship.*

According to a 2004 story in the *Chicago Sun-Times,*
"Attorney Edith Sampson, the first black woman to practice
before the U.S. Supreme Court, joined the Links in 1951.
Another early Link, who joined in the 1950s, was Olive
Diggs, a former editor of the African-American newspaper
the *Chicago Bee,* who later headed the Illinois Commission
on Human Relations. Anna Johnson Julian, the first black
woman to receive a doctorate in sociology and the widow of
prominent chemist Percy Julian, also was an active member."

The group has given more than $2 million to such caus-
es as Chicago Urban League, DuSable Museum of African
American History, and the Abraham Lincoln Center. The
Links also sponsored one of the nation's first Head Start
programs.

Current members of the club could not be reached for
comment.

✦ **The Girl Friends**, a New York–based national organization founded in 1927 (during the Harlem Renaissance), launched its Chicago chapter in 1953, according to the Harsh Library. The organization was founded by a handful of teenagers who were close friends that wanted to find a way to stay in touch "as they went away to college and encountered adulthood." According to a history on file at the Harsh Library, the Girl Friends by 1993 had grown to encompass 1,199 prominent women in 40 chapters from coast to coast.

A BLACK ATHLETIC CLUB?

The Harsh Library features a reference to an Ambassador Athletic Association organized on December 2, 1924, that was "the result of a merger between the Bon Vivant Osbie and the El Progresso Clubs." With a club photograph featuring a group of African-American men in business suits, the address is identified as 4336 S. Parkway, "in a palatial $35,000 clubhouse."

Sadly, the great frustration of researching African-American clubs is the paucity of information out there.

Sources:
Burris, Roland. Interview by author. 10 August 2005.
Flug, Michael. Interview by author. 13 August 2005.
Original Forty Club. *Original Forty Club*. Chicago: Original
    Forty Club, 1980.
Samuelson, Tim. Interview by author. 1 July 2005.
Taitt, John H. *The Souvenir of Negro Progress, Chicago,*
    1779–1925. Chicago: The De Saible Association, Inc., 1925.
White, Everett. Interview by author. 29 August 2005.

VI

WOMEN
. . . IN THE
CLUB?

———————

Hanna Holborn Gray, the first woman president of the University of Chicago, didn't intend to tear down the all-male bastion of private clubs when she took her new job. She was just trying to run a university.

"The president of the University of Chicago was automatically admitted to the Commercial Club upon appointment, and their meetings were held at the Chicago Club," Gray recalls. "Well, under their rules, I couldn't go in."

The year was 1978, and already a war had been going on for five years between activists and the city's male-only private clubs to get them to finally open their doors to women as full members. Indeed, once Gray's appointment at u of c was announced, the Commercial

*Hanna Holborn Gray.
(Courtesy of the University
of Chicago News Office.)*

Club saw the potential firestorm and moved quickly to stem the public embarrassment of leaving the head of a major university out on the sidewalk in her pumps. "They said, 'Just give us a little time,' and they apparently made something happen fast, because I was in," said Gray.

What had happened was a significant yet quiet breakthrough on the way to the last of the major male-only clubs going coed by 1987. It's unclear how important the Gray matter was in integrating the Chicago Club. The club's own history doesn't mention it, but it does note that by the end of that year the club had voted, fairly reluctantly, to allow women in the door *as guests.* In any event, as the Chicago Club went, so went the rest. By 1982 Gray and noted Chicago attorney Jean Allard would become the first women to gain membership in the Chicago Club. And despite many heated arguments inside those clubhouses, the rest followed by the end of the decade.

But we're getting ahead of ourselves.

For anyone safely over the age of 40 in Chicago with some knowledge of the city's private clubs, it wasn't so long ago when the wives, mothers, and daughters of the male club members or the rare female visitor coming for lunch or tea would typically have to enter the building through a separate "ladies' entrance." They

The women's entrance at the Union League Club of Chicago in 1940. (Courtesy of the Union League Club of Chicago Archives.)

would be allowed entry only during assigned hours and, unless accompanied by their husbands, fathers, or sons, would be kept within the confines of ladies' dining rooms or lounges. While some of these side entrances were nicely appointed with awnings and sometimes their own doorman, others were simple back doors shared with delivery workers and staff.

That world finally died in 1987, when the Union League Club of Chicago became the last of the major clubs to go coed. After that there were stragglers among the smaller clubs, but it was very much a done deal.

All in all, it wasn't an easy road getting there.

"MISS, YOU CAN'T GO IN THAT WAY"

Sheribel F. Rothenberg began her law career nearly 40 years ago, and she quickly got used to being the only female lawyer in an office where all the other women were legal secretaries. It didn't take her long to realize that the status of being a female attorney working alongside male attorneys didn't mean much at the male-only clubs.

"We had clients who had board meetings at the Chicago Club, and even if I was on the case, I couldn't join them because they

41

barred women entirely back then. Likewise, the University Club and the Union League had side doors and separate elevators to get upstairs at certain hours," Rothenberg recalls, laughing a little. "I'm from the neighborhoods, so what did I know about this stuff? You want to get inside a building, you walk in through the front door! But the first time I tried to walk in the front door at one of the clubs, I had a doorman at my arm politely leading me to the back entrance. That was not pleasant."

One too many incidents like that led to a conversation with Rothenberg's friend and fellow attorney Stephanie Kanwit in the early 1970s. The two attorneys had filed a lawsuit in federal district court a few years earlier against the city's four daily newspapers to get them to change their gender-specific "men wanted/women wanted" classified advertising. The suit was dismissed, but the newspapers, apparently seeing the handwriting on the wall, went ahead and quietly changed their policy to make their ads gender-blind. Rothenberg said that victory was the precursor to their later decision to challenge the clubs in court.

Yet it wouldn't be lawyers who got the ball rolling. It would be women reporters who were barred at the door of the Chicago Club, which in the early 1970s still had restrictions against both news media and women coming inside. On December 5, 1973, *Chicago Tribune* reporter Carol Oppenheim was blocked from entering the

CLUB NOTES

✑ REMEMBER THE E.R.A.? ✑

The early days of the club desegregation movement coincided with the contentious national debate over the adoption of the Equal Rights Amendment to the U.S. Constitution, which read in part, "Equality of rights under the law shall not be denied or abridged by the United States or by any state on account of sex."

The Amendment, originally proposed in 1923, finally gasped its last in 1982, three states short of ratification.

club when she arrived to cover a speech by Caspar Weinberger, then Secretary of Health, Education, and Welfare during the Nixon administration. (She had been invited by Weinberger's staff, which was apparently unaware of the Chicago Club's policy.) Within days the Chicago Club received notice from the Illinois Liquor Control Commission that it had allegedly committed a civil rights violation by not allowing women equal access to a club that had a city liquor license.

Rothenberg and Kanwit had been in touch with the *Tribune* during these incidents and finally decided it was time to make a move. They created a group called POWER (Professional Organization of Women for Equal Rights) and joined what would become a 15-year dance against the nation's private men's clubs in courts all over the country—even the U.S. Supreme Court.

The Chicago women joined a male attorney, Charles Davis, who wanted to see gender restrictions fall at the Mid-Day Club because he wanted his three daughters to have the chance to become members. The group came up with a strategy in 1972 to use the Illinois Liquor Control Act's civil rights provision formally in court against the Chicago Club. By 1974 POWER would add several other male-only clubs to the lawsuit including the Attic Club, Chicago Athletic Association, Covenant Club, Mid-Day Club, Union League Club, Tavern Club, and University Club of Chicago.

This initial court challenge would fail, and so would another one filed under the state's liquor law provisions, but the efforts had an important impact—the clubs started to loosen things up on their own. The Jewish-led Covenant Club in particular elected to drop its restriction on women members shortly after the lawsuit was filed, and although it would not confirm, the Standard Club dropped its restriction as well.

In notes from the now-defunct Covenant Club kept at the Chicago Museum of Jewish History, the club voted to admit women on October 28, 1974. Of the decision, then-president Leonard Server said, "Women have made a new place in the world. It's not the same. It's the trend today. We want to be among the first to make the change."

The publicity generated by the club desegregation effort over that 15-year period would put pressure on individual members who were in prominent public positions. One was Adlai E. Stevenson

III, who would eventually drop out of the 1985 Illinois governor's race against Governor James Thompson after Thompson attacked Stevenson for being a member of the Cliff Dwellers (of course, Thompson had previously been a member of the Union League Club, the last to go coed). It wasn't the first time Stevenson was called upon to explain himself on the "women issue." Back in June 1975 Stevenson wrote the following letter, on behalf of the Chicago Club, to two individuals and the entire staff of the Abraham Lincoln School in Oak Park. It comes from the Chicago Club's most recent history, published in 1995.

> Thanks for your letter about the membership policy of The Chicago Club. Women, Blacks, Jews—everyone, including men [is] entitled to assemble privately with those they choose, and they will remain free to do so for as long as this is a free country. Women maintain an all-women's club across the street from my recent home in Chicago. That is and should remain their right.
>
> If your concern is about discrimination in employment or other such economic opportunities—then it is a concern I share in full. . . .
>
> Between "public" and "private" a line must be drawn to protect the rights of all persons to equal opportunity, on the one hand, and to privacy and the right to assemble on the other. That line is not always easy to draw. Once drawn, the "right" requires enforcement or it is meaningless. Enforcement of a right to membership ultimately requires unenforceable quotas. If The Chicago Club, or some other club, were forced by law or pressure to open membership to all, it would probably remain subject to such pressure until it had demonstrated compliance with some objective test. Those tests are inevitably quotas for sexes, religions, races, etc. The quotas are not only unenforceable; they deprive us of individual rights.
>
> There are no easy answers to the questions raised by your letter; I would be less than honest if I said there were. I believe that private organizations such as The Chicago Club and the Eleanor Club are entitled to determine their member-

ship as they choose. If, however, an exclusionary policy deprives a citizen of an equal economic opportunity, the policy should be modified. If, for example, The Chicago Club continues to be a place for business meetings at which women are arbitrarily excluded and are thereby prevented from pursuing all their economic opportunity, and that has happened, then the policy should be condemned and changed. That does not mean that membership must be made open—but it does mean that women should not be excluded from business meetings because they are women. I would think that The Chicago Club, like others in Chicago, could arrange to make facilities available for such meetings, if they are to be held, so women can attend—without depriving men of their right to assemble socially.

What was interesting about the 1980 vote at the Union League, according to Nowlan's book, was that the leadership had actually surveyed the membership by postcard, and the numbers looked overwhelmingly positive toward approval. Yet the postcard campaign didn't take into account a particular faction of the club—the

CLUB NOTES

◦— NAKED BOYS SWIMMING! —◦

Sometimes if stories are repeated often enough, they take on a life of their own. Such is the case with naked swimming in the "baths," the early name for pool facilities at Chicago's oldest private clubs. There's no doubt that it happened, but as the years went on, the "boys just like to swim nude" refrain was often used as an excuse to forbid female membership in the clubs. "What if guys want to swim naked? You can't do that if women join!" was the refrain.

Emmett Dedmon's 1960 history of the Chicago Club offers a memorable description of how women were regarded in the affairs of the private male club back in the 1800s:

The windows were just above eye level and although the exterior was decorated with flower boxes and ivy, no proper Chicago lady ever lifted her eyes passing The Chicago Club. The younger children or grandchildren of members were not as inhibited. Kathryn Shortall, who later married Harry J. Dunbaugh, still remembers her experience as a 10-year-old when she waved to her grandfather, John D. Shortall, whom she saw sitting in The Chicago Club with Robert T. Lincoln. . . . That night at dinner, he took her to one side and said sternly, "My dear, when a lady passes the windows of a men's club, she never looks up."

Dedmon also points to a story told by Cornelia Conger, who had a similar experience waving to her uncle William C. Lyon at the Chicago Club. "He repeated the advice that Shortall had given Kathryn and added to it the epigram that 'when a gentleman is in his club, he is invisible.'"

While the effort to open Chicago's clubs continued, it would be a critical New York court decision in 1984 that would accelerate the end of the ban in the Windy City. The New York case took an interesting tack—focusing on the size and composition of the club as a trigger for desegregation.

The New York Supreme Court in the mid-1980s upheld a New York City law that prohibited discrimination by any private club that had at least 400 members and served meals. Because the majority of male-only clubs in Chicago fit that description, members started grassroots campaigns to end their respective bans voluntarily. In many cases these efforts created serious rancor that stuck with those clubs for years.

At the Union League Club, women were expected to enter on Federal Street and take the ladies' elevator up to the fifth floor, the lowest level women were permitted in the club until 1972, when rumors of a lawsuit were starting to surface. At that point women were allowed to go in the front door and circulate with their male hosts on the lower levels of the club.

By 1976 the University Club (which, according to Union League biographer James T. Nowlan, was the Union League's chief competition for membership) had dropped its bar to female membership as had several others (see page 50). Before finally admitting women in 1987, the Union League Club would have its first vote to accept women members in 1977, which failed, and another in 1980, which also died but with a flourish, seven years before the action that would finally open the ULCC to women.

athletic department, members who used the club's gym facilities every day and were the loudest voice against female membership. The pro-women forces thought they'd lock up the election by physically moving it to Orchestra Hall, thinking the opposition—many of whom worked down at the Board of Trade—wouldn't make the hike. As Nowlan wrote, the leadership was dead wrong. The traders hired a fleet of limousines to carry their contingent back and forth across the Loop to vote against the measure. When they got there they didn't bother to use the private voting booths. They grabbed their ballots and voted out in the open. The vote was 349 in favor of women joining the club, 721 against.

Particular heat followed that second election. In one of her first actions, Susan Getzendanner, the first woman appointed to the federal bench in Chicago, held a press conference to publicly reject the Union League's offer of membership privileges it afforded federal judges (but had declined to offer the first black federal judge, James B. Parsons; see Chapter 4) due to its decision on women members.

There was yet another effort in 1983 to try to put it to a vote, but this didn't even get that far. The *Chicago Sun-Times* managed to get a member to pen a story anonymously on July 14, 1983, with the headline "No Women: The Quest to Preserve the League's Century-Old Union." It featured the following quote from a member:

Susan Getzendanner.
(Courtesy of the U.S. District
Court/Northern District of
Illinois.)

"I go into the Wigwam [a club dining room] and there's a bunch of men talking men's talk. There are no women chattering," he said. "Then I go downstairs to the second floor and see no women—it's *great!*"

All this was great press through 1987, when the Union League voted for the third time on the issue—and failed again. This time dozens of club members resigned in protest, and the club took more hits in the press. The community activist Gail Cincotta said she might propose to the City Council an ordinance that would deny liquor licenses to clubs that discriminated against women.

The City Council took the bait. Aldermen David Orr, of the 49th Ward, and Edwin Eisendrath, of the 43rd Ward, representing two of the most liberal wards in the city, carried the ball on the ordinance. Don Harnack, who became president of the Union League in May 1987, was able to convince the council staff to delay the effective date of the ordinance until the end of July. According to Nowlan, Harnack, an attorney from Winnetka, didn't want to risk losing another membership-wide vote, which would cost not only more public goodwill but something arguably more valuable—the Club's liquor license. So Harnack managed an end run that essentially declared, at a membership meeting, that the city ordinance trumped the club's bylaws and the club would meet the city requirement for equal access to all facilities within six months.

The meeting turned angry, and Harnack simply adjourned it.

The women were in.

Eisendrath, who left the City Council in 1993 to work for the U.S. Department of Housing and Urban Development and in 2006, launched an unsuccessful Democratic bid for Illinois governor, recalled the ordinance flurry with a bit of amazement. "I had only been on the council for a few weeks, and this fell into my lap and David's. It had gone on long enough. It was degrading to women and to the city," he said. "Everyone thought it was such a big deal, but you know what? Social change is always late. We were at least ten years late on this one. Social change happens after everyone's OK with it."

Orr, now Cook County clerk, admitted the whole episode of allowing women into the clubs was important to the city, but with 20 years of hindsight, it was amazing the amount of rancor and

Edwin Eisendrath.
(Courtesy of Edwin
Eisendrath.)

emotion that went into beating it. Asked if he had ever belonged to any of the clubs then or now, Orr deadpanned, "Well, after all these years, I'm still with Bally's [health club]."

Sources:

Eisendrath, Edwin. Interview by author. 30 June 2005.

Gray, Hanna Holborn. Interview by author. 25 October 2005.

Nowlan, James D. *Glory, Darkness, Light: A History of the Union League Club of Chicago.* Evanston: Northwestern University Press, 2004.

Oppenheim, Carol. "Newswoman Left Out in Rain." *Chicago Tribune,* 5 December 1973, p. 2.

Orr, David. Interview by author. 6 July 2005.

Rothenberg, Sheribel F. Interview by author. 6 September 2005.

Wittebort, Robert J., Jr. *The Chicago Club,* 1960–1994. Chicago: The Chicago Club, 1995.

CLUB NOTES

～ WHO LET THE WOMEN IN . . . ～
AND WHEN?

The following serves as an incomplete chronology of when women were voted into full membership at Chicago's historic private clubs. Several clubs did not fully participate in answering questions for this book, so there are gaps.

Mid-America Club	1958*
City Club of Chicago	1962
Chicago Athletic Association	1974
Metropolitan Club	1974*
Standard Club	1974
University Club of Chicago	1976
Caxton Club	1976
Commercial Club of Chicago	1978
Executives' Club of Chicago	1980
Chicago Club	1982
Mid-Day Club	1982
The Cliff Dwellers	1984
Union League Club of Chicago	1987
Tavern Club	1987
Adventurers Club	1989
Chicago Literary Club	1995

*Women were admitted as members from inception.

VII

THE
LOST
CLUBS

———————

The number of clubs that have come and gone in Chicago will probably never be tracked to an exact figure, but they're definitely in the dozens. This chapter is a compilation of brief histories of notable clubs in the city's past, listed in alphabetical order. If both founding and closing dates are not available, only the founding dates are given.

Arché Club (1895): This literature club was founded by the top society ladies of the day, including Mrs. (Bertha) Potter Palmer. In 1916 the club sponsored a memorial fountain to Abraham Lincoln in Chicago Heights as a place of rest for cross-country travelers on the Lincoln Highway. The bust of Lincoln is flanked by several of his famous sayings.

Argo Club (May–October 1893): So much of Chicago's future was riding on the World's Columbian Exposition, and Chicago's top business leaders weren't sparing any expense on attracting the attention of the world. The Argo Club was a warm-weather spin-off of the Chicago Club, started by 50 of its members who wanted a cool place on the lake to entertain their friends during the summer months of the Columbian Exposition. The all-wooden clubhouse was designed by John W. Root in the shape of a Spanish caravel (just like the *Niña*, *Pinta*, and *Santa María*) and placed on stocks as if it were about to be launched.

The Argo was built on the Illinois Central pier because it was close to the Chicago Club and its members could pull their steam yacht—purchased just for the Exposition—up to the pier to ferry their guests back and forth from the lakefront fairgrounds. Getting into the club was a bit of a chore, as it could be accessed only by ladder. But inside it was outfitted with all the conveniences of a club—members could host dinner gatherings, play cards below, or sit on the deck and enjoy the scenery.

Chicago Club historian Edward T. Blair described the Argo as "the most expensive club ever started in Chicago" because it was in

The Argo Club, a lavish boat on dry land. (Courtesy of the Chicago Club.)

existence for only six months, vanishing at the conclusion of the Columbian Exposition on Halloween 1893.

Attic Club (1923–95): The Attic Club was organized in the Roaring Twenties by Paul E. Gardner, Charles F. Glore, and Henry A. Gardner as a way to gather together men who were on the rather long waiting list to join the Mid-Day Club. Its mission was strictly "social recreation," and until its closure in 1995, the Attic Club was based in the 43rd and 44th floors of the Field Building at 135 S. LaSalle Street in quarters that were designed by Chicago architect David Adler. During its 72 years the Attic Club was known for its fish chowder and chocolate macaroons. A table from the Attic Club was kept in the Mid-Day club, where most of its remaining members transferred their memberships. (The Mid-Day Club was closed in 2007.)

Builders Club: The dates for this particular club are spotty, but it was believed to have thrived through the Chicago building boom that resumed in the 1950s. The club was located at 228 N. LaSalle Street and its membership was made up of heads of construction companies that worked with commercial and residential developers throughout the city.

Calumet Club (1878–late 1800s): This private social club, formed in 1878 by a group of wealthy Chicagoans, provided some valuable

The Calumet Club. (From The Book of its Board of Trade and Other Public Bodies *by George W. Engelhardt, published* 1900.)

53

documentation of Chicago history. They took the Indian name Calumet because it implied goodwill. In 1885 the club assembled its old settlers' list, which included the names and addresses of all residents who had arrived in Chicago prior to its incorporation in 1837. That list was preserved in A.T. Andreas's *History of Chicago*.

Chicago Press Club (1880–1987): To say there was one Chicago Press Club for 107 years is inaccurate. Various incarnations of the organization moved around Chicago's various newspaper locations in the Loop. For a time members met on a lower floor of the old Medinah Athletic Club on Michigan Avenue, now the site of the InterContinental Chicago hotel. The last incarnation of the Press Club spent its last few years in the basement of the historic Wrigley Building before succumbing finally to the passage of time and indifference from teetotaling journalists. There used to be a nationwide market for press clubs and the convivial atmosphere they created for press agents, corporate PR types (most of them former journalists), and, of course, journalists themselves for the ten daily newspapers in Chicago at the turn of the last century. But over the course of time, PR people have gravitated to groups made up exclusively of their own. And journalists? Well, there are simply fewer media outlets, and today's scribes simply don't drink, smoke, or carouse to the level to support a member-supported private club. How boring.

Chicago Woman's Club (1876–1999): Before the public school system started picking up the tab for kindergarten, before there were school lunch programs and support for children whose mothers were incarcerated, there was the Chicago Woman's Club. This organization's membership included Jane Addams, Bertha Palmer, Helen S. Shedd, and other wives of the most important men in the city. Housed on the fourth floor of the building at 200 N. Michigan Avenue for the latter part of its history, the club also supported the arts, particularly by holding Shakespearean events and sponsoring speakers such as Carl Sandburg. Like the Woman's City Club of Chicago, the Chicago Woman's Club was an early activist organization that supported women's and children's rights long before women got the vote.

Dearborn Club (1861–63): Many of the earliest members of the Chicago Club came from this club, which met in humble wartime surroundings on State Street across from the first Palmer House hotel. From *History of Chicago* by A.T. Andreas: "The facilities for indulging in good dinners, ever a foremost club proclivity, were primitive. A Negro steward, who on his small stove in a die pantry could produce an occasional rasher of bacon and a cup of good coffee, represented the catering department. . . . With such limited facilities in war times, and with the true Club spirit scarcely as yet existing in the city, the Dearborn Club struggled along for two years before closing its doors in 1863." Among the names that spanned the Dearborn Club and the Chicago Club were Edward T. Blair; William B. Ogden, the first mayor of Chicago; and two presidents of the Dearborn Club, N.K. Fairbank, and Andrew T. Dickey.

Dill Pickle Club (c. 1910–20): Workers of the world, unite! Jack Jones, a member of the International Workers of the World (better known as the Wobblies), organized the Dill Pickle Club at 18 W. Tooker Place, near the Gold Coast. The place was a center of radical thought. Plays by August Strindberg, Ben Hecht, and Eugene O'Neill were performed there. The venue drew jazz dance, art shows, and as much bohemian entertainment as possible.

Farragut Boat Club (1880s): This Chicago athletic club gave birth to softball—and not just the 16-inch kind. The lore goes that a bunch of Harvard and Yale alums were waiting for the results of the Harvard-Yale football game in 1887, and once word came that Yale had won, a Yale alum picked up a boxing glove and threw it at a Harvard alum, who hit it back with a stick. That evolved into an indoor version of baseball that, over the decades, worked its way outside. Eventually, the boxing glove became a ball that was soft enough to be fielded without a glove. The Farragut Boat Club set officials rules for the game, which spread around the country.

Germania Club (1865-approx. 1986): German societies were rampant in the 1860s and were very patriotic as well. Built in 1888 and located at Germania Place and Clark Street, on the city's North Side, the Germania Club had a motto that reflected its patriotic

The Germania Club building, now renamed Germania Place. (Photo by Lisa Holton.)

values. It read, in part, "To foster admiration for the United States of America, its Constitution, laws, traditions and political institutions, and to uphold its independence." Many of the club's members were present at Lincoln's funeral. The club itself was formed in 1865, when a group of German-American Civil War veterans got together to peform a concert in honor of slain President Abraham Lincoln. The building itself was opened 24 years later.

In 1986, the club's quarters were purchased by Chicago-based Realty & Mortgage Co., private owners who rehabbed the space and reopened it as Germania Place in 1994 as rentable space for weddings, parties, and other events. In early 2008, a unit of Kimco Realty Corp., the New York-based shopping center giant, paid $9.3 million for the historic Old Town building.

The Germania Club successfully passed its 100th anniversary in 1965, but it is unclear exactly when the club vacated its location and closed up for good.

The club had to struggle during the heightened anti-German sentiment during both World Wars. On May 9, 1918, the Germania briefly changed its name to the Chicago Lincoln Club. Membership fell through the 1920s until 1935, when the club had to file for bankruptcy reorganization, from which it was able to successfully emerge in 1939. During World War II the club struggled to keep a low profile while trying to manage the sympathies of its members. According to its president, A.F.W. Siebel:

> Racial and religious hatreds are also rampant in the world today. It has been my purpose to steer an even keel so as not to upset our equilibrium in the center of such antagonistic sentiments and send us into fields of activities, which, once entered, would automatically compel continuous pursuit and eventually destroy us. Our club does not exist for such purposes. Its object is to foster and advance a taste for music and social gatherings and the refined enjoyment of life.

Hamilton Club (1890): One of the earliest Republican clubs in the city, the Hamilton Club was located at 14–26 S. Dearborn Street, the site of what is now known as Chase Tower.

Illinois Athletic Club (1907): Now part of the School of the Art Institute of Chicago, the old IAC has been refurbished for office and classroom space, though the school now rents out the old club's 1927 vintage ballroom.

Illinois Women's Athletic Club: See Chapter 24, "The Woman's Athletic Club."

Iroquois Club (1882): Politics was the main activity of the Iroquois Club, which was known as an organization of "silk-stocking Democrats." Located in the Brunswick Hotel at Michigan Avenue and Adams, the Iroquois Club was an early king-making organization for the Democratic Party. However, the Republican-leaning *Chicago Daily Tribune* didn't miss an opportunity to use the club's name to attack the club's opposition leanings:

> The Iroquois were once a strong tribe in New York, but as early as 1600, whenever they got into serious trouble, they migrated to Canada and carried on their hostile operations from that point. We need not make application further than to point out that the Democratic Party on more than one historical occasion has found Canada a convenient refuge from

The exterior of the Lake Shore Athletic Club after its opening in 1927. (Courtesy of Preservation Chicago.)

The club's current lobby. (Courtesy of Preservation Chicago.)

enforced service at home and from which to distribute the sinews of war to active partisans on the side.

Lake Shore Athletic Club (1927): As this book was nearing publication, this venerable Streeterville club on inner Lake Shore Drive had been saved from the wrecking ball. In late 2007, local preservationists and politicians successfully pressured the building's owner, Northwestern University, to drop a deal with a developer who wanted to demolish the structure to build a luxury condomini-

*The club's
pool, now
closed.
(Courtesy of
Preservation
Chicago.)*

um in favor of one willing to turn the existing structure into luxury senior housing.

Architect Jarvis Hunt—who is also responsible for the Michigan
Boulevard Building at 30 N. Michigan—designed the Lake Shore
Athletic Club in 1924 and opened it about three years later. The
club's indoor pool hosted the Olympic trials for the 1928 Games.
Northwestern bought the structure in the late 1970s and used it as
graduate housing, but stopped placing students there in 2005 in
hopes of a sale.

Before the worst of the Depression, the club had more than 400
members, with James R. Offield, son-in-law of William Wrigley, as
its first president. When the club closed, its membership was less
than half that.

Lakota Club (1893): The Lakota Club, with a membership limited
to 300, was located on the South Side at Calumet Avenue and 45th
Street. The social club chose the name Lakota because it signified
"a gathering of friends."

The Little Room (1898–1931): Before he founded The Cliff Dwellers,
Hamlin Garland founded the Little Room with fellow novelist
Henry B. Fuller, author of the novel *The Cliff-Dwellers*. The Little
Room was a rare coed gathering of men and women from the arts.
The name of the club (which met at the Fine Arts Building on

Michigan Avenue) was taken from the title of a short story written by Madeleine Yale Wynne, which appeared in *Harper's Monthly* in the 1890s, about a mysterious room where a visitor with the right frame of mind would find companionship and happiness. About 30 to 40 members would meet regularly on Friday afternoons for light music, drama, or some other presentation. Among the other members were George Ade, Hobart Chatfield-Taylor, Alice Gerstenberg, James T. Hatfield, Franklin Harvey Head, John T. McCutcheon, Anna Morgan, Allen Bartlit Pond, Henry Kitchell Webster, and Edith Wyatt.

M & M Club: This elegant luncheon and dinner club in the Merchandise Mart building closed in the early 1990s when the Merchandise Mart redeveloped its space, turning the first two floors into a shopping mall. For a brief period in the 1980s and early 1990s, it was home to the Traffic Club of Chicago. Sadly, the Mart's management has no information or photo archives on this club.

Guests of the InterContinental Hotel still get to swim in this pool that was initially described as follows: "The Swimming Pool, with its crystal clear azure water; with its ceiling of dark walnut; its beautiful carved stone architecture – is reminiscent of Venice although it approaches Modern Italian in its period." (Courtesy of InterContinental Chicago.)

In an original club photo, the caption reads: "Imperial Potentate Leo V. Youngworth and Imperial Chief Rabban T. Houston on a recent visit to Medinah Temple." The Medinah Temple was the ornate convention space built by Chicago-area Shriners at 600 N. Wabash. Today, it's the site of Bloomingdale's Home and Furniture Store. (Courtesy of InterContinental Chicago.)

Marquette Club (1886): This early men's club met at a location near the intersection of Dearborn and Maple.

Medinah Athletic Club (1929–34): Anyone visiting the InterContinental Chicago hotel at 505 N. Michigan Avenue knows they're standing in a special building. What they might not know is that this was one of the most opulent private clubs built before the Great Depression. The Medinah has been a hotel property for most of its time since closing, but the InterContinental used club records to complete its refurbishing of the property in 1988, right down to the detailing of draperies, carpets, and murals.

Merchants Club (1896–1907): See Chapter 12, "The Commercial Club of Chicago." In brief, this was the club that gathered the initial funds for Daniel Burnham's development and authorship of the historic *Plan of Chicago*, the blueprint for Chicago's rebuilding after the Great Fire.

Sunset Club (1889): Club founder W.W. Catlin, a member of the Chicago Board of Trade, saw the Sunset Club's mission as "to foster rational good fellowship and tolerant discussion among business and professional men of all classes." It was, at its heart, an informal debating society. In a *Chicago Herald* piece, Lyman J. Gage, president of the World's Columbian Exposition, said that what he liked best about the Sunset Club was "its wakefulness—it was ever abreast of the times on all subjects in which the people were interested."

The piece described the environment of the club this way:

> At one of the club dinners, a certain railroad official whose road had had serious trouble with its employees found himself at table with a walking delegate whose utterances and advice had been diametrically opposed to the interests of his company. Having opened a bottle of wine he sent a glass to the delegate with his compliments. Neither had ever met before, but each knew the other by reputation, and the railroad man had formed a most unjust conception of the delegate's character and disposition. He believed the man to be a boor and sent the wine to test his breeding. With perfect taste, however, the labor agitator raised the glass in his right hand, acknowledged the courtesy with a polite bow and at once emptied the glass. Since then the same delegate has several times spoken at the club meetings in the hearing of the railroad official, who now entertains a vastly different opinion of the laborers' champion.

The Sunset Club had a fairly lighthearted declaration of principles, which went as follows:

> No Club-House
> No Constitution
> No Debts
> No Contribution

The Lost Clubs

No Accounts
No Defalcations
No Bylaws
No Stipulations

No Profanity
No Fines
No Stealing
No Combines

No President
No Bores
No Steward
No "Encores"

No Long Speeches
No Dress Coats
No Late Hours
No Perfumed Notes

No Parliamentary Rules
No Personalities
No Dudes
No Mere Formalities

No Preaching
No Dictation
No Dues
No Litigation

No Gamblers
No Dead Beats
No Embezzlers from Foreign Retreats

No Meanness
No Vituperation

Simply Tolerant Discussion and Rational Recreation.

Twentieth Century Club (1889): According to the *Encyclopedia of Chicago*, the Twentieth Century Club was a cultural and literary club composed of members from the city's best families. Its mission was to help Chicago overcome "its reputation for coarseness." The club was created by Mrs. George R. Genevieve Jones Grant of Prairie Avenue and several of her friends in the mold of twentieth century clubs in New York and other cities.

Whitechapel Club (1889): The Whitechapel Club was the much crazier parent of the Chicago Press Club. The club was dedicated to Jack the Ripper; a life-size effigy stood inside the club on Calhoun Place, then an alley near LaSalle Street. If you believed a *Chicago Tribune* piece written in 1890, each table featured the "skull of a murderer." The paper offered this description of the clubhouse:

> The room is triangular. Long, narrow tables run through the center spaces. But this goes for little. It is the walls that give the 'Whitechapel Club' a distinctive character. There one finds the rope that hanged the three Italians who did that ghastly murder on the West Side.

Sources:
Blair, Edward T. *An Early History of The Chicago Club*. Chicago: The Chicago Club, 1898.
Dedmon, Emmett. *Fabulous Chicago*. New York: Athenaeum, 1981.
Dubin, Arthur Detmers. Interview by Betty J. Blum. Transcript. Chicago Architects Oral History Project.
"Death of the Chicago Press Club." Broadcast transcript. *John Madigan Views the Press*. WBBM-AM radio, 10 February 1987.
The Ernest R. Graham Study Center for Architectural Drawings. Department of Architecture, the Art Institute of Chicago.
Germania Club. *Germania Club 100th Anniversary Book*. Chicago: Germania Club, 1964.
Herguth, Robert C. "Women Admit Their Age: Charitable Club Closing Its Doors." *Chicago Sun-Times*, 13 May 1999, p. 5.

"Surpasses Them All. The Noted Sunset Club of Chicago: An Organization That Would Have Delighted the Heart of Mr. Pickwick — Brief History of This Unique Club and Its Remarkable Success." *Chicago Herald*, 26 April 1893.

"With Skulls for Bowls: A Night in the Suddenly Famous Whitechapel Club." *Chicago Daily Tribune*, 28 February 1890, p. 8.

PART II

THE PRESENT

The Big Four

———

VIII

THE
CHICAGO
CLUB

———◆———

The Chicago Club
Founded: 1869
Address: 81 E. Van Buren Street,
Chicago, IL 60605
Architect: John C. Bollenbacher and
Alfred Hoyt Granger (Granger and Bollenbacher)

Jim Farrell, retired chairman of Illinois Tool Works in Glenview, remembers the first time he went inside the Chicago Club. What impressed him most wasn't the stateliness of the historic surroundings or the fact he was in a place where so few get to go. This is how he described that first visit:

I was probably in my early 30s when I moved to Chicago, and I was a junior executive at ITW at the time. Back then the CEO of ITW was a man named Silas Cathcart, and one day Si took me to the Chicago Club to meet some people.

The Chicago Club's current club-
house, built on the site of the origi-
nal Art Institute of Chicago. (Photo
by Lisa Holton.)

W. James Farrell. (Courtesy of
Illinois Tool Works.)

Back then we were a couple hundred million in size, not the biggest company in the world by any stretch. And once we got there, Si looked at me and said, "Stay right with me, and if I don't say the person's name, stick your hand right out there and say yours so they'll mention theirs." Of course, Si never missed a beat—he knew everybody's name, and one by one, I met them. That day was one of my greatest lessons in how real leaders behave.

Much is made of the value of business networking in today's society, and there are plenty of places to do it—professional associations, industry conclaves, and, for many, even a coffee shop will do. But going back through the city's history, the Chicago Club is the only bricks-and-mortar club that has drawn and maintained a

The gilded lobby staircase. (Courtesy of the Chicago Club.)

The club's main lounge, facing Michigan Avenue. (Courtesy of the Chicago Club.)

consistent level of top social and business leadership from the day it began. While local politicians often visit, it is a temple to the other form of clout that matters in Chicago—old money mixed with the highest levels of corporate power.

The bottom line is that if you're a top executive, the Chicago Club is your number one target.

The Chicago Club has always drawn the city's elite families—it has merited a standing listing in *The Social Register*'s private club section for most of its history—but today it pulls a significant portion of its membership from top executive suites and next-generation talent at major companies and civic organizations. The clubhouse has hosted key national and international decision makers

71

through the years, even the ever-controversial Trilateral Commission.

The club has allowed journalists as members—most notably, Emmett Dedmon, a former top editor of the *Chicago Sun-Times* and the *Chicago Daily News*—but continues a lifelong restriction against media events inside the club. Therefore, the club is an excellent choice for secret meetings that need to stay secret.

Farrell's memory is a common one at the Chicago Club—one of older, experienced executives bringing younger executives through the door to see if they'll click, to see if they make a good fit to carry the club into the future. Farrell himself became a member a few years after that first visit. Women were finally admitted in 1982, and though the club won't state precisely when, members say that men of color first started getting invitations in the 1970s as pressure to integrate finally reached the corporate and civic ranks. Today Si Cathcart's exercise happens with a far more diverse base of membership than ever before.

Charles K. Bobrinskoy, vice chairman of Ariel Mutual Funds, is like most members of the Chicago Club—he holds other important invitation-only club memberships, including the Commercial Club and the Economic Club. He emphasizes that such memberships go far beyond the status they deliver, saying that the most elite clubs in the city still help time-pressed executives do more on the job and on the charitable activities that show up on most top executives' plates. He explains:

At this level, the need for networking actually goes up, not down. Historically, the senior levels of the Chicago business community also tend to be very active in the civic community, so a lot of us are on the same boards and we're dealing with the same issues. So I can see, for example, Jim Farrell at the Chicago Club, and he and I can talk about issues relating to the Museum of Science and Industry and to the Big Shoulders Catholic Schools in a five-minute conversation. And then he'll go see Andy McKenna, who's on five boards, the United Way, etcetera. Networking person-to-person is a way to develop relationships, but it's also a way to speed up the communication you need to have. Clubs put you in the center of that.

Charles K. Bobrinskoy.
(Courtesy of Ariel
Capital Management.)

THE CHICAGO CLUB . . . AND THE STANDARD CLUB

The Chicago Club's history describes it as "the pioneer club of the West," though it clearly wasn't the first aspiring elite men's club formed in the city. In fact, its first members were believed to have come from the former Dearborn Club that held its meetings across the street from where the current Palmer House now stands. The Marquette Club at Dearborn and Maple was another close competitor, but died soon after the Chicago Club was in operation.

In January 1869 a meeting was called in the club room of the Sherman House, at that time Chicago's leading hotel (the Palmer House wouldn't open until 1871), for the purpose of gathering men from the city's top families and institutions under one roof. To ensure that status, the initiation fee was a hefty $100.

Founding members of the Chicago Club included David and George Gage, among the first members of the Chicago City Council; prominent attorney Wirt Dexter; merchant C.B. Farwell, generally regarded as the man who gave Marshall Field his first big job in retailing; and railcar magnate George M. Pullman. Edward S. Isham, a partner of Robert Todd Lincoln in the now-defunct law firm that would become Isham, Lincoln & Beale, prepared the papers of incorporation. And in the years immediately following the Civil War, the club also counted General Philip H. Sheridan as a member.

The Sherman House. (From History of Chicago, *Vol.* 2, *by A. T. Andreas.)*

It should be noted that the Standard Club (see Chapter 10)—formed by the city's rising population of affluent German-American Jews—lagged behind the opening of the Chicago Club by only a few months in 1869. The Standard Club and the Chicago Club are significant because they are the two oldest full-service clubs that survive today, and really, the "who came first" question is much less interesting than the forces that caused them to open their doors.

Chicago's boomtown culture, with population growing exponentially in those early years, led virtually every ethnic and racial group in Chicago that was barred from majority club membership to gather and identify their elite through their own clubs and organizations. In the 1860s Jews were forced to develop their own clubhouse structure because the time when they would be fully welcome in the Chicago Club and other majority clubs was still years away.

In the Chicago Club's early system, the entire club would vote on candidates, and six adverse votes would expel the applicant. In Edward T. Blair's early history of the club, blackballing was a common revenge tactic for members who had gotten their own nominees tossed.

In the dirty, dangerous, and politically corrupt town that Chicago was back then, the Chicago Club, the Standard Club, and others helped settle and build the city and, to a great extent, a private-sector power base that exists largely to this day.

THE GREAT FIRE OF 1871 AND THE PANIC OF 1873

Prohibition and the Great Depression were events that coincided and endangered the lives of Chicago clubs in the twentieth century. In the nineteenth century there was a remarkable parallel—the Great Fire of 1871 followed closely by the Panic of 1873. Many of the early entrepreneurs who came to Chicago to make their fortune leveraged heavily to rebound from their losses in the Great Fire only to be wiped out when the economic downturn came.

The Chicago Club lost everything during the Great Fire—in fact, on the second day of the blaze, its first clubhouse (at the Henry Farnham mansion on Michigan Avenue between Adams and Jackson streets) caught fire. Members who had shipped off their families and had their businesses burned out in the surrounding areas had spent the night at the club draining the liquor cabinet and watching the fire advance until they had to flee to safety.

Weeks later the club moved into temporary quarters at a residence at 279 Michigan Avenue. (Michigan Avenue was contained south of the river, so there was no north and south until after Pine Street north of the river was renamed North Michigan Avenue.) Two months after the fire, the club spent two years in the Gregg House, at 476 Wabash Avenue.

The Farnham Mansion, once home to railroad magnate Henry Farnham and the Chicago Club's first clubhouse. It succumbed to the Chicago Fire in 1871. (Courtesy of the Chicago Club.)

As much as the Chicago Fire provided a tremendous opportunity for rebuilding, the immediate aftermath created a culture of lawlessness that for a time would reach inside the elite clubhouse. Thugs would hide out in the burned wreckage of the central city, waiting to prey on the rich businessmen heading for their clubs. Chicago Club members started carrying concealed pistols with them on the way to the clubhouse, and on one occasion the club's history reports that two members progressed from a loud verbal argument over a card game to drawn weapons. Typically, both members would have been expelled, but the nation's economic collapse created a serious need to keep every possible paying member in the club, so the president convinced the board to let them stay.

Between 1873 and 1875 nearly 100 of the Chicago Club's most prominent members resigned or were dropped for nonpayment of dues. It was time to do something quick. On February 1, 1875, board members scrambled to convince members that it was time to buy a new location for a centrally located clubhouse that would be more of an attraction. To afford the $35,000 asking price for Potter Palmer's land on Monroe across the street from the rebuilt Palmer House (where the historic hotel stands today), the club's leaders created a stock offering that every member was required to hold.

The Chicago's second official clubhouse at State and Monroe. (Courtesy of the Chicago Club.)

The new club location on Monroe—officially its second address—opened in July 1876 to great public fanfare, even though the club still couldn't afford furniture for its upper floors. As the economic fog began to lift, the Chicago Club's fortunes began to improve. On September 13, 1878, it hosted its first presidential visit, that of President and Mrs. Rutherford B. Hayes.

As mentioned, the city's victory in obtaining the World's Columbian Exposition set new building and construction plans into motion for the entire city, and clubs wanted to join the building boom by creating even more opulent clubhouses. By 1890 the Chicago Club decided its space on Monroe had gotten too cramped for a major club in a city with Chicago's aspirations.

So the Chicago Club's directors started to examine in 1890 what is now its current space on Van Buren, soon to be vacated by the newly named Art Institute of Chicago, which wanted its own world-class building across the street on Michigan Avenue. The Art Institute would share the cost of its current structure with the World's Columbian Exposition, which initially used the structure for the fair's scholarly congresses before turning it over to the Institute at the fair's conclusion. There was an important Chicago Club connection at the Art Institute. He was Charles L. Hutchinson, a powerful local banker and club member who would transform the Art Institute from a school run by artists to a world-class educational and exhibition institution run by the biggest money in town.

The club's real estate decisions were serendipitous. The Chicago Club sold the Monroe clubhouse to the Columbus Club for $220,000, and it began selling all its assets, including its sizable stockholdings in the Dearborn Club, to afford the $640,000 price tag for the new space it currently occupies at Michigan and Van Buren. During the Exposition Chicago Club members entertained more than 6,000 guests, going so far as to create a special club on the lakefront accessible by yacht to entertain high-society visitors (see the Argo Club discussion in Chapter 7).

Eventually, the club would replace the original Art Institute site and its annex with the structure that stands today. There was a near-tragic experience during this process. About a month after the renovation started in 1928, a club watchman reported for work at

*The first Van Buren
clubhouse, originally
the home of the Art
Institute of Chicago.
(Courtesy of the
Chicago Club.)*

4:30 on a Sunday morning and found the timbers over his head
creaking in an ominous fashion. He ran out of the club and called
a policeman. Both men rushed to seal off the entrances. They went
inside again, felt the walls shake, and luckily crawled out seconds
before the interior of the building collapsed.

If the disaster had happened on a weekday, a significant part of
Chicago's leadership class would probably have been wiped out.
Efforts to restore the building were deemed pointless, and the
remains were demolished and carted away, after which the current
version of the Chicago Club was built.

THE "LITTLE SONS OF THE RICH"

At the turn of the century, both the club and its members had
returned to robust financial health. A "millionaires' table" in the
northeast corner of the Chicago Club's main dining room was the
regular lunch stop for Marshall Field, Henry W. Bishop, and T.B.
Blackstone. A "railroad table" formed in the southeast corner of
the dining room, and a third table irreverently referred to as the
"Little Sons of the Rich" was a home for second-generation members of the club, including Walter Keith, Edward Tyler Blair,

*Interior of the collapsed
Chicago Club, June* 1928.
*(Courtesy of the Chicago
Club.)*

Watson Blair, Edward Doane, Stanley Field, James Walker,
Emerson Tuttle, and Richard T. Crane Jr., among others.

Dedmon's history interviewed Stanley Field, who reported that
although he did not sit at the millionaires' table, "Everything that
was to be done in Chicago was discussed by that group, and then
the word was passed out."

The turn of the century at the Chicago Club was particularly
notable because the giants were starting to die off. Philip D.
Armour and T.B. Blackstone died in 1900, and in 1902 so went
Edward S. Isham, J. Sterling Morton, Potter Palmer, and Perry
Trumbull. The club's average wait for new members was now ten
years, which was tremendous for the club's reputation but damag-
ing to the infusion of new blood. After the end of World War I,
members successfully lobbied to raise the Chicago Club's resident
member limit from 700 to 850 members.

But there was a bigger issue on the horizon—Prohibition. As
was done at most private clubs in the city, elaborate plans were
made to stockpile and hide liquor (see Chapter 3). Even today the
billiards room at the Chicago Club still features hidden trapdoors
in the paneling for a member to hide his cocktail in case of a
raid—of which, of course, there is no record. But there were other
ingenious solutions as well.

THE INNER CLUBS

Most of the major private clubs in Chicago featured clubs within a club. The Chicago Club's attempt at this idea served two purposes: it brought together men of like minds in special rooms decorated as mini-clubhouses and gave members a very private place to drink while the 18th Amendment flourished. There were as many as six Inner Clubs during their heyday, but after a recent addition for younger members known as Room 503, there are now five. These clubs are located on different floors near the lodging space of the club, marked by neat little signs mounted to the wall that only suggest what goes on inside.

The top Inner Club today is known as Room 100. It was established at a round table in the Chicago Club in December 1920 under the original name of the Slippery Elm Club. It was an eclectic membership-only group that featured one important benefit—the membership of Thomas W. Hinde, who owned a distillery in Kentucky and managed to keep the club full of good Bourbon during Prohibition. It is also the only one of the Inner Clubs to have published its own history and today is populated by CEOs and their guests.

Room 1871, an inner club, was formed in memory of the Chicago Fire and features firefighter memorabilia throughout the space. (Courtesy of the Chicago Club.)

Room 19, another Inner Club, has a railroad theme inspired by the early railroad magnates who were once leaders of the club. Lastly, there is an Inner Club in Rooms 800–803 of the clubhouse's lodging area, Room 1871 (which was founded for younger members in 1976), and a new group of associate members reforming a club from the 1920s in Room 503.

THE GREAT DEPRESSION

The club's history shows that few veteran members of the Chicago Club were hit hard by the Crash of 1929, but as the downturn deepened and started to poison business everywhere, mostly younger members took the blow. During 1932 the total number of resident members slid from 905 to 706, and nonresident membership dropped from 357 to 299. The much-envied ten-year waiting list evaporated. A letter-writing campaign was begun to keep selected members in the club who had resigned, offering them the chance to rejoin with a full forgiveness of past obligations. The club also developed its first associate and junior memberships at reduced fees. Northwestern Mutual Life Insurance Co., which held the mortgage on the new clubhouse, was worried as well—the lender helped force the changes in membership.

It was a survival move for an organization and a class of individuals that had never really faced a survival struggle before. But as any experienced club member will say, the most valuable asset for a club isn't necessarily the real estate or the bank account—it's the quality of the people inside.

Indeed, by 1937 the roughest patch seemed to be behind the club and the country. The club had about $7,500 in the bank when Stanley Field made the following statement at the 1938 New Year's Day luncheon:

Gentlemen. I have a small announcement I am going to make. We all know it has been a struggle here to keep this club going in pretty tough times, putting up legacy for your mortgages and everything, and I hear every day that the club is broke and is going to close. And I keep telling people it isn't. I would like to make a statement and here are the figures—

CLUB NOTES

The New Year's Day luncheon, a tradition at the Chicago Club, began in 1901. Members would arrive in morning coats, striped pants, and top hats, their carriages polished and horses specially groomed for the day. There was never a special program at the luncheon—just a few remarks by the president and some original songs led by one of the members. Today the morning coats are gone and the date of the luncheon has changed, too, to the Friday after New Year's Day—the latter thanks largely to the full roster of college football games that members prefer to watch from home. Even still, the date is probably the most important at the club, and it all has to do with a woman named Aunt Clara.

The tune, "Aunt Clara" was penned by member John D. Black. It's a ballad about a small-town choir singer who had left town in shame and was told the following:

. . . she'd live in the muck and the mud—

The redoubtable Aunt Clara.
(Courtesy of the Chicago Club.)

Yet the paper just published a snap
Of Aunt Clara at Nice with a Prince
of the blood
And a Bishop asleep in her
lap.
They say that she's
sunken, they say that
she fell
From the narrow and
virtuous path,
But her French formal
gardens are sunken as
well
And so is her pink marble
bath.

As Black would start the song, an oil portrait featuring a prim and proper spinster would be displayed for the crowd. But as the men joined in on the following chorus…

We never mention Aunt Clara
Her picture is turned to the wall
Though she lives on the French Riviera
Mother says that she's dead to us all.

The portrait would be flipped over to reveal quite the opposite vision of Aunt Clara, above. Today both portraits have a permanent home in Room 100.

the bills are paid and there is cash in the bank—and the club is not going broke. It's a permanent institution in Chicago. Now, I hope I don't have to repeat that again.

The club's history adds, "With his last words, there was a great cheer, everybody reached for his glass of champagne and there were more toasts to the success of the Club."

ON THE SUBJECT OF WOMEN . . .

As was the case in many other private clubs in Chicago, the admission of women was a longtime topic of controversy at the Chicago Club. In 1876 the bylaws were amended to allow women in the club on Thursdays. At some point (which is unclear from the records) the club stopped giving public receptions, and the doors closed to women again. Women were readmitted as guests in 1979 but were required to enter the club through a separate entrance until 1982, when women were admitted as full members of the Chicago Club. (The Chicago Club was a specific target of one of the lawsuits filed to open up the clubs in the 1970s. Much of the club's history in admitting women is covered in Chapters 6 and 8.)

There were but a few breaches during the 100 years or so when women were barred from the club. According to the club's history, Mrs. John B. Lyon was allowed three clandestine days in the club to nurse member Charles Rhodes back to health from typhoid fever. And Kate Buckingham, who in the mid-1920s donated $700,000 to the city for a fountain in memory of her brother Clarence, was actually brought into the clubhouse after slipping in front of the entrance and breaking her leg. (She got to stay inside until the ambulance arrived.)

But change was incremental. In 1978 influential members, including former Illinois senator Charles Percy, voted in favor of allowing women into the club *as guests*. Yet in his postcard ballot, Percy wrote a note anticipating the next hurdle: "Thanks for the study you have given this issue. I actually favor membership as well."

There was plenty of grumbling, but the club's records show only one resignation—S. Kip Farrington Jr., a nonresident member in

East Hampton, New York, identified as a well-known sportsman and author. He wrote to the club, "please accept this as my resignation from the Club. After being a member thirty-four years it is too bad to have to go out because of women. You will soon know you have made a serious mistake."

Others chose to echo Farrington's sentiments with, literally, a last supper. According to the club's history, "The atmosphere was funereal—or rather, a mixture between a funeral and an Irish wake. One member had caused several small but exquisite signs to be printed and framed; one read 'The Chicago Club R.I.P. 1978.'"

The club's Executive Committee in 1979 made a sweeping move—it rewrote the company's bylaws to remove masculine usages and in particular changed all occurrences of the word *servant* to *employees*. Much more quietly, it granted itself the ability to appoint members it found suitable, thereby enabling the committee to essentially open the door to women members in 1982 without so much as a membership vote. In one fell swoop, the club named two women concurrently to membership: Jean Allard (a leading Chicago attorney and former vice president of the University of Chicago) and Hanna Holborn Gray (then president of the University of Chicago).

One last point. When women were admitted as guests and, four years later, as full members, the club reported that revenues immediately headed up. With the extra money in the bank, the club was able to launch a renovation in 1980.

As it turned out, women were good for business at the all-business Chicago Club.

THE CHARACTER OF THE CLUB TODAY

Farrell's comments back at the beginning of this chapter reflect what the Chicago Club is today. At its founding it was regarded as a social club for men at the highest level of society. Today the club is most commonly referred to as the city's most elite business club.

While social events—weddings, conferences, receptions, and parties chief among them—hosted by members go on at the Chicago Club all the time, the nature and purpose of the club is strictly corporate. Longtime names familiar to Chicago society are still members, but it is not a club like the Woman's Athletic Club, The Casino, or The Fortnightly, where lineage is still seen as a major consideration for membership.

Unlike the other Big Four clubs, the Chicago Club has not invested heavily in gym and spa facilities. Also, its total square footage for lodging and meeting space is probably the smallest among the top clubs given the size of its building. But it doesn't seem to matter, even though Chicago has lost a significant number of its earliest headquarters companies since the 1980s. Farrell explains:

> We're looking for leadership, and that doesn't always mean that someone has to have the letters *CEO* behind his or her name to join. We're looking for people who are going to take an active interest in the employment and cultural future of the city. We like to describe ourselves as "active but reserved." I almost dare to say that with very few exceptions, there are no egos that are that big. People are too busy getting things done.

Are there any top leaders who wouldn't be welcome in the club today? Farrell pauses and then responds:

> I don't say anyone gets blackballed, I won't go that far, but you are definitely looking to maintain the character of the kind of people who have always been in the club. We don't want anyone who is egregious in terms of personality — like a Donald Trump.

Sources:
Blair, Edward T. *An Early History of The Chicago Club.*
    Chicago: The Chicago Club, 1898.
Bobrinskoy, Charles. Interview by author. 23 June 2005.
Dedmon, Emmett. *A History of the Chicago Club.* Chicago: the
    Chicago Club, 1960.

Farrell, James. Interview by author. 28 June 2005.
Wittebort, Robert J., Jr. *The Chicago Club*, 1960–1994. Chicago: 1995.

IX

THE
UNION LEAGUE
CLUB
OF
CHICAGO

The Union League Club of Chicago
Founded: 1879
Address: 65 W. Jackson Boulevard,
Chicago, IL 60604
Architect: William Le Baron Jenney

The Union League, long before the name was associated with elegant private clubs in Chicago, New York, and Philadelphia, was a crafty little spy organization born in downstate Pekin that first fought for the Union cause during the Civil War and helped build the Republican Party.

The nation was crazy for such organizations back in the 1800s because they offered pomp and circumstance and a certain amount of tantalizing secrecy, particularly in wartime. In James D. Nowlan's book about the Union League Club, entitled *Glory, Darkness, Light: A History of the Union League Club of Chicago,* he points out that the war between the states only added fire to the mystery, intrigue, and ritual already inherent in these groups.

The ULCC'*s current clubhouse. (Photo by Lisa Holton.)*

Amelia Earhart (center) was invited to join women guests of the ULCC *in 1936. (Courtesy of the Union League Club of Chicago.)*

Members of the Union League made it their mission to keep a close watch on such groups that featured Southern sympathizers, particularly the Knights of the Golden Circle and their more militant arm, the Sons of Liberty, both active in Northern territory.

Union League chapters spread quickly, not only for patriotic reasons but because they had direct—and secret—funding from the White House. The Lincoln administration's secret support of the Union League was a political masterstroke. The administration's dollars not only supported a neat little populist war intelligence function but also created a powerful political action committee that successfully secured Lincoln's reelection in 1864. Union Leagues were filled largely with wealthy conservatives with one important twist—they urged freed black slaves to vote and accepted freedmen as Union League members.

The Union League supervised war relief efforts, including the training and supply of nurses, and helped build the first Union regiments of freed slaves. As the war's fortunes gradually turned in favor of the North, the Union League focused its attention mainly on local and national politics. The Union League's outreach to African-Americans was a significant factor in locking up the early black vote in favor of the Party of Lincoln. That's not to say, however, that the Republican Party—or the Union League Club— would consistently maintain their close initial ties to the African-American community.

Those very Republican, patriotic roots are still very apparent in the Union League Club of Chicago, something of an anomaly in the center of one of the most Democratic cities in America. It is a club that, like its crosstown rival the Standard Club, celebrates the memory of George Washington. But unlike the other leading clubs in Chicago that tend to relish their privacy, the Union League Club has waged a notably high-profile public agenda since its formation. Its Public Affairs Committee has taken action on major civic and legal issues ranging from the fight to convict Al Capone to its most recent effort to convince Illinois and support former governor George Ryan (also a Union League member) to suspend the death penalty in 2000.

To this date, the club's motto is "commitment to country and community." That commitment has taken interesting turns

The ULCC *'s main dining room. (Courtesy of the Union League Club of Chicago.)*

Boardroom meeting space for members. (Courtesy of the Union League Club of Chicago.)

throughout its history. Jonathan McCabe, the club's general manager, explains:

> The Union League Club was put together as a civic organization rather than a social club. Its founding members were Jews, Catholics, and Protestants, which in the 1870s and 1880s was unheard of in a club but de rigueur in business. Its social club aspects really evolved later, and it was very ecumenical in the beginning.

Like most private clubs in Chicago, the Union League Club did not always stay ecumenical. It wavered on its Jewish membership

and admitted its first African-American member only after a bruis-
ing membership battle in 1969 (that member, Frederick C. Ford,
would eventually become the club's first African-American president). It also worked notably hard to keep its all-male status late
into the 1980s. In fact, even as public outcry over the admission of
women put extraordinary scrutiny on the club, the Union League
was still the very last of the major men's clubs to go coed and had
to be threatened with permanent loss of its liquor license to seal the
deal.

But its ability to crusade and change, however late in the game,
has made it a survivor among Chicago's most historic private clubs
with a unique sense of purpose that exists to this day.

FROM THE UNION LEAGUE TO THE UNION LEAGUE CLUB

Chicago had survived the Civil War, the Great Fire, the economic
crisis of 1873–79, and the labor riots of 1877 more or less intact.
But as noted earlier in this book, the club movement wasn't so
much about creating a sanctuary for the rich from the mass disorder in the streets, finance, and government. Instead, it served to
create a new power structure that would bring that disorder to
heel. Chicago in the immediate aftermath of the Great Fire was a
lawless, devastated piece of land that held despair for many and
incredible potential for only a chosen few. Particularly in desperate
times, the "chosen" in America have tended to ruthlessly define
themselves.

That was definitely the case for "Long John" Wentworth. The
two-term Republican Chicago mayor was a former journalist and
proclaimed reformer known for the unusual tactic of raiding and
burning out North Side shantytowns that had become full of squat-
ters during the 1850s. Two decades after his political zenith,
Nowlan writes, Wentworth found himself adrift in the 1870s and
was looking for a new bully pulpit. Owen Salisbury, a Union
League member who was looking for a job, saw potential in
Wentworth's quest for a comeback and convinced him of the need
for a new patriotic men's club in Chicago that would make a fine
"marching club"—essentially, a local political action committee—
for the third presidential campaign of Ulysses Grant. Grant's run

would fail, and Wentworth never made it to the top of the political heap again, but it forged an early alliance of younger men on the make who aspired to local leadership but didn't quite have the bloodline or wealth to make it into the elite the Chicago Club.

As club biographer Nowlan put it:

> The Chicago Club had been started a decade earlier and was reserved for the small number of very wealthy leaders of business and society—those who had already made it. The Union League was going to be a club who was *going* to make it.

CLUB NOTES

⤙ THE $500 MONET ⤚

The Union League Club, with more than 750 separate paintings, sculptures, works on paper, and decorative arts pieces, has probably the most extensive art collection among any of Chicago's private clubs.

In 1895 the club's Art Committee managed to buy a painting, called *Pommiers en Fleurs (Apple Trees in Blossom; Le Printemps; Springtime)*, from a then barely known Claude Monet for $500, roughly one-third its value at that time. John H. Hamline, the club's president at the time, had the painting put away. He reportedly commented, "Who would pay $500 for that blob of paint?" It's obviously worth in the millions today.

*The ULCC's art collec-
tion includes contempo-
rary American and
Native American artists,
and pays special atten-
tion to patriotic art. In
1997, the Club estab-
lished an on-site con-
servation laboratory
and added a paintings
conservator to the staff,
making it the only club
in Chicago with a full-
time curator and an in-
house paintings conser-
vator. (Courtesy of the
Union League Club of
Chicago.)*

A NEW CLUB IS BORN

In its first year, the Union League Club of Chicago spent most of its
time arguing in rented meeting space in the Sherman House about
what it really wanted to be—a political club or a social club. The
political approach certainly worked in 1880 when the Republican
Convention came to town. But what would come afterward?

The answer was something quite different—a club that would
be a very public hybrid of business, politics, and civic endeavor. In
the late 1880s the prevailing concept of a men's club was exclusively social, meaning that it would exist as a refined, exclusive haven
away from business, politics, and the strains of home (read that,
the demands of wives and children). This was not to say that business, politics, and dramatic actions weren't discussed behind closed
doors in all men's clubs—what else was that interesting to talk
about, other than sports?

But transparency certainly wasn't the goal at the Union League
Club of Chicago, which was different from the start. In fact, for a

William LeBaron Jenney, noted architect and member of the club, designed the first Union League clubhouse, which opened in 1885. (Courtesy of the Union League Club of Chicago.)

club to state publicly that business or political issues would be an active part of a club's agenda was considered unusual at best and gauche at worst in those times. Nevertheless, the new Union League Club of Chicago wasn't shy about wearing its historic political and patriotic mission on its sleeve. Its articles of association read as follows:

+ To encourage and promote by moral, social and political influences, unconditional loyalty to the Federal Government, and to defend and protect the integrity and perpetuity of this nation.
+ To inculcate a higher appreciation of the value and sacred obligations of American citizenship, to maintain the civil and political equality of all citizens in every section of our common country, and to aid in the enforcement of all laws enacted to preserve the purity of the ballot box.
+ To resist and oppose corruption and to promote economy in office, and to secure honesty and efficiency in the administration of national, state and municipal affairs.

CREATING A PUBLIC AGENDA IN A PRIVATE CLUB

The club's Public Affairs Committee has produced plenty of news and controversy at the club and incited much change in the public sector.

In 1912 the club played a key role in election reform by pushing for the expulsion of U.S. Senator William E. Lorimer after it was revealed that his election to Congress involved bribery. The club's effort was a factor in the creation of the 17th Amendment, which required that U.S. Senators be chosen by popular vote rather than designation by their state legislatures.

And in 1919, after the Chicago race riots that left many dead, club members worked to bring police, prosecutors, and courts to task for discriminatory handling of cases involving African-Americans.

THE "SECRET SIX"

Throughout its history, the Union League, like its compatriots at the Commercial Club and the City Club of Chicago, has fought hard for cleaner elections and cleaner government, a battle that remains joined today.

The scathing 1894 book *If Christ Came to Chicago*, by British minister William T. Stead, drew the world's attention to the corrupt city on the lake with a detailed portrait of Chicago's crooked aldermen, gang crime, and failed government. The Republicans at the Union League Club, frustrated with their crooked Democratic counterparts, began working to eradicate the criminal elements at City Hall and the wards.

The Union League Club has always been heavy with attorneys and prosecutors—law enforcement was always a ready topic of conversation. The scourge of the Capone era was particularly irksome to the club, which saw local government as corrupt and the federal government as do-nothing. Julius Rosenwald, president of Sears, Roebuck and Co. and a rare Jewish member at the Union League and other leading clubs of the day, started pouring his millions into the Chicago Crime Commission as far back as 1919.

Rosenwald, who was once hauled into court on a phony tax evasion charge by officials angry with his public meddling, helped create and fund a secret task force to eradicate Al Capone from Chicago before Chicago's Century of Progress Exposition opened the city to international scrutiny. In addition to Rosenwald, the group, to be called the Secret Six, was made up of Union League club members Frank Loesch, William Barnard, and Ed Gore, as well as utilities magnate Samuel Insull (who would later face sensational fraud charges of his own that he was later acquitted of—see below) and George Paddock. The Secret Six financed and ran what would become a major spy effort to gather information on

SPOTLIGHT

SAM INSULL'S DOWNFALL

Chicago's business aristocracy has had its share of big leaders who have fallen from grace. But Samuel Insull's downfall happened on the world stage.

Insull was critical in the birth of two important business institutions—one international, one local. He was an early builder of General Electric Co. and Commonwealth Edison. He also helped create the Chicago Transit Authority. He foresaw the linkage between modern energy and modern transportation, and it transformed the country.

Insull, born in London in 1859, came to the United States at 22 to become a disciple to Thomas Edison. He later ran Edison's first electrical factory in Schenectady, NY—one of General Electric's first operations.

According to the CTA's own history, when financier J.P. Morgan took over Edison's power companies in 1892, Edison was out and Insull was sent to Chicago to rescue the struggling Chicago Edison Company (later Commonwealth Edison). Insull was a visionary who not only put electricity into homes, but he harnessed its power to create Chicago's elevated transit system.

In the early days of electrical and phone utilities, the landscape was dotted with small, inefficient providers. Insull cleaned up the mess at Chicago Edison and started buying up as many small competitors as the company could get his hands on. According to the CTA, by 1907, all of Chicago's electricity was being generated by Insull's newly named

Capone to feed to the feds and the eventual task force led by Elliot Ness. They even set up a speakeasy called the Garage Café in Cicero—Capone territory—where they could watch the enemy.

THE DEATH PENALTY MORATORIUM

In the 1990s club member William J. Nissen, a partner at Sidley, Austin, Brown and Wood, was the court-appointed lawyer for serial killer John Wayne Gacy. He was left with lingering concerns over the death penalty after Gacy was executed in 1994. As a member of the club's Public Affairs Committee, Nissen proposed that they

Commonwealth Edison Company. At the same time, he leveraged his energy management into unifying rural electrification and in supplying gas.

His fate—which will follow—is ironic given his skill at fighting off the more corrupt businessmen of his time, notably Charles Yerkes and his crooked allies in city government. Yerkes attempted but never succeeded at foiling Insull's efforts to get into the public transportation business. And Insull also ended up controlling Commonwealth Edison by outwitting a trio of crooked politicians (led by former Chicago Mayor John Hopkins) who formed the early utility under that name. Insull would also come to control key rail lines that are now part of the Metra system.

By the time the Great Depression arrived, Insull was one of the top captains of Chicago industry and a member of most of its clubs. A month after the crash, his face appeared on the cover of *Time* magazine as "financial father of the Chicago opera." Yet what most of his colleagues didn't realize was how heavily he was leveraged. Insull had sold low-price bonds and stock to more than a million Americans. Those bonds became worthless after the 1929 market crash. Insull fled the country with a debt of over $16 million by 1932. He was charged with fraud, tried in 1934, and acquitted, but it was too late. His reputation was destroyed and eventually he and his wife left the country for Paris, where he died, supposedly penniless, in 1938.

study the death penalty issue when the Anthony Porter case came up in 1999. (Porter was an Illinois death row inmate whose sentence was commuted after a team of Northwestern University journalism students confirmed his innocence.) Nissen explains:

> Our point was we very well could have had a divergence of interest in the club on whether or not the death penalty is a good thing, but we felt we potentially could have a consensus that the system in Illinois was broken and that it would be best to stop executing people while we took a look at it.

Eventually, club member and former governor George Ryan, after creating a task force that took the Union League's position into consideration, commuted the sentences of 156 inmates on death row in Illinois.

Nissen, who was a Vietnam veteran, says that he was attracted to the club originally for its Armed Forces Council, which provides outreach on many military issues. "We were not looked on with favor in the civilian community when I got back home," comments Nissen. "The Union League looked at me differently."

Indeed, the Union League has a history of supporting and building the U.S. military presence in the Chicago area. Most notably the club helped rehabilitate a depleted National Guard after World War I. At that time Illinois Governor Frank Lowden named 13 members of the club to a commission to revive the National Guard. They went to banks and other businesses in an effort to draw more recruits, and in 1920 the Union League Company was sworn in as Company E of the First Infantry Regiment of the Illinois National Guard.

CHARITABLE WORKS

The Union League has long had specific philanthropic efforts that it has kept operating for decades. The club has operated four Boys & Girls Clubs serving 8,000 inner-city youths and a 250-acre summer camp for kids in Salem, Wisconsin. The club also has two scholarship organizations. The Chicago Engineers' Foundation provides scholarships to college-bound engineering students to help launch their academic careers. The Civic & Arts Foundation provides scholarships and grants to further the creative efforts in art, music, performance, civic endeavors, and academic affairs.

Sources:

McCabe, Jonathan. Interview by author. 23 June 2005.

Nissen, William J. Interview by author. 9 June 2005.

Nowlan, James D. *Glory, Darkness, Light: A History of the Union League Club of Chicago*. Evanston: Northwestern University Press, 2004.

SPOTLIGHT

❧ NO TIPPING ALLOWED! ❧

Many of Chicago's private clubs to this day restrict tipping employees, and it's not about the stinginess of members.

Well, mostly not.

Tipping today is a common activity for most everyone who walks into a restaurant or valet parks a car. But in the early days of the club environment, tipping was regarded as a way to unfairly monopolize the services of club staff with money.

Here's the logic as explained in a letter from one particular club's House Committee to the membership in the mid-1990s:

Again it is time to bring to the attention of our members the fact that tipping of employees is not only a serious violation of Club Rules, but it tends to break down the standard of service rendered by the employees by neglecting some members and favoring others.

It shows lack of consideration for the rest of our membership who wish to abide by the rules and it is embarrassing to the employees, who, when hired, are strictly instructed not to accept tips. Members may show both their generosity and their appreciation by contributing as liberally as they please to the Employees' Annual Holiday Fund, which is distributed among all the employees.

In the club environment, no tipping means no favoritism.

With the rise of workplace laws that started pressuring companies to offer benefits to workers, there came clout to the no-tipping movement. As Christmas funds, pension plans, and eventually, health insurance were provided for club staff, members became doubly adamant about tipping. After all, benefits were expensive enough.

So before you go as a guest to a private club, ask your host about tipping—what's appropriate and what's not.

X

THE
STANDARD CLUB

———— ✦ ————

The Standard Club
Founded: 1869
Address: 320 S. Plymouth Court,
Chicago, IL 60604
Architect: Albert Kahn

The character of the Standard Club is extremely private, as Peter Borzak, the club's 2005 president, will tell you. He acknowledges that the club's low profile was a necessity at first but is more of a preference today. Chicago's Jews, like the city's other minorities, were ever mindful of bigotry that seemed to ebb and flow through the decades. Borzak, a third-generation member, notes:

> The Standard's history, as a Jewish club, was obviously due to business segregation. While there were some Jewish members welcomed in the other clubs, our community became large enough where we needed a dedicated place that welcomed us so we could meet and do business. In those early days and at

later times, there were good reasons to keep out of the public eye. Those reasons are generally gone today, but we keep a low profile because that's what our membership is comfortable with, and after all this time, it's part of our character.

The Standard Club, like all traditional men's clubs in the city, is now open to women, minorities, and, of course, gentiles, though it doesn't keep track of its demographics.

• • • • • • • • • • • • • • • SPOTLIGHT • • • • • • • • • • • • • • •

⌒— THE JEWS OF CHICAGO —⌒

According to author Irving Cutler, Jews began arriving as soon as the city was incorporated in the 1830s. However, the first authenticated Jewish settlers arrived in Chicago in 1841 from Bohemia and Bavaria, which became part of a united Germany in 1815. Among the first Jews on the city's rolls were Benedict Shubart, Philip Newburgh, Isaac Ziegler, and Henry Horner (grandfather of the Illinois governor who served from 1933 to 1940).

These early German Jewish settlers, known as the first wave of Chicago's Jewish migration, made their initial fortunes at Lake and Clark streets. They mainly started as street peddlers and laborers, but it wasn't long before many worked their way up to running prosperous landed businesses in all major industries of the city.

Chicago's German Jews became Chicago's Jewish aristocracy in that purely American way—they got here first. And the reign of the German Jews would affect Chicago's club life for decades to come.

These men would form the Standard, now one of the nation's oldest Jewish clubs at nearly 140 years of age. Its name was taken from a George Washington quotation: "Let us raise a standard to which the wise and honest can repair; the rest is in the hands of God." With America having narrowly avoided the destruction of the Union during the Civil War, Washington's accomplishments were getting a second act at Chicago's clubs in the wave of patriotism that followed.

But at The Standard, Washington's role was particularly meaningful to

The Standard Club—originally named The Standard at its founding—was opened just a few months after the Chicago Club, and the parallel history of both organizations is an interesting commentary on the beliefs and biases that built the early club system in Chicago. The Chicago Club was founded by the wealthiest Protestant business leaders in Chicago, who generally restricted Catholics, Jews, and other ethnic minorities from joining.

Meanwhile, the Standard Club was founded by German Jews who saw themselves as the first settlers and therefore the leadership

its immigrant founders. According to the club's century yearbook, published in 1969:

All in all, (the founders) were men greatly devoted to the meaning of America. Also, they were of a time when men like themselves did not take America's finest meaning lightly. Especially not those of the group who had come from abroad in their youth.

In its early years, the city's free-for-all environment posed relatively few social barriers for Jews—certainly compared to life in Europe. Chicago after the Great Fire was a city in critical need of a speedy rebirth, and all white people with capital and vision were welcome to play.

The earliest Jewish settlers actually found their way into city politics even before the Great Fire. Abraham Kohn, an early settler, became city clerk under Mayor John Wentworth in the 1860s. Jacob Rosenberg, one of the principals of Rosenfeld and Rosenberg, one of the city's earliest retailers, became a Chicago alderman.

Yet The Standard wasn't the first Jewish club. Though records are spotty, there appear to have been three earlier: the Harmonie Club, Phoenix Club, and Concordia Club. It is unclear when these three folded, but the Concordia Club was notable for a piece of Civil War history. The club formed and helped fund a volunteer Union company of Jewish soldiers named the Concordia Guard. Out of the city's 1,500 Jewish residents, 96 men went off to fight in the unit, which was later named Company C of the 82nd Illinois Volunteer Infantry Regiment. Its members fought in the battles of Fredericksburg, Chancellorsville, Gettysburg, and Chattanooga and eventually joined Sherman's march to the sea.

class in Chicago's Jewish community. They also considered themselves ahead of Jews from Poland and Russia who followed them within a few years. The rivalry became institutional. Eastern European Jews, who tended to be far more religious, ended up founding their own synagogues and clubs (see the section on the Covenant Club below).

BIRTH OF THE STANDARD

New clubs are often created by disgruntled members of old clubs, and that's how the Standard was born. Though the club's own records make no note of member strife at the Concordia, Cutler's version states that the Standard was created in part by breakaway members of the Concordia. The Standard was incorporated under Illinois law on July 7, 1869, only two months after the Chicago Club opened its doors.

Its founding members dubbed themselves the Sixty-Niners, named for the year the club was founded and the original membership limit. Among the founders were the following:

✦ Dankmar Adler, Louis Sullivan's legendary partner who helped design the Auditorium Building in 1889. He was also one of the first Jews to earn club membership at several of the majority clubs.

CLUB NOTES

◦— CHICAGO'S FIRST SYNAGOGUE —◦

Standard Club members notably founded Chicago's first synagogue, Kehilath Anshe Ma'ariv (K.A.M.), which eventually was located at 3301 S. Indiana Avenue in a building designed by Louis Sullivan and his partner Adler. The building housed the Pilgrim Baptist Church from 1922 until a fire in early 2006 gutted the landmark building. This ecumenical site was the birthplace of gospel music in the 1930s. Among those who sang here were Mahalia Jackson, Sallie Martin, James Cleveland, and the Edwin Hawkins Singers.

+ Nelson Morris, founder of one of the first meatpacking companies at the Union Stock Yard. His company went nationwide in direct competition with the Swifts and Armours and was a leading manufacturer until it was merged into Armour & Co. in 1923.
+ Bernard Kuppenheimer, who founded his men's clothing manufacturer in 1876. His company was sold to Hart, Schaffner & Marx (now Hartmarx) in 1982. The Kuppenheimer operation was sold again in 1997 and is now part of the Men's Wearhouse suit retailer.
+ Simon Florsheim, a local corset manufacturer whose family members started the Florsheim Shoe Co. in 1892.

The Standard built its first clubhouse at Michigan Avenue and 13th Street in 1870. In addition to having beautiful ballrooms, the first clubhouse also had a bowling alley, thanks to Chicago's Brunswick family. With its success it would move to a second, larger location, at Michigan Avenue and 24th Street, in 1889.

The Standard Club's first clubhouse (left), stood at Michigan Avenue and 13th Street. The second (right) stood at Michigan Avenue and 24th Street. (Courtesy of the Standard Club.)

The Standard Club's first clubhouse didn't see much immediate clubhouse duty because of the Great Chicago Fire. The blaze left most of the city's clubhouses and hotels uninhabitable or burned to the ground, but because of its near South Side location, the Standard Club was one of the few private clubs to survive the destruction. The clubhouse was seized for a year by the government to use as the command post for General Philip H. Sheridan, who directed firefighting, public safety, and reconstruction.

A LAUNCHPAD FOR JEWISH CHARITY AND POLITICS

Standard Club members created much of the Jewish philanthropic infrastructure that exists in Chicago today, most importantly, the Jewish Federation of Metropolitan Chicago and Michael Reese Hospital, Chicago's first Jewish hospital. Before the twentieth century, both Jews and African-Americans generally operated segregated hospitals.

During the Civil War, the Standard men were usually fervent Republicans and pro-Union, according to the club's history. They also denounced the Fugitive Slave Law, which fined or imprisoned anyone harboring escaped slaves. Member Michael Greenebaum had helped a slave escape seizure via the Underground Railroad. He and his children became powerful in the city's Democratic party.

The former Pilgrim Baptist Church, originally built as Kehilath Anshe Ma'ariv (K. A. M.), Chicago's first synagogue. It was designed by Louis Sullivan and Dankmar Adler, one of the founders of the congregation. The landmark building burned in 2006. (Courtesy of Bob Thall and the Commission on Chicago Landmarks.)

The interior of the former Pilgrim Baptist Church, still displaying ornamentation of Synagogue K. A. M. *(Courtesy Bob Thall and the Commission on Chicago Landmarks.)*

Members of the Standard Club had important roles in the World's Columbian Exposition but were generally not allowed in the front ranks of the team that got the fair to Chicago. Dankmar Adler and Louis Sullivan designed the fair's Transportation Building, which was controversial for going against the Romanesque style of the fair.

In the building boom that would abruptly stop before the Depression, the Standard Club opened its current clubhouse in 1926.

The Standard was like many of the clubs that were heavily mortgaged at the time of the stock market crash—it nearly failed. Its board of governors voted that "the Club seek such financial relief under Section 77B of the National Industrial Recovery Act as may be necessary or desirable to accomplish the proposed reorganization." The club was allowed to rescue itself with the issuance of $1 million in certificates of indebtedness and 15 years in leasehold bonds in the principal amount of $782,000.

THE HOLOCAUST

Though the Standard Club had always made a point of keeping its political and civic activity quiet, it veered from that course during

The Standard Club involved family members in activities throughout the club from its earliest days. Every year, wives, sons, and daughters participated in an annual Washington's Birthday musical (above); sons got to participate in regular gym classes while their fathers spent time at the club (below). (Courtesy of the Standard Club.)

World War II to address the extermination of Europe's Jewish community. Five years after the Nazis came to power in 1933, Hitler's forces launched their infamous Crystal Night (in German, *Kristallnacht*), the attacks that destroyed Jewish shops and sent more than 17,000 Polish Jews across the German border back to Poland. Board member Albert D. Lasker called a special meeting after the tragedy and launched a relief fund with his own $75,000 check to start.

Though all of Chicago's clubs stopped many regular activities to aid in the war effort, by 1941 "all club activities stopped save for Thursday evening dinners," according to the Standard's history. More than 100 members of the club went into military service during the war.

The Standard Club's current building on Plymouth Court. (Courtesy of the Standard Club.)

THE CURRENT CLUB

Beyond the book marking its 100th anniversary, the Standard Club itself has not kept much of an archive on its activities. But Borzak points out that the club's traditions of entertainment, community service, and intellectual development continue on. Like the Chicago Club, the Standard has its own rules about opening its facilities to the public and particularly the press, so he and other members are not terribly forthcoming about anecdotes and other club lore. He explains that it's all part of protecting the atmosphere.

> Our members know this is a quiet and interesting place where they can sit and read a paper and they won't see their name in it—that they were spotted at the Standard Club. But it's bigger than that. You now have generations of families that grew up in this place, and it truly does give a sense of belonging to something larger, to our history in this city and our history with each other. And we're actually seeing younger members coming in, and I think that's because they want that, too.

The club's ballroom, second-floor living room, a typical guest room, the club's "Wall of History" featuring mementos of the Standard Club's past, and the club's library. (Courtesy of the Standard Club.)

Until 1986, *this familiar building at* 10 *N. Dearborn was the Covenant Club's headquarters. But it does have a few of the old touches inside. Now an office building, one of the tenants has taken space in the club's old ballroom. (Courtesy of* HSA *Commercial Real Estate.)*

CLUB NOTES

⌐ THE COVENANT CLUB ⌐

Cultural friction between Chicago's German Jews and Eastern European Jews created a second, and at one time larger, Jewish club in the city of Chicago—the Covenant Club.

The Covenant Club's headquarters still stands at 10 N. Dearborn, though the club's 69-year history ended in 1986. The Covenant Club reflected the wants and needs of its membership—a close community with a religious infrastructure.

The Covenant Club was formed October 1, 1917, for Chicago members of the B'nai B'rith Organization. Morton A. Mergentheim was its first president, and initial club dues were $50 a year. It's often been said that the Covenant Club was formed in response to the Standard Club, which took a more secular approach to its Jewish identity.

In an early document on file at the Chicago Jewish Archives at Spertus Institute of Jewish Studies, the club stated its mission: "The CC membership recognizes no caste, no aristocracy except the fundamental aristocracy of Jewish integrity." For the first ten years of its history, no one but B'nai B'rith members were allowed to join.

The club first occupied the top two floors of an earlier building at 10 N. Dearborn, but by 1922 the club had outgrown the quarters and began the effort to raise $1 million to build what would be an eight-story Italianate skyscraper.

Among its members were Polk Bros. founder Sol Polk, former Cook County Sheriff Richard J. Elrod, and Bears football legend Sid Luckman. Guests over the years included Danny Thomas, Harry Truman, Richard M. Nixon, Eleanor Roosevelt, Israeli diplomat Abba Eban, David Ben-Gurion (Israel's first prime minister), and Judy Garland.

Club activities always had a strong family focus, and it never segregated dining by gender (rare among clubs in its day). The Covenant Club said in its literature:

The average private social club is notoriously misogynistic; and even though Jewish life is characterized by deep family devotion, many Jewish clubs follow the general custom. Not so the Covenant Club. Jewish to the core, the Covenant Club provides a generous welcome for its member's wife and children. There are facilities and programs for the women, the youngsters, the youth. There is a specific interest in the welfare of the growing generation and the definite effort to develop character in the young people.

The Covenant Club held an annual children's party for Chanukah, as described in this way in its newsletter: "On Sunday, grown-ups are taboo. Hostesses are hired to watch them and cut meat as mother might do were she near by. But she isn't. For grownups are strictly taboo."

The club also held an annual Sons-Daughters dance, held every year in the club during the mid-winter school vacations. It was traditionally a formal affair with attendants wearing tailcoats and evening gowns, though during the war people came in "less formal dresses and suits."

The club adopted full membership for women in 1974, but by the, mid-1980s, total club membership had slipped to about 600 from its 1940s height of 1,200. The club decided to shut its doors in 1986, and while the Standard Club doesn't have exact records of how many Covenant Club members it accepted, it confirmed that many did come over.

Sources:

Andreas, A. T. *History of Chicago*, Vol. 2. Chicago: A. T.
  Andreas, 1885.

Borzak, Peter. Interview by author. 3 June 2005.

Cutler, Irving. *The Jews of Chicago: From Shtetl to Suburb*.
  Champaign: University of Illinois Press, 1996.

The Standard Club of Chicago. *The Standard Club of Chicago,*
  1869–1969. Chicago: The Standard Club of Chicago, 1969.

Covenant Club records, 1924–78. Chicago Jewish Archives, collection #59.

XI

THE
UNIVERSITY CLUB
OF
CHICAGO

The University Club of Chicago
Founded: 1887
Address: 76 E. Monroe Street,
Chicago, IL 60603
Architect: Martin Roche

What was the most dominant alma mater when the Midwest's first private club celebrating university men opened? Northwestern? The University of Chicago?

Try Harvard.

As much as Chicago considers itself today a defiantly Midwestern metropolis, the city began—as the club movement did—at the hands of rich, homesick Easterners longing for a touch of the old tradition and exclusivity that they saw as their birthright. In 1885 discussions began between a handful of Chicago-based Harvard graduates about building the Midwestern incarnation of university clubs then springing up in major cities around the country.

The University Club of Chicago's building at Michigan and Monroe (above). The club's library (below). (Courtesy of the University Club of Chicago, Hedrich-Blessing.)

The University Club of Chicago was the first notable club started by Chicago's second- and third-generation wealth—the young whippersnappers, if you will, armed with fresh Ivy League degrees and a desire to do things just a little differently than Dad. Ostensibly, the main qualifications for admission, as today, were an accredited university degree and recommendations from existing members. Like all of Chicago's bricks-and-mortar clubs, the University Club was founded to serve members who were male, wealthy, and white, but it had the distinction of being the second of the Big Four private clubs in Chicago to break the gender line—its first women members were admitted in 1976. (The Standard Club confirms it admitted its first women members in 1974 in tandem with the now-defunct Covenant Club. See Chapter 10.)

Yet at the start, when it came to a true open-door policy for the upstart institutions of higher learning springing up across the prairie, the apples really didn't fall far from the tree.

The club's own golden anniversary history in 1937 takes a humorous look at how tough it was to shed that upper-crust, Ivy League veneer—clearly, not just any university education would do for membership in the early days of the University Club of Chicago. In a document called "The Reading of the Minutes," prepared for the club's golden anniversary celebration in 1937, the following conversation, "which never took place exactly as reported," according to the history, describes the less-than-welcoming atmosphere for colleges on the prairie:

CARPENTER: Has anybody talked with any of the Western college men?

HUBBARD: Of course not! Why would we?

CARPENTER: Well, why not?

FURNESS: Carpenter, have you forgotten what we said when the Chicago University gang invited us down there? (This refers to the defunct Chicago University, predecessor to the University of Chicago.) You know very well we had to decline, because it would have meant we would have been obliged to entertain them.

HUBBARD: It was unthinkable!

CARPENTER: Anyway, what about Michigan?

FURNESS: What about what?

CARPENTER: I said Michigan—Michigan—at Ann Arbor.

FURNESS: O-h-h! Ann Arbor, of course! Why didn't you say so? I believe we can ask the Ann Arbor fellows. Some of 'em aren't half bad.

DE WINDT: You may be right, but if we take in one Western college, aren't we likely to take in others?

HUBBARD: Of course we are, and I, for one, don't intend to stand for any of these fresh-water colleges with tin roofs.

CARPENTER: Northwestern and Beloit and Knox are satisfactory to me.

FURNESS: Yes, and there may be others if we dig deep
enough. . . .

It should be noted that their reference to "Western" colleges
meant all schools apparently to the west of Cambridge,
Massachusetts. Northwestern University, the Chicago area's first
major school, 14 miles north, was also lumped into this "Western"
ghetto.

Yet the club makes clear that the admission process got considerably friendlier as the young club's fortunes began to founder
within a few months of opening its doors in 1887. According to the
club's 1987 history:

> You can afford to look down your nose only if you can keep
> your head above water, and it became quickly apparent that
> the Club's chief early problem was simply sustaining itself. . .
> For all the social uppiness of the 15 founding fathers, they
> all had the good sense to add 300 men to their ranks—as
> charter members—by 1887.

Out of those 300 new members, 34 were graduates of those so-
called Western institutions. They included the University of
Michigan, Northwestern University, Beloit College, Western Reserve
(now known as Case Western Reserve), Knox College, Kenyon
College, and Lombard College.

THE FIRST CLUBHOUSES . . . AND
THE PLANS FOR A LANDMARK

The University Club had two homes before Roche built its palace at
Michigan and Monroe. The first was the now-vanished Henning &
Speed Building at 22 W. Madison, one of the first new constructions
after the Great Chicago Fire. It had its problems. The club rooms,
gymnasium, and kitchen had to accommodate not only members
but a population of rats that never quite moved out. Club history
shows that a giant rat even earned a name, Lulu.

A decade after its founding, the club chose a second home, at 30
N. Dearborn in the four-story Hansen Block building. There the

club started taking on more of its current personality. It was a much better location for social functions and general relaxation. Members started their first committees on literature and art, though according to the club's history:

> ...it must be noted that the members seemed to thrive more on political than on literary or artistic subjects, judging from the intense attention focused on various phases of the Spanish-American war and from dinners staged in honor of such visitors as the hero of that contemporary conflict, Admiral George Dewey (1900) and a precocious 27-year-old member of the British Parliament named Winston Spencer Churchill (1901).

In Chicago, where politics has always been a blood sport, that made perfect sense.

But by the turn of the century, a movement had begun to find the club its permanent landmark home. Though the club's records are fuzzy on the exact date when members started their efforts, an independent corporation called the University Auxiliary Association was formed to build the skyscraper and own the lease on land owned by the one-time agricultural giant International Harvester Co. (once a big property owner on Michigan Avenue) at Michigan and Monroe.

It was decided that a whopping $1.1 million would have to be raised to complete the project, literally the city's first skyscraper private clubhouse.

Yet club president William C. Boyden assembled a team that crafted an unusual financial structure for the project so members would own the capital stock of the association and the club would incur no financial responsibility for either the land or the building—it would only pay rent. The stock would become a fully paid, nontaxable security paying regular dividends for 196 years—the length of the lease on the land with Harvester. Boyden would be supported in his efforts by Victor F. Lawson, former publisher of the *Chicago Daily News* (and namesake of the Lawson YMCA on Chicago Avenue); architect William Holabird; and John P. Wilson, the attorney who oversaw it all.

It wasn't all smooth sailing. The Panic of 1907 — the New York credit crunch that spawned the Federal Reserve System — slowed funding of the new building to a crawl. Yet the Burnham Plan was moving toward completion in the front yard of the new clubhouse, and Boyden and his team used the development of Grant Park and the lakefront as the selling tool that kept the membership on focus. The project continued, and the clubhouse opened April 3, 1909. The club's 1987 history describes the opening this way:

> The night was clear, the air bracing, and the ballads, cheers and marching songs to which we gave voice as we paraded through the streets echoed and reechoed off the hard fronts of the big commercial buildings that made up Chicago's downtown district. When we arrived at our new clubhouse, we tarried long enough downstairs to divide into units representing our respective colleges and universities and changed from our dress suits to a variety of academic costumes. Then we ascended to the ninth floor and processed into Cathedral Hall. There again we closed ranks and paraded, the colors of our academic flags bobbing and weaving in moving contrast to the stately black of our robes, the whole spectacle cradled generously within that dark and glorious space.

The club's history also quotes a *Chicago Record* report on what happened next:

> Finally, the hall was crowded and then suddenly from a balcony at the rear the blue flag of Yale was thrust forth to view. Instantly, the crackling Yale yell rang out while a half-hundred blue-capped "old grads" crimsoned to the ears with the unwonted vocal effort. Then there were Yale songs and at last a pause.
>
> Out flaunted the Harvard banner and a big group of Harvard men in crimson hats and sashes burst forth in full cry until the roof seemed coming off. "Fair Harvard! Thy sons to the jubilee throng," sang the glee club, pausing finally when Michigan's pennant appeared. Then there was more yelling and more singing. Thus in turn Princeton,

Northwestern, Cornell, Chicago, Williams and Wisconsin got their just meed of song and glory until as a finale, the Stars and Stripes flashed forth to the music of "The Star Spangled Banner," and with the aftermath of such a torrent of tigers as would have made the most exacting patriot proud.

CLUB NOTES

∾ SOUP'S ON ∾

There wasn't a lot of controversy at the University Club—well, except for the night when one of its kitchen workers almost murdered Archbishop George Mundelein.

In 1916 radical political sentiments were raging in the final months of World War I, and the club staged a major banquet to welcome the new archbishop of Chicago. A cook's helper, identified in the club's history as Jean Crones, "a strange little man described by those who knew him as a loner and a hothead," who apparently belonged to "several radical anarchist groups," managed to dump a healthy load of arsenic in the soup.

Apparently, the archbishop and at least a couple hundred people were saved by the fact that nearly 100 members showed up unannounced for the dinner. The chef, realizing that there wasn't enough soup to go around, gave orders to dump gallons of water into the broth.

Crones was never caught, and how his soup terrorism was discovered is unclear, but it made national news, including this reference in the *San Antonio Light*:

Had it not been for the water—and the very poor soup—there would have been a wholesale job for the coroner. This is a matter for wide congratulations, but it also has served to prove the fact that the exclusive University Club of Chicago has some exceedingly reprehensible practices when it comes to making soup.

THE CLUBHOUSE

While all of Chicago's historic private clubs have some jaw-dropping aspects to their clubhouses — most of them aesthetically pleasing, some not so — the University Club's clubhouse is put in a particular class for several reasons. First is the simple matter of timing. William Holabird and Martin Roche were both University Club members (Holabird a charter member) and principals of Holabird & Root, the Chicago architectural firm that helped establish the modern skyscraper.

Roche would become the clubhouse's architect, and there would be no doubt that it would become Chicago's first true skyscraper clubhouse, 12 stories in all.

Few would disagree that the University Club's Cathedral Hall is the definitive knockout among Chicago's clubhouse spaces. The membership took its cue from Crosby Place, a manor home in London's Chelsea neighborhood that included a banquet hall with an intricately carved wooden ceiling. Roche duplicated it in this space, which features an eastward view of Lake Michigan (the same view shared by four other clubs — the Cliff Dwellers, the Chicago Club, and the now-closed Chicago Athletic Association.) The club's Michigan Room, a slightly smaller ballroom space, features some of the best work of muralist and member Frederick Clay Bartlett, including dozens of individually drawn ceiling panels depicting various medieval and historic scenes encased in carved wood. Bartlett, a major art collector and benefactor of the Art Institute of Chicago, also designed thousands of feet of gorgeous stained glass throughout the building.

There's art throughout the clubhouse, dating from the thirteenth through the twentieth century. The names start with Bartlett but include Roger Brown, Ed Paschke, Leon Golub, William Conger, Richard Hull, and Martin Roche himself. The club also has rotating monthly exhibits of local artists in its gallery on the 12th floor.

Most of Chicago's clubhouses had ladies' days or dedicated ladies' areas where female family members could use the club — polite segregation being the rule. The University Club converted its

The Cathedral Hall windows.

Cathedral Hall, the major dining and ballroom area of the club.

The Michigan Room, with its famous ceiling panels designed by Frederick Clay Bartlett.

The Monroe Room, part of redesigned space on the second floor for corporate and social events.

The President's Bar features portraits by nationally known Chicago artists, including the late Ed Paschke.

(Courtesy of the University Club of Chicago, Hedrich-Blessing.)

old Ladies' Dining Room to the Monroe Room, now a general reception area for functions in the Michigan Room.

Also, the University Club continues to operate another longtime luncheon institution, the Tower Club, in the Lyric Opera building. The Tower Club was formed in 1916 as the Chicago Electric Club, a business group focused on science and technology.

THE SOCIETIES

University Club members keep connected to the liberal arts side of their college careers with frequent lectures on literature and the arts and sometimes with performances. The club also has specialty groups known as societies dedicated to specific areas of interest, including cigars, civic affairs, classical music, diving, garden, golf, investments, art, wine, and target shooting (Wing & Clay).

· · · · · · · · · · · · · · SPOTLIGHT · · · · · · · · · · · · ·

✌ WHAT'S IN A NAME? ✌

Maybe the equivalent of getting Oprah Winfrey to join your club back in seventeenth-century England was signing up a king or someone like that. But especially today celebrity membership sells—to the paying customers, that is.

In the world of private clubs, honorary members get in free, but only because their name has significant marketing value to attract prospective members. That's why in Chicago, Mayor Richard M. Daley—just like his father—is probably the most ubiquitous non-dues-paying, honorary club member in town.

Mayor Daley may never have seen the inside of many of the clubs where he's listed on the membership roster—City Hall won't say for sure—but the listing of a popular politician or today's celebrity gold standard, the talk show host, is a long-standing ritual at private clubs.

124

UPDATING FOR THE FUTURE

General Manager John F. Spidalette knows as well as anyone that the club business is changing, that nonexclusive alternatives exist for many of the services the old private clubs used to have a lock on—gourmet dining, health clubs, and meeting space. "People used to belong to full-service lunch clubs for a reason—there was nothing out there that came close. Today that's changed, and we have to change, too," he explains. That's why the University Club recently completed a multimillion-dollar renovation of the club, including updates to its dining options (for example, by hiring a chef from the Four Seasons) as well as renovating guest rooms and other spaces.

"We are nonprofit and we are exclusive, and we have a member-ship to serve. We're not here to serve the general public," Spidalette adds. "But you have to make an option like ours attrac-tive to the general public who may want to join, and that's why we constantly have to reassess our business model."

Spidalette points out that all clubs are entertaining more outside business and events—brought in by members, of course. It is much easier for outsiders who know someone within the club to pay to use the club's facilities for meetings, events, parties, and weddings. Such flexibility is going to be more necessary for clubs in the future.

Sources:

Schulze, Franz. *A Heritage: University Club of Chicago*,
    1887–1987. Chicago: University Club of Chicago, 1987.
Spidalette, John. Interview by author. July 2005.

THE
BUSINESS/
PUBLIC POLICY
CLUBS

XII

THE
COMMERCIAL CLUB
OF
CHICAGO

·

The Commercial Club of Chicago
Founded: 1877
Address: 21 S. Clark Street, Suite 3120,
Chicago, IL 60603 (office only—no clubhouse)

For as much influence as the city's leading bricks-and-mortar clubs have had since the city's founding, it is still hard for most to compete with the level of civic accomplishment achieved by the Commercial Club of Chicago since its inception.

The Commercial Club—an organization created by 17 businessmen over a dinner in 1877—helped change a dirty, disorganized, and corrupt city in an indelible way and continues to work for civic change. Most notably, its founding members—George Pullman, Marshall Field, Cyrus McCormick, George Armour, and railroad executive–turned–regional planner Frederic Delano among them—underwrote member Daniel Burnham's 1909 *Plan of Chicago*, the blueprint that created the city's park system, uncluttered lakefront, and easy-to-navigate street grid.

The founding members of the club collected $3,000 to bring members of the Boston Commercial Club to Chicago to give them a shape for their organization. The East Coast group inspected the city's businesses, grain elevators, and stockyards; the Chicagoans in turn picked their brains about their organization and the civic value it provided. Within weeks of that experiment, the host committee officially founded the Commercial Club of Chicago on December 17, 1877.

The Commercial Club became an extremely powerful group without the benefit of a trophy address. Back then, as today, the invitation-only club meets in rented space and funnels its considerable member talent and financial resources into the investigations and research studies that have made it famous.

In the late nineteenth Century, the Commercial Club was so exclusive, writes Muriel Beadle in her book about The Fortnightly Club:

"Indeed, forty of the sixty members of the exclusive Commercial Club lived within a six-block area centered on Prairie Avenue between Sixteenth and Twenty-Second Streets, and Prairie Avenue came to be called 'the sunny street which held the sifted few.'"

A PRECURSOR TO THE BUSINESS THINK TANK

All the major men's clubs were full of business and political leaders, but very few made their discussions of public issues in those exclusive forums public. They were considered social clubs, after all. However, from the start, the same players formed the Commercial Club to unite the city's business sector so it could publicly analyze and define solutions for the serious urban problems that have faced Chicago from its beginnings: taxation issues, crime and corruption, street repairs, schools, and employment.

After the 1886 Haymarket Riots raised concerns about the lack of military might in the immediate Chicago area, members of the Commercial Club donated land in north suburban Highwood to build Fort Sheridan, which eventually opened in 1890. The Commercial Club's main rival, the Merchants Club, donated more

President William Howard Taft attends the first graduation at the new Great Lakes Naval Academy in October 1911. The Commercial Club helped finance Great Lakes, a project started by the Merchants Club before both organizations merged into the Commercial Club. (Courtesy of the Great Lakes Naval Museum.)

than $171,000 to quietly buy up lakefront property in Lake Bluff that would be turned over to the government to build what is now known as the Great Lakes Naval Training Station. The two clubs merged in 1907 under the Commercial Club's name.

During the Progressive Era at the turn of the twentieth century, the Commercial Club worked to create vocational training programs for poor youngsters. It founded the Chicago Manual Training School and supported similar "practical education" projects, including the Illinois Training School Farm at Glenwood and the St. Charles School for Boys. The club also sponsored and translated studies of vocational education in Europe for an American audience.

THE CREATION OF THE BURNHAM PLAN

Daniel Burnham, a protégé of William Le Baron Jenney, father of the skyscraper, was partner to John Wellborn Root; their firm designed the Monadnock, Reliance, and Rookery buildings that still stand in the Loop. After Root died suddenly in 1891, Burnham solidified his reputation as a city planner by leading the design and

Michigan Avenue looking south as pictured in Daniel H. Burnham and Edward H. Bennett's Plan of Chicago, *commissioned by the Commercial Club of Chicago. (From* Plan of Chicago *by Daniel Burnham.)*

construction of the World's Columbian Exposition in 1893, the first critical test of Chicago as a world-class city.

Burnham was as much a celebrity architect of his time as Frank Gehry or Rem Koolhaas today. He was a hot draw on the elite city club circuit—a great speaker with an unmatched portfolio of work to fire the imaginations of the rich and powerful. In the early 1900s—in the aftermath of the wildly successful World's Columbian Exposition that Burnham also directed—he spoke to the Merchants Club about his vision for a revised plan for the city that would create an orderly, expandable metropolis flanked by beautiful parks and gardens. In 1906 the Merchants Club asked Burnham to develop a complete plan for Chicago. He offered his own services for free but accepted $30,000 to hire a staff and build workrooms on the roof of the Railway Exchange Building, today known as the Santa Fe building, at 114 S. Michigan Avenue.

Burnham envisioned a metropolis stretching 60 miles from its core through the suburbs and the satellite cities of Elgin, Aurora, and Joliet. He unified the city's railroad network and diverted traffic away from the center of town, relieving the unwieldy city's terrible congestion problems and freeing the lakefront from shore-line development.

Burnham coauthored the *Plan of Chicago* with architect Edward H. Bennett, and the Commercial Club published it in 1909. The creators understood that to sell the plan, it had to be a striking document. To supplement the prose, Burnham and Bennett enlist-ed painter-illustrators Jules Guerin and Fernand Janin, who creat-ed the 143 colorful and detailed illustrations filling the book. Commercial Club member Thomas Donnelley's Lakeside Press supervised the production of the book with a run of 1,650 num-bered copies. Some have been donated to local libraries—they're definitely worth a look.

The plan's illustrations and paintings were displayed at the Art Institute, which got the public on the bandwagon. The Chicago City Council acted quickly, creating the Chicago Plan Commission (which still exists today) to implement it. The Commercial Club's connections were there, too—member Charles Wacker would chair the first Plan Commission. Michigan Avenue was widened as sug-gested with a double-deck bridge across the river, and Burnham created Chicago's gold standard of parks with Grant Park and the south lakefront as a continuous band of greenery. Forest preserves were acquired, Navy Pier was built, and the chain of museums still around today began construction.

It's unclear whether the following words were actually spoken at a London planning conference in 1910. According to *Respectfully Quoted*, a publication of the Congressional Research Service, Burnham's words were spruced up by Willis Polk, Burnham's San Francisco partner. But real or apocryphal, Burnham's words cap-ture his contributions to Chicago and gave weight to the mission of the Commercial Club:

Make no little plans; they have no magic to stir men's blood and probably themselves will not be realized. Make big plans; aim high in hope and work, remembering that a noble, logical diagram once recorded will never die, but long after we are gone will be a living thing, asserting itself with ever-growing insistency. Remember that our sons and grandsons

*The Museum of Science and Industry, a venture of the Commercial
Club of Chicago launched by member Julius Rosenwald. It saved the
Palace of Fine Arts building from the World's Columbian Exhibition
from demolition. (Courtesy of the Museum of Science and Industry.)*

are going to do things that would stagger us. Let your watch-
word be order and your beacon beauty.

After the success of the Chicago Plan, the Commercial Club
never looked back. It had committees investigating everything from
rail terminals to education and high-pressure water systems. In
1910 the club sent a former Chicago Public Schools superintendent
to study European vocational schools and later published two text-
books on the subject. That gave birth to the city's vocational
schools the Commercial Club helped create. Another effort involved
John V. Farwell Jr., who launched a 16-year club campaign to bring
reform to the Federal Reserve System. He helped draft the Federal
Reserve Banking Act of 1913, which gave the Federal Reserve
responsibility for setting the nation's monetary policy.

In 1911 Commercial Club member Julius Rosenwald, then president of Sears, Roebuck and Co. and a member of most leading
clubs in the city, got inspired after visiting Munich's Deutsches
Museum, one of the oldest science and technology museums in the

world. Rosenwald and his eight-year-old son were inspired by its hands-on displays and public-friendly exhibits.

Rosenwald never abandoned the memory, and ten years later he proposed to club president Samuel Insull that Chicago should have a similar place according to the club's history, "a great Industrial Museum for Exhibition, in which might be housed, for a permanent display, machinery and working models."

At that time the old Palace of Fine Arts built for the Columbian Exposition in 1893 was condemned and headed for the wrecking ball. Because it was the last major building left vacant after the fair, various groups and politicians had dwindling hopes and ideas for its reuse, none of which suited Rosenwald. He raised an initial donation of between $1 million and $3 million in 1915 to prevent the site from being chopped up into a mixed-use civic development. With the aid of several Commercial Club members, he won the battle. A museum board of trustees was formed, eventually including 17 Commercial Club members.

In the proposal stage it was known as the Rosenwald Industrial Museum. But it made its debut as the Museum of Science and Industry in 1933.

THE GREAT DEPRESSION

All of Chicago's private clubs had their own war with the 1930s, but for high-profile civic groups, the burdens were unique. Granted, the Commercial Club had none of the overhead issues that forced many clubs near bankruptcy and closure, but it was wrestling with a time when so many of the city's problems seemed insurmountable.

In 1931 the Commercial Club merged again, this time with the Industrial Club of Chicago, which added new blood. But the club was up against the administration of William "Big Bill" Thompson, who was closely aligned with organized crime. The club's Committee on Crime issued an update with the rather obvious and overly diplomatic summary, "crime will increase/decrease in inverse proportion to the character and competence of those holding public office." Large-scale projects never got much traction through the 1930s, but meetings continued for networking—and commiseration.

A SLOW REAWAKENING

Given all the development Chicago has seen in the last quarter-century alone, it's hard to believe that no major buildings were constructed downtown from 1934 to 1955, when the original Prudential Building was completed. The postwar boom ushered in the years of Richard J. Daley, who brought in billions of dollars in federal aid to build rapid transit lines, highways, public buildings, and public housing. Times weren't perfect, but the city was growing—and the Commercial Club was apparently lulled by it.

In a 1986 speech recorded in the club's history, former club president Donald Perkins, chairman of the former Jewel Foods, said, "In all honesty, the Commercial Club's contribution to our community has been too often nonexistent in the most recent 50 years of its Rip Van Winkle history."

Perkins's statement was a wakeup call to the historic organization, and the Commercial Club began to re-grow its teeth during the Reagan era.

In 1983 the Commercial Club created the Civic Committee, a nonprofit organization representing a cross section of the greater Chicago area's top public- and private-sector leadership from organizations large and small. The Civic Committee's first assignment was to examine the future employment picture for Chicago in the go-go '80s.

Made up of 315 members with 75 Commercial Club members on board, the Civic Committee members served on 15 committees and subcommittees to dissect the metropolitan situation. Instead of a rosy picture that reflected the building and economic boom going on in the city at that time, the committee's report released in 1984 showed a very different picture.

Jobs for Metropolitan Chicago showed that metro Chicago's job growth in 1984 trailed the nation in virtually every industry sector, most notably a 10 percent decline in manufacturing jobs while the sector gained 11 percent nationally. Wholesale and retail trade was growing at half the national rate, and finance, insurance, and real estate still trailed the national average. It was a bombshell report that dominated civic discussion for years and put the Commercial Club back on the map.

In 1983 Mayor Harold Washington was elected, and in the midst of the "Council Wars" fracas that brought Chicago embarrassing national acclaim, the city's first African-American chief executive asked the Civic Committee to create a report on the city's finances and, in particular, the health of Chicago's public school system. Since Washington had so few allies inside city government, he decided to build an unprecedented alliance with a business community that was never particularly outspoken during previous administrations—particularly that of the first Daley administration.

In response, the Civic Committee teamed with Chicago United to form a new subgroup, the Financial Research and Advisory Committee (FRAC). The Commercial Club's own history quotes a member as saying, "We told Washington that we were willing to do the study, but only if we could report exactly what we found without any political interference. He gulped hard and said okay."

The preliminary 1986 report—completed by a blue-ribbon team of lawyers, accountants, bankers, and businessmen on loan from Civic Committee member companies—predicted a city deficit of $500 million by 1991 with suggested improvements. After Washington died suddenly in 1987, FRAC continued to work with Mayors Eugene Sawyer and Richard M. Daley to implement cost-saving measures in real estate, energy, fleet management, and other key resource areas where the system was overspending. Today FRAC has been succeeded at the Commercial Club by a new group called the Civic Consulting Alliance, which matches consultants from private industry to city projects.

The club's renaissance in the 1980s made it a more diverse and powerful organization. The Civic Committee was well funded by local corporations and tackled a wider variety of projects, including the creation of a small business assistance center for manufacturers and an information industry council to nurture telecommunications and software businesses.

THE CURRENT AGENDA

After 30 years of support for the expansion of O'Hare International Airport, the Civic Committee decided to launch a more aggressive campaign in the fall of 1999. It hired consulting firm Booz Allen & Hamilton to conduct an independent assessment of O'Hare, its economic impact on the regional economy, and the potential benefits of expanding the airport. The study, which was released in April 2000, reported that O'Hare contributed about $37 billion annually and more than 400,000 jobs to the economy. The O'Hare modernization bill, which was endorsed by the Civic Committee, received bipartisan support in the Illinois legislature and passed both chambers in 2003.

At this writing, the club is carrying out the work of its 1999 report *Chicago Metropolis* 2010, an ongoing project examining Chicago's future regional planning from the key mileposts of education, housing, taxation, transportation, infrastructure, health care, and industrial development. The project was based on the premise that the City of Chicago and the surrounding area—Cook, DuPage, Lake, McHenry, Kane, and Will counties—constitute a single region and that the pressing public policy issues it faces are interdependent.

Sources:

Beadle, Muriel, and the Centennial History Committee. *The Fortnightly of Chicago: The City and its Women:* 1873–1973. Chicago: Henry Regnery Co., 1973.

Commercial Club of Chicago. *Together for Our City: A Brief History of the Commercial Club of Chicago.* Chicago: Commercial Club of Chicago, 1996.

Commercial Club of Chicago research collection, Chicago History Museum.

XIII

THE
CITY CLUB
OF
CHICAGO

———◆———

The City Club of Chicago
Founded: 1903
Address: *360 N. Michigan Avenue, Suite 903,*
Chicago, IL 60601 (office only — no clubhouse)

The City Club of Chicago was born in the midst of the Progressive
Era, and Chicago was definitely ready for reform—as it always
seems to be. Then as now the organization remains open to all who
are interested in civic responsibility, public issues, open political
debate, and networking opportunities. At 104 years of age, the City
Club is the longest-running weekly lunch forum in Chicago.

The club's early history is steeped in turn-of-the-century corruption and political unrest. The City Club was born within a 15-
year span that created private clubs that for the first time pushed
a very public agenda outside private club walls. The Union
League Club of Chicago, the Civic Federation (see "The Genesis
of the City Club" a little later in this chapter), and its spin-off

organization, the Municipal Voters' League (MVL), all started during this period.

Chicago has long had a habit of attracting world attention for the wrong reasons. The City Club was inspired by 1894's landmark book *If Christ Came to Chicago*, which embarrassed the city fathers by shoving the rampant political corruption and social injustice right in their faces.

James L. Merriner's centennial history of the City Club points out that Chicago's earliest reformers had a take-no-prisoners approach to cleaning up city government. Knowing that government officials on a state and local level were on the take and therefore useless to their cause, these reformers had the money and clout to hire private investigative help to root out problems, making the then-Chicago-based Pinkerton National Detective Agency the number one private crime-fighting squad in the country. Of course, among the problems that the Pinkertons helped solve were labor strikes at the same businessmen's companies, which earned them a reputation for violence and suspicious undercover tactics against organized labor.

The City Club is also interesting because of a parallel organization that grew up alongside it, the Woman's City Club of Chicago. The WCCC was an example of another club formed because its demographic wasn't fully welcome in the majority club—at least for some time. It would have been interesting to see the results had the City Club men actually welcomed their female counterparts into their organization as full members from the start, given that both genders had their focus on the same problems, if not always the same solutions. The Woman's City Club featured the leading women activists of the day: Jane Addams, Louise de Koven Bowen, Harriet Vittum, Julia Lathrop, Grace and Edith Abbott, Alice Hamilton, and Lea Demarest Taylor.

SPOTLIGHT

⌒ CORRUPTION IN THE 1890S ⌒

As much as scandals surround the Chicago City Council today, most of Chicago's current aldermen and women are angels compared to their counterparts in the 1890s. During that time a group of aldermen known as the Gray Wolves were so named because they preyed on a defenseless electorate with elaborate frauds and other schemes. They were led by "Bathhouse" John Coughlin and "Hinky Dink" Michael Kenna of the notorious First Ward and Johnny Powers of the 19th Ward. They not only controlled various rackets and prostitution, but they also got control of the award process to private companies of electricity, gas, phone service, and mass transit.

Bribes were almost quaint during this period. The Gray Wolves were true artists of political thievery. One of their more notable schemes was to create a fictional company known as Ogden Gas Co., which forced the existing legitimate franchise holder to buy up the rights to the fake company's gas holdings. Once that money changed hands, it went into the pockets of the aldermen and crooks along the food chain.

The various scandals—and the high-profile First Ward Ball that brought together a cross section of the city's business and crime elite at the biggest party in town—led to the formation of the Municipal Voters' League (MVL), which begat the City Club of Chicago.

THE GENESIS OF THE CITY CLUB

Attorney Walter L. Fisher, secretary and later president of the MVL, saw an unmet need among all the reform organizations built so far. The MVL, which had cleaned up the City Council to an admirable degree, wanted to keep its focus there. The Civic Federation, which would start as a corruption fighter and eventually zero in on municipal tax policy, had more of a research agenda. There was something missing in the middle—a newsmaking forum that would embrace the purpose of the earlier groups but create a networking function as none of them had. Today the City Club is part reform organization, part social club, part public forum.

In a genetically Democratic town, Chicago's reformers were generally middle- to upper-middle-class Republican, white, and Protestant—the historic loyal opposition in the city. They tended to come from the private sector—lawyers, businessmen, even a few politicos working for a progressive Republican agenda. The City Club was no different.

The club's first meeting, according to the club's history, occurred on December 3, 1903, at Vogelsgang's restaurant. The group was exclusively male and white. By 1912, however, the organization had dropped any resistance to men of color as members or presenters. Soon such prominent blacks as Booker T. Washington were invited to speak at meetings. Politicians were restricted from membership until 1914. But it would take until 1962 before women could join as full members of the City Club.

The City Club's first major investigation was the "Piper Report" in 1905 which looked into corruption at the Chicago Police Department.

A TRADITIONAL CLUB, A TRADITIONAL CLUBHOUSE

The clubhouse movement during the teens and 1920s had virtually any club that operated looking for a nameplate on a building—no matter how much it cost. The City Club built a clubhouse of its own at 315 S. Plymouth Court in 1911 at a cost of $211,000. The clubhouse was designed by the architectural firm of Pond & Pond. According to John Marshall Law School, which has occupied the

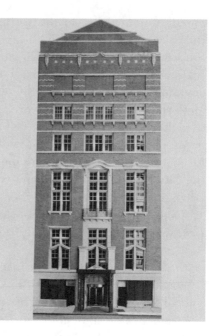

The City Club of Chicago established its clubhouse at 315 S. Plymouth Court but lost the building during the Depression. Today it is the headquarters of the John Marshall Law School. (Courtesy the John Marshall Law School.)

building since the club had to sell it in 1934, "The architects claimed that the building did not 'conform strictly to any of the established styles,' but that it could be described as a 'free Renaissance treatment not devoid of gothic suggestions.'" At the time the club occupied it, one entire room was used as a humidor.

The City Club, like many others, was always beset with some sort of revenue crunch, and the bricks-and-mortar responsibility didn't help. Since it was forced to relinquish the John Marshall property in the 1930s, it hasn't operated a clubhouse and all meetings have been held in public spaces. In 2007 the club held its weekly meetings at Maggiano's Banquets at 111 W. Grand Avenue.

THE CITY CLUB—A COMMUNIST FRONT?

The City Club was never terribly popular for its open-minded attitude on race and reform causes—at least among certain people.

Enter Joe McCarthy. His Red-baiting rampage of the 1950s found its way to the City Club's door in the person of one Theodore W. Miller, a patent attorney and supporter of the Wisconsin senator's efforts to root out Communist sympathizers wherever he sup-

posedly found them. In the spring of 1949, the infamous Broyles
Bills were introduced in the Illinois legislature to prohibit any person who was "directly or indirectly affiliated with any communist
[or] communist front organization" to hold any governmental or
civil service position in the state of Illinois. During the height of the
McCarthy era, these bills were passed every two years, though
Governor Adlai Stevenson vetoed them.

Miller, in writing his support of another Broyles Bill coming up
for a vote, identified 11 Communist-sympathizer groups, including
the City Club, the Independent Voters of Illinois, and the Chicago
Bar Association.

According to Merriner's book *The City Club of Chicago: A
Centennial History*, Miller said this about the City Club:

"The Club has long been a focal point of Communist infiltra-
tion and recruiting ground for Communist Party members. Its
board of directors includes Edgar Barnard, Communist Party
member referred to above in connection with the board of the
American Civil Liberties Union, and John A. Lapp, whose
Communist Party Activities date back to September. 17, 1934,
or before. I have in my possession a photostatic copy of a
memo bearing the signature of John Lapp verifying a quotation by Gill Green, State Chairman of the Communist Party of
Illinois made to the *Herald-American* on July 13, 1948,
denouncing the Chicago Civil Liberties Committee on behalf
of the Communist Party."

And he went on, targeting Lapp a little more and even dragging
in legendary former Chicago alderman Leon Despres, whom he
identified as "a member of the Trotskyite faction of the Communist
Party."

DECLINE AND RECOVERY

Merriner's book details the club's continuation of its reformist
agenda from the postwar era through the tumultuous 1960s, when
it fought for better housing conditions for the city's poor. At a City

Club forum on March 14, 1967, Mayor Richard J. Daley was asked what the city was doing about the poor conditions of public housing, and the mayor said, "No one has taught [many] of them to make a bed, to sweep a room, to keep out rats by covering up food. . . . It's not just Negroes. There are people from Appalachia and Puerto Rico. . . . They have a background of a rural environment."

City Club member Charles Swibel, the then-two-decade chief of the Chicago Housing Authority, fought back against City Club members who attempted to criticize his leadership and reform the system. Fellow member James S. Fuerst coauthored some of the most scathing studies against the agency, thereby eventually helping to oust Swibel in 1982. A 2001 *Chicago Sun-Times* story on the state of the system singled out Swibel's reign as the reason the CHA was "run into the ground."

Even so, during the 1960s and 1970s the media generally ignored the club. By 1976 there was talk about closing it down. Larry P. Horist, a public relations consultant, was named to manage the club and started the tough work of turning it around. He began with the basics—financing and fund-raising, the quality of food at meetings, and then, what many consider the most important move, getting Thomas F. Roeser involved. Roeser, a conservative Republican and at the time head of governmental relations for Quaker Oats, was convinced to take over as president of the City Club in 1977.

Immediately, programming got better and members started coming back to the meetings. Merriner explained that Quaker began funding breakfasts under Roeser's leadership, and the club even kicked off 1977 with its annual meeting at the freshly vacated Playboy Mansion at 1340 N. State Parkway, which got more than a little attention. Members brought guests, and membership and revenue began to rise. In 1980 then presidential candidate Edward M. Kennedy spoke, drawing a sellout audience. Roeser, who would steer the club for nearly 20 years—and make a media celebrity of himself in the process—turned the City Club back into a leading salon for public policy on the local, state, and national scale.

Today the club's policy breakfasts and luncheon forums continue with a constant flow of newsmakers from the public and private sectors, all focused on city issues. The club, which dwindled to a few hundred members when it was near extinction, now stands at more than 1,000 with a reasonable annual individual membership fee of $50.

Sources:

Grossman, Kate N., and Curtis Lawrence. "CHA 's Big Gamble." *Chicago Sun-Times*, March 25, 2001.

Merriner, James L. *The City Club of Chicago: A Centennial History*. Chicago: The City Club of Chicago, 2003.

XIV

THE
MID-DAY CLUB

The Mid-Day Club
Founded: 1903
Address: Chase Tower, 21 S. Clark Street, Chicago, IL 60603
Architect: Walter Frazier (current clubhouse, Chase Tower)

Author's Note: Just before publication, the Mid-Day Club announced its plans to close by yearend 2007, allowing its members to transfer to other clubs including the University Club of Chicago, the Tower Club (a unit of the University Club), the Union League Club, or the Cliff Dwellers. For this reason, there is no listing for this organization in Appendix A.

At the turn of the twentieth century, every ambitious man had to have a club membership. At that time most Chicago clubs had waiting lists because the alternatives — loud, overcrowded restaurants filled with wage slaves and vendors of questionable street food — clearly were not suitable environments for the conduct of important business.

As has probably become obvious throughout this book, multiple club memberships — often freely subsidized by employers looking to grow and make connections — were commonplace among these individuals. One wonders where they got the time to visit them all. Of course, most club members probably didn't visit their clubs all that often, because the real value, you see, was not in being present but in being listed on that gilded nameplate in the front hall-way of the club. If you were on that wall, you had arrived—even if you never set foot in the place.

Which brings us to 1903 and the growing population of bankers and lawyers downtown just west of State Street. There were 15 movers and shakers in this group who wanted to start, yes, one more club. Their names were William Gerrish Beale, Fredrick Seymour Winston, J. Lewis Cochran, Henry Dibblee, Charles Wacker, Fredric Adrian Delano, John Farson, Hiram R. McCullough, Henry H. Porter, John Dupee, John J. Mitchell, John Alden Spoor, Harry Gordon Selfridge, Arthur Meeker, and Herman Henry Kohlsaat.

According to the Mid-Day's history, Beale was the club's first president and the attorney that drew up the will of Marshall Field as a name partner of Isham, Lincoln & Beale. Lincoln, meanwhile, was Robert Todd Lincoln, son of President Abraham Lincoln and a serial club member in his own right.

John Farson was a self-made millionaire and financier who helped promote Chicago as an industrial growth center in the post–Great Chicago Fire era. According to the club his "penchant for all things red included everything from cars to pajamas to over 175 neckties, of which most were red." As one of the first presidents of the Chicago Auto Club, he lobbied for an increase in the eight-mile-per-hour speed limit.

Harry Gordon Selfridge started in Chicago but claimed his greatest fame in Merrie Old England. At age 15 Selfridge went to work for Field, Leiter & Co., predecessor to Marshall Field's. In 1909 he came out of semiretirement and established the first retail-er in Europe to practice American-style department store mer-chandising. The store, Selfridge's on Oxford Street in London, still thrives today. Selfridge eventually settled in London, remaining an honorary member of the Mid-Day until he died in 1947.

Like most club cofounders, these men all knew each other from their homes on Astor Street, in Lake Forest, and, during the sum-mer months, in Wisconsin. Others knew each other through their mutual club memberships at the Chicago Club, Union League, University Club, Chicago Athletic Association, Merchants Club, or Commercial Club. They shared the same vision—the creation of a

*The first home
of the Mid-Day
Club, at the Daniel
Burnham-designed
First National
Bank Building
(now demolished).
(Courtesy of the
J.P. Morgan Chase
Archives.)*

prestigious luncheon club serving great food to the most respected individuals in the Chicago business community.

THE FIRST CLUBHOUSE

On December 4, 1903, the Mid-Day signed a five-year lease at $20,000 annual rent at the Daniel Burnham-designed First National Bank Building. With lunchtime business its main focus, it was dubbed the Mid-Day Club.

The doors officially opened on March 6, 1904, with 400 members each paying annual dues of $50. Within the first year membership had to be capped at 525. The reputation of the club preceded it. Novelist Edna Ferber wrote about the club under the fictional name Noon Club in *So Big* (1924):

From the start [Dirk] was a success. Within one year he was so successful that you could hardly distinguish him from a hundred other successful young Chicago business and professional men whose clothes were made at Peel's; who kept their

*The Mid-Day Club's last home
on the 56th floor of Chase
Tower. (Courtesy of the J.P.
Morgan Chase Archives.)*

collars miraculously clean in the soot-laden atmosphere of the
Loop; whose shoes were bench made; who lunched at the
Noon Club on the roof of the First National Bank where
Chicago's millionaires ate corned beef hash whenever that
plebeian dish appeared on the bill of fare.

The club's famous corned beef hash remained on the menu. But
other popular dishes in the 1930s and 1940s—fowl livers en bro-
chette, clam juice cocktails, ox joints, and blood rare sirloin sand-
wiches—didn't stand the test of time, according to the club's history.

Club membership had grown to well over 700 by the time First
National Bank had moved into its new Perkins & Will–designed
headquarters (now called Chase Tower) in 1969. The Mid-Day
Club followed, moving to its final location on the 56th floor. Even
in a more modern facility, the club was able to move and install
most of its artwork and furniture, as did the Cliff Dwellers when it
moved to the Borg-Warner Building at 200 S. Michigan Ave.

A CLUB OF CLUBS

In its final years, the Mid-Day Club was able to keep its membership over 700 by taking in clubs that had given up clubhouse
space. The Mid-Day got a big assist when it welcomed the members

of the Attic Club, which vacated its old clubhouse space in the early 1990s.

The Mid-Day Club has provided a home to many smaller clubs throughout its history, some of them clubs within a club made up of the Mid-Day Club's own membership. According to the club's history, they include the Bandar-Log, Law Club of the City of Chicago, and the Loyal Legion Club. Here are descriptions of these clubs from the Mid-Day Club's own history.

THE BANDAR-LOG

Founded in 1922, the Bandar-Log was made up of members who were "independent and reasonably tolerant thinkers of varied careers and civic pursuits who discuss matters of current interest in an untrammeled way, with nobody being quoted, and with there being no tête-à-têtes, The Bandar-Log meets in round-table fashion," surrounding two prized silver engraved bowls. It took its name from author Rudyard Kipling's monkeys in *The Jungle Book*. Al Meyers, a member of The Mid-Day Club, wrote to Kipling advising him of the name and received "an appreciative reply."

According to this smaller club's charter:

Members must be able to absorb a reasonable amount of mental punishment in respect to fixed convictions, and all carefully chosen members can say their piece and be heard. . . . We have no bylaws, no membership committee, no constitution, officers, initiation fees, or dues—Forever we are very careful who joins, and, occasionally, we look at our two silver bowls and one of our steady waitresses will polish them.

THE LAW CLUB OF CHICAGO

The Law Club of Chicago was founded in 1883 to be "an association of members of the bar of the City of Chicago, for the purpose of advancing, by social intercourse and a friendly exchange of view, the condition of the law and the interest of its practitioners in this City." By 1900 the Law Club had 112 members. An early president of the Law Club is said to have suggested that "the old fellows had pretty well got control of the Chicago Bar Association and the Illinois State Bar Association, and the young fellows didn't have much of a chance." To be eligible for membership, one had to be a lawyer in good standing, active in the profession, and not more than 40 years of age at the time of election to membership. Membership became so coveted that the age of 40 became the minimum age for membership; that remains the case today. There is no record of when the Law Club commenced its longstanding practice of holding regular monthly dinner meetings and regular monthly luncheon meetings of its Executive Committee at the Mid-Day Club. Former trustee John K. Notz Jr., having been a guest at meetings prior to 1972, became a member when he was first eligible and was its president in 1989–90. In about 1998 the Law Club of Chicago merged with the Legal Club of Chicago (a slightly younger, similar organization that customarily has met at the University Club of Chicago) into the Lawyers Club of Chicago. Its meetings are divided between Mid-Day and the University Club.

THE LOYAL LEGION CLUB

Very few early records of this club remain, but there is documentation that the Loyal Legion Club was one of the first clubs to hold monthly meetings at the Mid-Day Club. The Loyal Legion was formed by three Union Army officers on April 15, 1865, after the assassination of President Lincoln, in an effort to thwart future threats to the federal government. By 1899 the Loyal Legion had more than 8,000 Civil War officers on its roster. As the members aged, the rules were changed to permit "Heredity Companions" (descendants of eligible officers). Starting in 1905 all the Loyal Legion meetings were sponsored by the Mid-Day Club's charter member and former trustee John Black of Winston, Strawn, Black & Towner. Black was the son of Brigadier General John C. Black, a Civil War hero who had received the Medal of Honor. Two Mid-Day Club members, Charles Gates Dawes and Rufus Dawes, attended these meetings because their father, Rufus R. Dawes, was a Civil War general serving as commander of the Wisconsin Iron Brigade. While its records are skimpy, it's believed that the monthly meet-

ings of the Loyal Legion Club may have been held at the Mid-Day
Club until 1952, seven years before the death of John Black.

THE CLOSING OF THE MID-DAY CLUB

During the summer of 2007, the leadership of the Mid-Day Club
was informed that it would lose its lease at Chase Tower since its
landlord JPMorgan Chase wanted the 56th floor space for its own
use. A search immediately ensued to find new quarters. After a
review of 32 potential locations, the club decided the build-out of
new space (including build-ins of the club artifacts) and the loss of
catering opportunities (an increasingly important part of all clubs'
income) would make moving unaffordable. Mid-Day Club members
would be given the option of transferring to the other clubs mentioned at the introduction of this chapter.

Indeed, other outside clubs that met at the Mid-Day—such as
the Caxton Club and the Traffic Club of Chicago—would also be
looking for new homes by the end of the year.

Sources:
Card, Jill. *The Mid-Day Club, Our First* 100 *Years* (1903–2003).
    Edited by John K. Notz Jr. Virginia Beach: Donning
    Company Publishers, 2005.

SPOTLIGHT

∽ WHO BLACKBALLED UNCLE SAM? ∾

The private club industry did not have a good tax year in 1993. As part of the Revenue Reconciliation Act of 1993— and increasing discontent in Washington with the deductibility of business expenses in general— Congress zeroed in on the deductibility of club dues as fringe benefits. This was a true blow to the club industry, because club memberships as a fringe benefit for management talent at all levels was the engine that kept membership rolls high. For all the tax geeks out there, here quoth the IRS:

CLUB MEMBERSHIPS—
Effective since calendar year 1994, § 274(a)(3) provides that no deduction is permitted for club dues. This includes all types of clubs, including social, athletic, sporting, luncheon clubs, airline and hotel clubs and "business" clubs for all amounts paid or incurred after 1993. Regulations § 1.274-2(a)(2)(iii) and (e)(3) (ii)(b) clarifies that the purposes and activities of a club, and not its name, determine whether it is covered under the disallowance

provision. The employer has the choice of either including the value of the club membership in the employee's income or forgoing any deduction for the club dues. IRS § 274(e)(2). Put another way, the company can deduct the cost if it treats the club dues as compensation includable in gross income and wages. However, if the employer's deduction for club dues is disallowed by § 274(a)(3), Regulations § 1.132-5(s) provides that the amount, if any, of an employee's working condition fringe benefit relating to the employer provided membership in the club is determined without regard to the application of § 274(a) to the employee. To be excludible as a working condition fringe, however, the amount must otherwise qualify for deduction by the employee under §162(a).

Note that the requirements of § 274(d) must still be met (i.e., time, place and business purpose must be established). See Regulations §1.132-5(s)(3) for examples applying these rules.

Although many corporations are aware of the law regarding the deductibility of club dues and mem-

bership fees, they will often make such expenditures and disguise the deduction. Club memberships have been distributed to departing executives through severance agreements. The value of a club membership distributed to executives upon departure is wages. Close scrutiny should be afforded employment contracts and severance agreements for executives.

In reality the 1993 ruling hit social, athletic, and sporting clubs the hardest, unless tax advisors could help their clients justify that their dues contributed to the active conduct of their trade or business. City clubs took less of a hit because they have always drawn the power suit crowd, and if anything, the 1993 ruling got clubs to increase their business services and facilities to make it easier for club members to make those numbers work.

The bottom line? If you're thinking about joining a private club, call your tax professional first.

155

THE
ECONOMIC CLUB
OF
CHICAGO

The Economic Club of Chicago
Founded: 1927
Address: 177 N. State Street, Suite 404,
Chicago, IL 60601 *(office only—no clubhouse)*

*Author's Note: The Economic Club of Chicago declined to be
interviewed for this book. Therefore, much of the information you
see here comes from the club's brief history and other sources.*

First of all, the Economic Club of Chicago was not created to wor-
ship what Thomas Carlyle called "the dismal science." In fact, very
few economists belong to the club, which instead opts for top
officials and up-and-coming executives in the city's business, nonprofit, and public-sector organizations. It is also a gathering place
for some of the most powerful people in the world. The Economic
Club has hosted such luminaries as former Federal Reserve chairman Alan Greenspan; Presidents Ronald Reagan, Jimmy Carter,
Herbert Hoover, John F. Kennedy (when he was a U.S. senator),
and Richard M. Nixon; Tony Blair, the British prime minister; and
Microsoft chief Bill Gates.

While press coverage of the club's events is covered on local cable TV access, the group itself is genuinely private about its own history. In fact, the club's 75th anniversary history book, published in 2002, is light on narrative and essentially a compilation of guest speeches throughout its history.

The Economic Club is an invitation-only group, what the club itself describes as the "Who's Who and Who's to Be" of Chicago's business and professional elite. Further, it states:

> The Economic Club's membership policies explicitly seek to establish lasting inter-generational relationships so as to insure a continuum of knowledge and traditions within Chicago's civic and business community as the torch of leadership passes from one generation to the next.

The coed organization holds four black-tie speaking events each year, usually featuring major heads of state or corporate chieftains.

Sources:

The Economic Club of Chicago. *History's Witnesses*, 1927–2002. Chicago: The Economic Club of Chicago, 2002.

XVI

THE
EXECUTIVES' CLUB
OF
CHICAGO

———◆———

The Executives' Club of Chicago
Founded: 1911
Address: 8 S. Michigan Avenue, Suite 2500,
Chicago, IL 60603 *(office only—no clubhouse)*

Author's Note: The Executives' Club of Chicago declined to be
interviewed for this book. Therefore, much of the information you
see here comes from the club's brief history and other sources.

Part speakers forum, part professional development organization,
the Executives' Club of Chicago was formed in 1911 as an organization for men "holding an executive position, either as owner, partner, department manager or official of the company he represents."
The club describes itself as "the oldest business forum in the
Midwest." Today the club is coed, though membership is by invitation only.

The club's speakers over the years haven't all been strictly from
the world of business or politics. The club has hosted speakers as
diverse as film director and producer Cecil B. DeMille (who spoke
in 1947 on the topic "Are the Movies Infested with Commies?") and
Katharine Graham spoke on Ladies' Day on February 15, 1974. The

announcement of her speech included the headline "Lady Publisher."

Today the club not only hosts a diverse range of speakers but sponsors several committees within the club, dealing with civic affairs, communications, finance, real estate, and technology. Another committee is for young leaders.

The club's staff and leadership are shy about talking, but the group continues to be one of the most sought-after memberships in the city. In December 2007, the Executives' Club's management fell under criticism by *Crain's Chicago Business* for not reporting salaries and fees paid by the organization pursuant to Internal Revenue Service rules. Club management would only say that the Executives' Club was "in the black and had net assests of more than $1 million as of mid-2007."

Sources:

The Executives' Club of Chicago. *The Executives' Club of Chicago: 90 Years and Counting.* Chicago: The Executives' Club of Chicago, 2003.

XVII

THE
CHICAGO NETWORK

———————

The Chicago Network
Founded: 1979
Address: No clubhouse;
meetings held at various locations.

It would be another eight years before the last of the major men's clubs finally knocked down the gender barrier, but a group of Chicago businesswomen found themselves at dinner in 1979 and began to hatch a plan. This group, which dubbed themselves the Good Old Girls and were part of the first generation of women to reach middle management in major corporations, had been meeting socially for a while. But they started to wonder what it would be like to increase the size of their group over time.

The group hired a professional researcher to help find the leading women in metropolitan Chicago. They pared their list from 1,000 to 113 invitees, established a Founding Board, and wrote and mailed the invitations. Ninety-seven women accepted the invitation to meet for the first time on the 67th floor of the Sears Tower in the Metropolitan Club.

And thus the Chicago Network was born.

"It started very slowly, and very quietly," recalls Amy Osler, the Chicago Network's executive director. "Women function on a variety of levels very quickly. But this was a way to gather up the highest-ranking women in a variety of fields, not only representing business, but hundreds of civic boards. No one had really attempted to gather a group like this in Chicago before."

Among the organization's past and current members are Jean Allard, first woman partner at Sonnenschein, Nath & Rosenthal (and one of the first women members of the Chicago Club); former Chicago mayor Jane Byrne; former Illinois state representative Susan Catania; and mystery novelist Sara Paretsky.

Now more than 25 years old, the group has 350 members and is one of the cofounders of the National Women's Forum. It continues to conduct groundbreaking research on the progress of women in corporate leadership.

Based on a joint 2006 survey, the news hasn't been great. Among the findings:

The number of women directors decreased nearly one percentage point to 13.8 percent after a 2005 increase.

The number of women executive officers decreased to 14.6 percent after an increase the previous year.

Thirty-seven companies (74 percent of the total) have no women top earners, up from 35 in 2005.

Today the group has an even more diverse membership, including mathematicians, TV producers, educators, doctors, lawyers, sculptors, art historians, scientists, computer programmers, psychiatrists, and painters of buildings and of canvas. On the corporate side, club members head ad agencies, construction firms, not-for-profit organizations, medical groups, messenger services, theater troops, museums, public relations companies, international divisions, and their own businesses. They don't make political endorsements and in fact have only one absolute rule: each member must return a fellow member's phone call or e-mail within 24 hours.

Sources:

Osler, Amy. Interview by author. 15 June 2005.

XVIII

THE
TRAFFIC CLUB
OF
CHICAGO

The Traffic Club of Chicago
Founded: 1907
Address: 600 Enterprise Drive, Suite 106,
Oak Brook, IL 60523 (office only — no clubhouse; meetings
are held at various locations, around the city and suburb.)

Transportation has always driven the growth of Chicago. First it was water, then rail, then auto and air. The Traffic Club of Chicago is probably one of the best surviving examples of an industry-themed club that's held on despite great change in the business that created it.

Most of the city's clubs have gone through sweeping changes culturally as members from different professions entered and left. Not the Traffic Club. It's always been about transportation, one of Chicago's most enduring industries if not always the most stable.

"You'll see corporations and industries come and go, but Chicago has always been about moving things from one place to the other," says Bill Fors, who has been the club's general manager since the 1970s. "Transportation is still a lifeblood industry in this city, though people don't think about it as much. We're still the rail hub of the country, and that continues to be the reason that so much of this industry is still here — air, water, and highway transport all fit in together with the rail lines, even today." Indeed, for freight and passenger traffic, nowhere in the country, not even New York, comes close.

According to Fors, the Traffic Club harkens back to a day when the captains of industry were in direct, often face-to-face contact with the leaders of the country. Relationships were very personal and driven by the almighty dollar, and politicians came to them, not the other way around. Not only were members of the Traffic Club — and other clubs besides — able to pick up the phone and have presidents, senators, and congressmen come when called, but these powerful people were regular visitors at the clubs when they came to town.

"President Taft used to come here all the time," Fors remembers. "The clubs back then were extraordinary centers of power. Obviously, government and business have a much more distant relationship now by comparison."

Still, presidents depending on the transportation health of the country came to the Traffic Club. The club hosted not only Taft but also Coolidge, Hoover, Eisenhower, and Reagan. The Traffic Club also welcomed Captain Eddie Rickenbacker, America's first air ace of World War I, as well as Amelia Earhart and Will Rogers Jr.

THE BEGINNING

Frank T. Bentley, a traffic manager for the Illinois Steel Co., got the idea that there should be a specific networking group for manufacturers and the transportation companies that got their goods from point A to point B. After an informal dinner at the Auditorium Hotel on March 28, 1907, the Traffic Club of Chicago was formed.

The first board of the Traffic Club featured Bentley and a variety of other business leaders, including John Stockton, manager of the Joseph Stockton Company, as secretary; M.S. Connolly, general Western freight agent for the Pittsburgh, Cincinnati, Chicago & St. Louis Railway, as treasurer; and three vice presidents: Darius

Miller, vice president of the Chicago, Burlington & Quincy Railroad; Frank S. Spink, traffic manager of the National Packing Company; and G.H. Ingalls, freight manager for the New York Central Lines.

The club's first lunchroom was established in the Grand Pacific Hotel, with the stipulation "open to all members and their friends on the Dutch Treat plan, unless you wish to open your hearts and wallet to entertain as at any other place."

As the Traffic Club grew, it kept moving on to bigger quarters. In 1909 it moved into the 18th floor of the newly built LaSalle Hotel, where it would remain for 20 years. Then the Palmer House came calling with a sweet deal for 20,000 square feet. The club would pay nominal rent, and the hotel would operate the food and bar service, leaving the organization without significant headaches from managing overhead.

The club moved out of the Palmer House in the early 1990s for a brief and unhappy stay in the old M&M Club in the Merchandise Mart. That club's open-door policy toward CTA workers left some pieces of the Traffic Club's priceless art collection damaged, Fors maintains. After the M&M Club closed a few years later when the Mart redeveloped the club's second floor space into its current two-story mall area, the Traffic Club decided to centralize its management quarters in Oak Brook but let its meeting space roam. Through 2007, it was holding many of its downtown meetings at the Mid-Day Club.

TODAY'S WORKER, TODAY'S CLUB

The days of the railroad magnate and robber baron long since over, Fors notes that the Traffic Club has had to change considerably with the times. He explains:

> To be a member of the Traffic Club once carried a lot of weight. We don't kid ourselves now—we are a group that enables networking for a very important industry, and that's that. We used to declare honorary members at 20 years and retirement; now it's ten years and retired. Today nobody's working for a company forever—they're lucky to stay in the

same industry for a career. We have members who have worked for three companies in the last three years!

According to Fors, clubs need to adapt to the environment their members work in and want to play in. The club life is now primarily one of lunch with important industry speakers and the occasional golf outing or ball game. The after-work drink is gone and weekend activities are largely gone.

"In the end, the importance of a club is solely decided by its membership and its leadership," Fors says. "And at nearly a century old, we have people who are very serious about making sure this club survives."

Sources:
Card, Jill. *The Mid-Day Club, Our First* 100 *Years* (1903–2003). Edited by John K. Notz Jr. Virginia Beach: Donning Company Publishers, 2005.
Fors, Bill. Interview by author. 23 February 2006.
The Traffic Club of Chicago. www.traffic-club.org. Accessed March 2006–March 2007.

THE
SOCIAL CLUBS

XIX

THE
CASINO

———

The Casino
Founded: 1914
Address: 195 E. Delaware Place,
Chicago, IL 60611
Architect: Walter Frazier

Author's Note: The Casino declined to be interviewed for this book. Therefore, much of the information you see here comes from Oasis in the City: A History of The Casino *(1997), by Kevin M. Callahan. There is no listing for this organization in Appendix A.*

In the 1950 book *Chicago Confidential*, authors Jack Lait and Lee Mortimer said its building looked like an Exaggerated Beetle. True, it looks particularly bug-like next to one of the world's tallest sky-scrapers, the John Hancock Center.

But The Casino—not The Casino Club—holds a special place in Chicago's club history. Founded in 1914, it was a loud, boisterous coed social club founded by society women at a time when the only proper clubs being formed by women were literary in nature and more than a little staid. It was proof that if you gathered the rich-est women in the city—particularly the youngest ones on the brink of flapperdom—and let them design a club, it would become the one place everyone had to get into.

*The Casino, at 195 E.
Delaware Place, is one
of only four city clubs
regularly listed in
The Social Register.
The others are the
Contemporary Club
(housed at The
Fortnightly, itself a
historic women's club),
the Chicago Club,
and the Racquet Club.
(Photo by Lisa Holton.)*

THE VISION OF LUCY McCORMICK BLAIR LINN

According to Kevin M. Callahan's book, *Oasis in the City: A History of The Casino*, Lucy McCormick Blair was inspired by travel. A visit to New York got her to start Chicago's first Junior League chapter "to give a sense of their social responsibility to young debs and provide funds for various philanthropies." She was 20 at the time. Two years later on a trip to France, she was enthralled by the sophistication of French resorts to borrow those ideas and create a French-inspired social club in Chicago, where, as Kevin M. Callahan writes in *Oasis in the City*, "men and women could gather for tea, parties and dinners."

She proposed the idea to Mrs. Joseph Coleman and Rue Winterbotham Carpenter, society ladies who, like her, were part of Chicago's oldest families. According to Callahan:

> They met at Mrs. Carpenter's, and initially they named the new club The Blue Bird after Madame Maurice Maeterlinck's book called *The Children's Blue Bird*. Initially, they had trou-

blc finding room because they wanted to keep fees cheap for younger members. Initially, the Blue Bird did not survive as a club. They renamed it The North Side Casino, which the *Tribune* said would give the club an "air of permanence." And at that time, members decided to build their own clubhouse.

Where did it get the name? Callahan notes that the first known organization called The Casino was the Newport Casino built in 1879 by *New York Herald* publisher James Gordon Bennett Jr. Then there was the Sconset Casino on Nantucket, which exists today for theater and tennis. There was also a building known as The Casino at the World's Columbian Exposition. It was essentially one of the world's first food courts.

A CLUBHOUSE LIKE NO OTHER

Blair's idea was to create a clubhouse with cutting-edge design that would be a clear departure from sedate places like the Lathrop House (home of The Fortnightly) and other brownstones that housed ladies' organizations. But they had to get the land first.

The land The Casino sits on was part of the original parcel controlled by the infamous Captain George Wellington Streeter. Because his boat was parked a block east on the lakefront, he declared squatter's rights on millions of dollars worth of property and actually began to sell lots for a hefty profit. Yet the real owner of what would become The Casino property was the Palmer family, which wrested their piece of land away from Streeter so they could lease it to The Casino. In a lease signed May 1, 1914, The Casino was to hold the property for a period of 30 years and could use the adjacent grounds until somebody bought the property.

Callahan's book repeats the *Chicago Tribune's* description of its clubhouse:

It would be a one-story stucco building of Spanish influence accompanied by long French windows which opened into iron-railed balconies. Rue (Winterbotham) Carpenter [the top celebrity interior designer of her day] did the interior design, but was also surprisingly powerful with the exterior design as well.

The first Casino building (more on that below), was a standout in Pepto-Bismol pink.

The book details the interior of the later club building in 1997:

Inside, the painted plumage of Nicholas Remisoff, famous Russian muralist of the day. Floral murals were done by Casino member Bill Moulis...The Biedermeier furniture, the Aubusson rugs and the taffeta curtains have all retained the distinct style of Rue Winterbotham Carpenter who designed the Club's interior in 1929. . . Tradition dictates that a woman test the slenderness of her figure by slipping between the legendary gold painted double columns.

On the left is the fountain room with mirrors on the walls, cast iron tables on the terrazzo floor, and retractable walls on each side that open into private dining rooms (quite an innovation for 1929). Beyond is the cocktail lounge, decorated in mahogany and velvet with foil-engraved pictures of various actors adorning the walls. Towards the front of the building stands the ladies' card room, small but comfortable, carpeted in forest green, and the larger drawing room with its Biedermeier couches, parquetry tables, elephant-form chenets and a rose medallion punchbowl.

THE MOST INFAMOUS CLUB IN TOWN

The Casino opened impressively enough, but the Roaring Twenties made it infamous. Young women bobbing their hair, raising their hemlines, and tucking away flasks during Prohibition didn't impress the dowagers of the club. According to Callahan:

This division never revealed itself beyond the confines of the Club until 1921, when the activities of the Club became cannon fodder for the latest volley of sensational yellow journalism. In October 1921, three leaders of what was called 'The Younger Set' were expelled from the Club and soon rumors were flying about Chicago. 'Strange things,' reported the sensationalist newspaper the *Herald American*, 'occurred within the club while the eyes of the older generation were turned away.' According to the paper, young men in evening clothes were to be seen emerging from The Casino at unseemly hours in laggard condition, 'bursting snatches of queer songs from their lips.'

The parties got so out of control that The Drake Hotel complained.

The last straw seems to have come in 1921 with something called the Harem Party. Traffic jams formed so onlookers could watch drunken revelers staggering and being carried from the building on stretchers. Eventually, the club got raided, though it made it through the ordeal in time for 1926's "Hard Times" party. Callahan describes:

The dance took place in December. It was cold, it was windy. There was snow on the streets. Charlie Walker chose to come in a barrel. The barrel was attached across his shoulders with purple suspenders nailed firmly into place. Underneath the barrel, Charlie wore B.V.D's, socks, and dancing pumps only. Dilemma? How to get to The Casino? He hailed a cab. Of course the barrel would not go through the cab door. So what did our outrageous hero do? He stood on the running board . . . therefore, suspended in this fashion, with his barrel swinging, Charlie Walker rode to the front door of The Casino . . . in time to win first prize.

In 1926 the Palmers wanted their money out of the land beneath the club — actually very good timing considering the crash was less than three years away. So the club had to move. There was some talk of putting it in a high-rise at Lake Shore Drive and Pearson and another plan to put it in the George Isham house, which eventually became the Playboy Mansion. Yet the owner of the property at Delaware and Seneca — directly west of the original Casino — put his parcel up for sale and the club bit. At the time, the land cost a whopping $30,000.

HANCOCK? WHAT HANCOCK?

Because The Casino was generally open to the city's ultrarich, there were no stories about near-bankruptcy that were common at the other clubs during the Great Depression. So until the 1960s not much really happened at The Casino except for the good times.

That is, until Skidmore, Owings & Merrill made plans a few feet west of The Casino's clubhouse. Big plans, in fact. Writes Callahan:

> Everything seemed just right for the [John Hancock Center] except for the fact that there was this little building, probably unseen from 95 stories in the air, which was sitting on the Hancock block. This little building had a peculiar design. It employed circular shapes and odd angles. This one-story oddity seemed to defy the metropolis of the future rising so high above its roof. Clearly, this little building had seen its day.

Somehow, with all the clout gathered within the walls of that little building, the Hancock people backed off. And The Casino is still there.

Sources:
Callahan, Kevin M. *Oasis in the City: A History of The Casino.* Chicago: The Casino, 1997.
Lait, Jack, and Lee Mortimer. *Chicago Confidential.* New York: Crown Publishers, 1951.

XX

THE
FORTNIGHTLY
OF
CHICAGO

The Fortnightly of Chicago
Founded: 1873
Address: 120 E. Bellevue Place, Chicago, IL 60611
Architect: McKim, Mead & White for original owner Bryan
Lathrop

*Author's Note: The Fortnightly declined to be interviewed for
this book. Therefore, much of the information you see here comes
from* The Fortnightly of Chicago: The City and Its Women *(1973),
by Muriel Beadle, and other sources at the Newberry Library.
There is no listing for this organization in Appendix A.*

Kate Newell Doggett came to Chicago to open a private school for
girls and ended up founding one of the most exclusive and important women's clubs in the country.

The Fortnightly was both a social and literary club for upper-
class women in the city. Unlike other women's organizations that
started afterward, it stayed away from publicity and out of the
public fray. They continue that tradition today—contacts with
current members indicated a general unwillingness to talk about
their club. Said one who didn't want her name used, "That's just
the way we like it to be."

Today, the club is a center for quiet meetings, classical concerts,
and general socializing. Then as now, it's not a center for political

The Fortnightly clubhouse is located in the Lathrop House, 120 E.
Bellevue Place. (Courtesy of Barbara Crane for the Commission on
Chicago Landmarks.)

discourse or activist thought despite the advances for women over
the past 130 years. Those activities—particularly in the early days
of the suffrage movement—were better left to organizations like
Chicago Woman's Club, which spun off from The Fortnightly in
1976 but contained the same blue-blooded membership.

In 1873 there was only a handful of upscale women's clubs in the
entire nation. Among them were Friends in Council (located in
Quincy, Illinois), which had been meeting weekly since 1866. The
Sorosis in New York would eventually spawn a Chicago branch. Yet
until Kate Doggett created The Fortnightly in 1873, there was no
dominant white woman's literary club in Chicago—though by that
time, there were a number of men's and women's literacy societies
among the top African-American families in Chicago.

The Fortnightly was an association for its first 50 years and
became a society thereafter. Beadle writes that The Fortnightly, like
The Standard (later the Standard Club) didn't attach "club" to
their name because, "in some circles, 'club' may have had a vulgar
or sporting connotation."

Initial members of the organization were the top women in
Chicago society. They included Katherine Medill, Kate S. Isham,

Isabella F. Blackstone, Elizabeth W. Skinner, Cornelia Gray Lunt, and Jessie Bross Lloyd. Lunt became most identified with her family's philanthropic work in Evanston, Illinois, while Lloyd would eventually make her home in Winnetka.

From the beginning members presented papers and essays with such titles as "Thee Material Life and Social Conditions of the Greeks in the Time of Homer," "Ovid," and "Roman Jurisprudence," which were presented between 1875 and 1880.

The first paper, according to Beadle, was written by member Ellen Mitchell, entitled "Culture for Women." Beadle's description follows:

> [The paper] reflected both [poet and critic] Matthew Arnold's thinking and the flowery rhetoric of lesser writers of the day. Culture— 'the best that has been thought and said in the world'—improves one's judgment when combined in a fair mind with fresh knowledge, Mrs. Mitchell said. . . . Finally, Mrs. Mitchell said, 'Would that the aims of women for culture. . . might be as high as the everlasting hills, as broad as the fields of Paradise and as deep as the fathomless sea!

If that seems a bit precious, Beadle stresses that The Fortnightly, particularly in the nineteenth century, provided a haven for women who were recognized for no other reason than their service as wives and mothers:

> First, [The Fortnightly] had conferred respectability upon club activity for women. Second, it had provided organizational experience, procedural training and practice in public speaking for the first generation of Chicago's clubwomen.

Beadle reports that after the launching of The Fortnightly in Chicago, other cities borrowed the name and started similar organizations throughout the country, though some like The Fortnightly Club of Redlands, California, founded in 1895, were actually started by men.

LIFE INSIDE THE CLUB

Again, the failure to get current comment inside the club makes this description dated and inadequate, but here's how Muriel Beadle described life inside the club in 1973:

> For almost all of its history, Fortnightly meetings have been held in the afternoon. The early pattern was to begin at two or two-thirty, with tea following the program. In the club's 'middle years,' luncheon preceded the meeting and tea followed. During the 1960s, the teas were discontinued except following a program given by a member. During the 1970s, a few morning meetings have been scheduled with luncheon afterwards. But the traditional, and still predominant, pattern of a Fortnightly day is one that clears the ballroom after luncheon and allows the members to finish their conversations—or start new ones—in the other rooms of the house; and then reassembles them in the ballroom, for the program.

> As a preamble, the president stations herself in the drawing room, with a board member or an honored guest at her side, to 'receive' the members. Out in the entrance hall, the ladies at the end of the line click open their purses and extract the white gloves they have brought specifically for the ceremony. A few have forgotten to bring any. Perhaps they dip into a drawer in the Biedermeier commode where a supply of white gloves is kept for just this emergency; perhaps they proceed bare-handed; perhaps they bypass the line and guiltily duck into the bathroom. Some of those wearing the gloves feel sheepish. 'The ritual is an anachronism,' they say to others of like mind—and in truth it is. Yet it persists.

Sources:
Anonymous Fortnightly members. Interviews by author.
    2005–2006.
Beadle, Muriel, and the Centennial History Committee. *The Fortnightly of Chicago: The City and its Women: 1873–1973.*
    Chicago: Henry Regnery Co., 1973.

XXI

THE
ADVENTURERS
CLUB

———◆———

The Adventurers Club
Founded: 1911
Address: 714 S. Dearborn Street, Unit #6,
Chicago, IL 60605

There was once a time when adventure travel meant so much more than going online and plunking down a credit card for a prepackaged trip complete with four-star hotel accommodations. In 1911 the world was still a relatively unknown place. It was three years before Sir Ernest Shackleton would launch his legendary *Endurance* mission to the Antarctic. It would take 42 more years for Edmund Hillary and Tenzing Norgay to reach the summit of Mount Everest.

Shackleton, Hillary, Thor Heyerdahl, and many of the other greatest adventurers in the last century's history have stopped in for a drink and a retelling of stories at a strange little Chicago clubhouse full of hunting trophies, shrunken heads, and edged weapons. It's the Adventurers Club, a nearly 100-year-old testament to men with fortunes who bypassed the golf course and spent their spare time off on safaris, trekking up mountains, and trudging to either pole.

Howard Rosen, president of the club in 2007, quotes the club motto, "To provide a hearth and home for those who have left the beaten path and made for adventure," as he explains the relevance of the club today. "It's easy in today's world to forget that seeking out adventure is what makes an interesting life. That's what this club is all about."

Marlin Perkins, the former Lincoln Park Zoo director and friendly host of the old *Wild Kingdom* TV series, was a former president of the club. Theodore Roosevelt, an adventurer and conservationist in his own right, was the club's first honorary member, and a congratulatory note from the 26th President is displayed in a prominent frame.

Millionaire balloonist and aviator Steve Fossett is a recent marquee name on the honorary list. (In September 2007, Fossett went missing after piloting his personal aircraft over Nevada.)

Reached via e-mail during 2005 while he practiced his record-breaking run at the longest distance flight in aviation history, Fossett responded, "The Adventurers Club represents a grand tradition in the spirit of the adventurers of the nineteenth and early twentieth century. I have taken particular pride in being an Honorary Member."

That's another change—adventurers have e-mail now.

The Adventurers Club has taken its hits over the years, if not for the stuffed seven-foot whale penis over the bar (yep, you read that right), then for other aspects of its decidedly unreconstructed male outlook on the world. A front-page *Wall Street Journal* piece from 1983 still sticks in Rosen's craw because it made a little fun of how rugged one of his South American fishing safaris wasn't and featured a subhead that said "Adventure Gone Soft."

"I don't think she [Laurel Sorenson, author of the *Journal* story] really understood us," says Rosen, a financial executive who in his 50s is one of the younger members of the club. "But not everybody does." Whatever the criticism, Rosen refuses to give up on his romance with a club he aspired to join as a young kid growing up in the suburbs. He just loves the lore.

"An adventurer today admittedly isn't the person he or she was at the beginning of the last century. But to try something that few people have tried, that's what makes life worth living," declares Rosen, whose main love is fishing in remote areas. The club's latest improbable headquarters—members have lost track of exactly how many times it's moved—is located in the middle of Printers Row.

IN THE BEGINNING, THERE WAS TEDDY

The club was started by Robert Foran, an Associated Press correspondent attached to President Theodore Roosevelt's African big-game expedition of 1909–10. After he got to town, Foran got to know Charles Dawell, the proprietor of St. Hubert's Old English Grill, where a number of locals who were big-game hunters, explorers, and military men had been meeting informally.

According to club materials:

> Bob, author and journalist, with his background of adventure that included big-game hunting, ivory poaching, military and police service, was a welcome addition to their group. It was during one of these informal meetings that our club came into

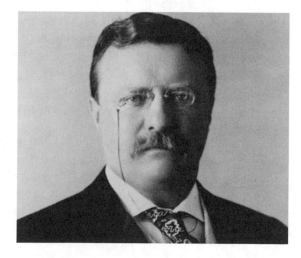

Theodore Roosevelt, 26th President and inspiration for the Adventurers Club. (Courtesy of the Adventurers Club.)

The long tables are intended to bring friends and strangers together during regular meals at the club. (Photo by Howard Rosen, the Adventurers Club.)

being—when Major Foran proposed its organization and all those present enthusiastically approved the idea.

The first of the club's many homes was opened in 1912 in the old Chicago Press Club Building at 26 N. Dearborn Street. As so many clubs have done, the Adventurers Club reached out to other similar-minded clubs, like the Savage Club of London, with which it still has a reciprocal agreement today. In 1914 the Adventurers Club moved to the Boyce Building at 40 S. Clark Street, to River North in 1997, and back to the South Loop in late 2006.

A SAVAGE CLUBHOUSE

Visitors walk in from the South Loop neighborhood into a room filled with plenty of taxidermy and the lingering smell of cigar smoke. Dozens of hunting trophies, including a grizzly bear at full height and Gertrude the gorilla in a crouch, surround the room. There are cases filled with shrunken heads and frightening-looking weapons that make you happy they're under glass. A long table for at least 20 sits in the middle of the room with smaller tables scattered around and the "Sign of the Whale" (we've already been over that) Bar in the corner. It's not a place for the squeamish or the smoke-averse.

On the ceiling, however, is the real sense of history—the flags.

The flags—200 of them—are banners awarded to members of the club who complete trips that qualify as adventures by the club. According to the club's literature:

> If the plan meets with our stringent standards of travel, adventure, uniqueness and daring-do, then the committee will order that two flags be made. When the member departs on the trip, the flags will accompany him or her. When—and if!—he or she returns, one of the flags will be presented back to the Club President, usually at a special dinner upon the Long Table (known as "Flag Dinners"), during the course of which the tales of the adventure will be recounted to the membership. The returned flag will proudly join its brothers

Tiara in place, Gertrude the Gorilla sits in the corner of the club. She was the trophy of a club member. (Photos by Howard Rosen, the Adventurers Club.)

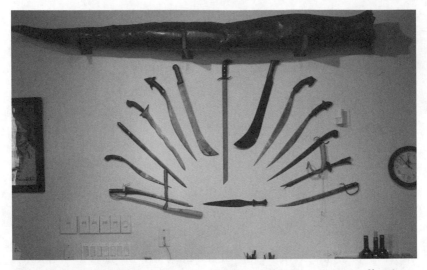

The aforementioned whale penis above a rather impressive collection of edged weapons at the club's bar. (Photo by Howard Rosen, the Adventurers Club.)

and sisters, to hang in the rafters as a memorial to the Adventure. The second flag is retained by the Member, to do with as he or she pleases.

It's a jocular environment, and wives and girlfriends are always part of major events. Women have been members off and on for the past few years. But for anyone who dislikes at least symbolic evidence of machismo from an earlier time, this may not be the place for you.

Mike Lane, a triathlon runner and head of a real estate technology company in Chicago, joined because he liked the camaraderie, the evening lecture series (running the gamut from hunters to anthropologists), and the general sense that he was part of history. How did he find out about the Adventurers Club? He saw it on the WTTW series *Wild Chicago* a few years back.

"Every member has an interesting story to tell," Lane says. "We really do have all sorts of people here: people with a lot of money, people with very little money who scrape together whatever they can to go around the world and try new things."

CLUB NOTES

⟫ SO . . . WHAT'S AN ADVENTURE ⟪
ANYWAY?

In case you're in doubt about what constitutes adventure in the twenty-first century, the club provides a list:

Racing (boat, plane, car, horse, etc.), rock and ice climbing, mountaineering, travel to remote areas of the world not readily accessible by guided tour, hunting and fishing, remote photography, white water rafting, extended stay in remote areas (Peace Corps, wildlife experts, ex-military), extended balloon or glider trips, sailing, skydiving, hanggliding and kite surfing, scuba diving in remote areas or great depths, environmental testing, space exploration, test pilots, ultralight plane flight, survival gear field testing, treasure hunters, spelunkers, astronomers, astronauts (we take cosmonauts these days as well), extreme sports enthusiasts, base jumping, adventure racing, mountain biking, orienteering, archaeologists, anthropologists, paleontologists, zoologists, extreme skiing, snowboarding.

Sources:
Adventurers Club. Membership materials, 2006.
Rosen, Howard, and Mike Lane. Interview by author. Summer 2005.

XXII

THE
CHICAGO ATHLETIC
ASSOCIATION

———◆———

The Chicago Athletic Association
Founded: 1890
Address: 12 S. Michigan Avenue, Chicago, IL 60603
Architect: Henry Ives Cobb

Author's Note: On August 24, 2007, the Chicago Athletic
Association finally closed its doors after agreeing to sell out to
developers hoping to turn the Michigan Avenue landmark into
hotel and residential space. The last managers and officers of the
club refused to be interviewed for this book, but certain historical
information was made available. Because the club has closed,
there is no listing for CAA in Appendix A.

Before the multibillion-dollar business of pro sports was born, there were city athletic clubs with rich members who sponsored talented teams of amateur athletes in a variety of sports, particularly the fast-growing game of American football in the late nineteenth century. One of the leading football clubs was sponsored by the Chicago Athletic Association. The CAA was a bustling place from the moment of its founding, with leaders like William Wrigley, Henry Ives Cobb, Cyrus McCormick, Marshall Field, and their descendents. These men were just as interested in securing the coming World's Columbian Exposition as they were in this fledgling megasport that would capture Americans' attention on the high school, college, and pro level during the next century. The Chicago Athletic Association was always a unique mix of sports and clout.

*The Chicago
Athletic
Association's club-
house. (Photo by
Lisa Holton.)*

The original articles of association of the Club state that these men founded the CAA "to encourage all sports, to promote physical culture, and to cultivate social intercourse and friendly relations among the members of the Association."

Chicago has always been a sports town, and the Chicago Athletic Association made a sizable contribution to this legacy. In its last years, the club has been less about competitive athletics, more about relaxation, and mostly about trying to ensure its survival. Since 2000, members had begun to feel the weight of falling membership and rising costs, so they began to consider various alternatives including a sale of one or more of its properties.

Despite its enviable location, the CAA has been strapped for cash for years. In 2003, the club attempted to bring in a new source of cash with a restructuring that established two classes of members. Class A members would pay a one-time fee of $2000 for a voting membership, while all who declined would continue to pay current membership rates and fees as non-voting members while not retaining any ownership rights if the club were to be sold. At the time, it was seen as just another Band-Aid move the CAA has attempted during its history.

By 2005, reports had surfaced that CAA was considering selling all or part of its space to shore up its troubled finances. In October 2006, the *Chicago Sun-Times* reported that several developers were talking with the CAA about buying at least part of its property and redeveloping it into hotel or condo space while preserving the bulk of the historic club space. While the CAA's management and officers have never commented publicly on its financial and ownership status, club members in November 2006 approved a proposal to sell the buildings to Ohio developer Snider-Cannata Interests for $28.6 million. Snider-Cannata plans a 185-room hotel, with a working name of Millennium Park Hotel.

Yet by November 2006, 21 Class B members sued the association, its president, and the CAA's directors, alleging they breached their fiduciary duties to Class B members by failing to keep them informed of the true value of the property and by refusing to let them become Class A members after the real value became known. On June 11, 2007, the club filed for bankruptcy protection mainly as a way to put off lawsuits while the sale took place. And true to the club's code of secrecy, the club's initial bankruptcy filing did not detail total assets versus liabilites, listing them only as being between $1 million and $100 million. At the time, however, the club's headquarters, its primary asset, had been priced at $31 million while its debts were estimated at $8 million.

It was revealed that Atlanta-based Songy Partners LLC and Snider-Cannata Interests LLC of Cleveland bought the landmark 114-year-old two-building property—at 12 S. Michigan Ave. and 71 E. Madison—for that $31 million. The developers have said they'll spend $100 million to convert the buildings to a 300-room Omni hotel, ballroom, and athletic facility.

Again, at press time, Landmark activists were concerned about what Songy would do to preserve the architectural integrity of the building, particularly since the developer plans to attach a 19-story tower to the CAA's historic facade. Whatever becomes of the CAA's future, its past made it one of the most unique venues in Chicago's world of private clubs.

HOW IRISH WAS THE CAA?

The CAA has long carried the label "Chicago's Irish club" as much as the Standard Club was considered Chicago's Jewish club and the Chicago Club the vault for the best Protestant bloodlines in town. Clear majorities of those groups still dominate each of those clubs, but society has largely eliminated the need for exclusivity. No longer do Irish Americans have to form their own clubs, nor do Jews or women for that matter—well, maybe the power elite does, but the law and society have pried opened the doors more than a little at all private institutions.

Today Chicago's private clubs may not be singular models of total diversity, but compared to 100 years ago? There is no comparison.

Like most of the clubs, the CAA had its roots in the Eastern establishment—Boston, to be precise. But it's unclear whether the "Irish" reputation of the CAA was warranted at the start, though it has certainly developed over time. Chicago businessman Nick Farina, who has belonged to the CAA for more than a decade, comments:

> I joined because I wanted a place where I could exercise and have a quiet place to have lunch, either alone or for business. Each club has its own personality. The Chicago Club is probably most elite. The Standard Club, as I understand it, is mostly Jewish. The Union League is LaSalle Street, WASPish. The University Club was easy to get into yet more formal than the CAA. The CAA is athletics-oriented and has tons of Irish lawyers.

Member Mike Houlihan reflects the longtime Irish heritage of the club. He says he literally grew up at the club, playing basketball and taking boxing classes at the CAA in the junior program as a kid. "I fell in love with the atmosphere then." A former Mount Carmel High School football player, Houlihan jokes that the CAA is a place where former high school and college athletes can recapture a bit of lost glory. "It's my hangout. For anybody who was a high school jock, well, maybe you weren't the greatest athlete, but you miss it, and here's a place where you can combine sports with eating and drinking. It's great!"

Though the CAA allowed women to become full members in 1972—making it one of the earliest male-only clubs to do so—it didn't move into the future painlessly. In fact, there are still members who grumble a bit that the ladies pretty much ended the long tradition of nude swimming at the CAA.

THE EARLY CLUB

Like most of Chicago's major private clubs, the CAA was designed by a member—Henry Ives Cobb. The property was originally leased from Marshall Field, another founding member, and the club was eventually able to buy the land beneath the club in 1929, mere weeks before the Great Depression began. In 1907 the CAA added a new 18-story structure. The Madison Building connects to the northwest corner of the original structure, which has come to be known as the Michigan Building.

The club's sports legend dates back to 1896, when the CAA Pigskin Squad defeated Harvard, Yale, and dozens of other universities and clubs to take the National Championship. It continued into the early 1900s, when the club sponsored Frank Ross in the 1920 Olympic Games, where he shattered the world pole vault record. It continues today, with active internal clubs including the Tankers, Boxing Club, Basketball Teams, and the Runners.

In the Club's final months, Chicago was named the United States's entry as host city for the 2016 Olympic Games. This might have stirred some memories for CAA members—their forebears had been instrumental in a narrowly failed attempt to get the Olympics to Chicago in 1904. Back then, the CAA worked hard to wine and dine the Olympic Committee and extol the virtues of Chicago, as its members were still glowing from their success in helping secure the 1893 World's Columbian Exposition. Yet in the end the Olympics went to St. Louis for an all-too-familiar reason in Chicago—politics. The club's own history notes that President Theodore Roosevelt had little use for then-alderman William Hale "Big Bill" Thompson, a CAA member who was elected Chicago's mayor in 1915.

THE CUBS LOGO . . . OR THE CLUB'S LOGO?

When CAA member William Wrigley Jr. bought the Chicago Cubs, he needed a logo for the team. This was in the 1950s, a time well before lawyers would have seized on the opportunity to enforce the organization's trademark as they might today. So, Wrigley just "borrowed" the CAA's logo and stuck it on the Cubs' jerseys, where it has remained in slightly altered form ever since.

Sources:

Anonymous CAA members. Interviews by author. June–August 2005.

Chicago Athletic Association. Brochures on the club's history.

Chicago Athletic Association. www.chicagoathletic.com. Accessed November 2005–March 2007.

Roeder, David. "Athletic Assn. could lock horns with clout-heavy Walshes." *Chicago Sun-Times*, 4 October 2006.

Frisbee, Tom, and David Roeder. "It really is the end of an era." *Chicago Sun-Times*, 12 January 2007.

"Newcastle Limited Selected by the Chicago Athletic Association to Conduct a Sealed-Bid Offering for South Michigan Avenue Property." Newcastle Limited press release, April 2005.

XXIII

THE
RACQUET CLUB

———◆———

The Racquet Club
Founded: *1924*
Address: *1365 N. Dearborn Street, Chicago, IL 60610*
Architect: *Andrew N. Rebori*

Author's Note: The Racquet Club declined to be interviewed for this book. Therefore, much of the information you see here comes from The Racquet Club of Chicago: A History *(1994), by Peter T. Maiken. There is no listing for this organization in Appendix A.*

It's easy for the plebiscite to confuse the game of racquets with squash. After all, practically anyone plays squash these days.

Of course, if you made that mistake, you have no business being in a place like the Racquet Club. Upper crust and secretive to the core, the octogenarian club on North Dearborn continues to celebrate a rare sport in a rarefied atmosphere.

Created by members of the elite Chicago Club and the old Lake Shore Athletic Club, the Racquet Club was intended to be a show-place for a sport that had its start in, of all places, British prisons. Modeled on the game fives—essentially, handball—racquets follows similar rules only with the addition of a 30-inch wooden racket and a hard, white ball made expressly for that purpose. It's not an inexpensive or common sport.

The Racquet Club. (Photo by Lisa Holton.)

Like handball, racquets is played against a wall and sidewall, and only the server can score; the receiver gets to be server after winning a rally. The game is fast and potentially dangerous. Games go to 15 points, and matches are usually the best of five games.

That's the game. Here's the club.

Peter T. Maiken's 1994 in-house anniversary book on the club, the primary resource for this chapter, tells the story of an elite club with a sense of fun:

> The legend passed down to one long-time employee held that origins of the club were traceable to long Saturday luncheons at the old Lake Shore Club, where a circle of enthusiastic men made ambitious plans for the new facility at Schiller and Dearborn.

> Chicago architect Albert B. Dewey Jr. acquired a piece of property at the southeast corner of Schiller and Dearborn in 1922. The property was deeded to the club on February 9, 1923, for $66,000. Later the organizers bought additional land to the south at a cost of $33,000. All organizational meetings were held at the Chicago Club.

The history describes the décor of the club at its 1924 opening:

The appointments were decidedly masculine. It was, after all, mostly a place for men. Dark paneled walls, heavy wood beam ceilings, a stone fireplace of baronial dimensions—those were typical of the character lines it presented.

There was also a club room, lounge, and kitchen for the use of wives and daughters of members. "This was the women's department, a small club within a club, mostly segregated from the main operation. Still, there was an overall unity," Maiken writes.

WOMEN WELCOME, EXCEPT . . .

The relationship with women at the club was liberal at first. According to Maiken:

The women felt that their department should be developed into an athletic center as well as a place where wives could rendezvous at noon with one another, or to which they could invite their husbands to lunch or tea.

Dinner would not be served, although the department would remain open until 8 P.M. to accommodate women, especially those from Lake Forest who needed a place to dress before going out in the evening. They suggested giving daughters over 18 access to the quarters. As for the athletic facilities, they wished to use the swimming pool for 2 1/2 hours each morning, the racquets and tennis courts for one day each week, and the gymnasium in the mornings for fencing. They also asked that they be allowed to bowl with the men in the evenings and thought that occasional dances in the gymnasium would be a good idea.

Lest the women get out of hand, the men "offered thanks to the women" but "reduced the morning swimming time to 1 1/2 hours and stipulated that "bathing suits for women using the swimming pool must be uniform and can be purchased at the club." The governors also noted that the wives and older daughters would have exclusive use of the lower singles squash court.

However, women were kicked out of the club in 1928 after "friction developed as the women seemingly encroached upon male territory. Their use of the pool in the mornings, for instance, upset those gentlemen who wanted to swim in the buff." There were a few more infractions besides that. Eventually, the women stopped using the women's department—probably at their husbands' requests—and it was finally shut down on April 1, 1929.

RACQUETS IN CHICAGO

At one time Chicago had a total of seven racquets courts. The Chicago Athletic Club opened two in 1894, the University Club followed with two more in 1909, and in 1913 Harold F. McCormick gave a court to the University of Chicago. This particular court, located under Stagg Field, is the subject of controversy, but not for the reason you'd think. It is indeed the court referred to as the site of the first atomic chain reaction—nobody disputes that. But the argument is over what kind of court it really was. Maiken insists that McCormick donated a racquets court, not a squash court, as u of c's press materials insist.

The debate continues.

Sources:
Maiken, Peter T. *The Racquet Club of Chicago: A History.*
  Chicago: The Racquet Club, 1994.

XXIV

THE
WOMAN'S ATHLETIC
CLUB

———

The Woman's Athletic Club
Founded: 1898
Address: 626 N. Michigan Avenue, Chicago, IL 60611
Architect: Philip B. Maher

*Author's Note: The WAC declined to be interviewed for this
book. Therefore, much of the information you see here comes
from* The Woman's Athletic Club of Chicago, 1898–1998:
A History *(1999), by Celia Hilliard. There is no listing
for this organization in Appendix A.*

While so many valuable blocks of Michigan Avenue have been
gobbled up by high-rises, mall space, or the occasional megastore
of the moment, there's a stately older building on the northwest
corner of Michigan Avenue and Ontario Street that has sat quietly
through it all—the Woman's Athletic Club (WAC).

It might be easy to write off this longtime fixture of *The Social
Register* as nothing more than a private haven for rich ladies and
their daughters. That it certainly is, and bloodline is reportedly
still a big factor in getting in. But the WAC's formation and longevi-
ty are a testament to a group of women who used their money and
power to create something entirely new—the first women's athletic club in the country to rival the facilities, exclusivity, and status
of those founded by men.

The Woman's Athletic Club. (Bob Thrall for the Commission on Chicago Landmarks.)

While their husbands scratched their heads in their powerful clubs south of the Chicago River, the women of the WAC actually foresaw the real estate gold mine that was to become the Magnificent Mile (then a developing but otherwise unremarkable strip of road near Streeterville known as Pine Street).

Its founder, Paulina Harriette Lyon, actually envisioned a future for the WAC that sounds very much like the health club chains of today. On her overloaded drawing board sat a proposal for the WAC to become a chain of upscale clubs in major cities. Though the chain concept never happened and Lyon eventually found herself forced out when the club fell into financial trouble after 1910, the WAC was something truly different in the sea of women's literary and social clubs that existed at the time.

And it remains so today.

PAULINA LYON'S VISION,
MEET MRS. ARMOUR'S CHECKBOOK

The club's own history notes that in 1896 there were 66 women's groups registered in the city, "earnestly devoted to issues ranging from clean streets to prison reform to the proper understanding of Tolstoy." Lyon, whose father, John C. Burroughs, had been the first president of the University of Chicago, was part of that crowd of notable society ladies. But she wondered why only men had the advantage of private clubs where they could exercise, socialize, and enjoy a relaxed meal with friends. "There was no such haven for women in Chicago, or, in fact, anywhere else in the country," Hilliard writes. "One quiet afternoon [Lyon] sat down in her study with paper and pen, and when she emerged several hours later she had drawn up a plan to create the Woman's Athletic Club of Chicago."

Lyon took her idea to the Prairie Avenue mansion of meatpacking king Philip D. Armour, "and when some of the women present complained of fatigue after yet another week of committee meetings," she described her vision of a club that would "minister to the needs of the whole woman, a retreat where health, grace and vigor could be restored."

Belle Ogden Armour was convinced, and she got the ball rolling with a $50,000 check — a sum equivalent to about $1.2 million today. Lyon immediately sent invitations to 1,000 leading women of Chicago to meet at the Auditorium Theatre to hear plans for "a handsome new club."

Unfortunately, only 13 of the invitees showed up.

So Lyon and Armour tried the one-on-one approach as only Mrs. Armour could. They eventually won the support of Mrs. William H. (Medora) Thompson, a wealthy widow who held extensive downtown real estate holdings. (Her father, Steven Gale, was one of 38 incorporators of Chicago in 1833.) Another was Mrs. C.K.G. (Blanche) Billings, married to the head of People's Gas Light and Coke Co. Her husband, known as America's Horse King, had just inherited $20 million and was considered a worthy target. Third was Mrs. William R. (Nellie) Linn, "a cordial South Sider who liked to bet friends she would wear the same little beret all winter if they would make a substantial contribution to her favorite charity."

Maybe it was the beret that did the trick. Sixty-three resident members were in the fold by 1898. The founding list of members was a Who's Who of Chicago society, including such names as Blair,

Caton, Clow, Crane, Cudahy, Donnelley, Drake, Henrotin, Hutchinson, Laflin, Lowden, McCormick, McNally, Noyes, Palmer, Pike, Pullman, Ryerson, Selfridge, Smith, and Swift.

GETTING STARTED

The WAC was formally incorporated on September 13, 1898. Its first clubhouse, at 150 Michigan Avenue, was part of a row of townhouses that were once home to Mrs. Bertha Palmer when she was a girl. The first life members of the WAC paid a then-hefty $500 to join (well above the inaugural fees at many men's clubs of the time) and at their death had the right to pass the membership on to an heir for a $100 transfer fee.

The first clubhouse featured luxury appointments including a white marble pool, a two-story gymnasium, and a bowling alley. Most of the early members had never been in a pool, much less a bowling alley. The club's parlor had "deep cushioned sofas and long tables tacked with recent issues of *Scribner's* and *Ladies Pictorial*." Around the club were small writing desks with stationery; though the telephone was certainly available at the time to the moneyed set, notes were still a major form of local communication. There was also a hairdressing parlor, manicure tables, and "retiring rooms" so women could take a nap after their new strenuous activities. Vases of daffodils were everywhere.

Full meals were served throughout the day, and husbands were welcome, but alcohol consumption at least initially was confined — tongue inserted firmly in cheek — "to the infirm." In the earliest days of the WAC, the club history lists its adult beverage policy as follows:

If fortified by a prescription from a doctor, a member could imbibe something "medicinal" in the seclusion of a private dining room.

Many of the husbands weren't crazy about the sizable amount of cash their wives were spending to get this venture off the ground. Hilliard writes:

This new enterprise was a big gamble, and more than one husband was heard grumbling that the punching bags in this ladies' establishment must be made of solid gold.

The media were also having a field day with the WAC. From the start, according to Hilliard, the project was dogged by "unrelenting masculine ridicule." She continues:

Scrappy reporters ran stories predicting the women would shortly plant pod lilies in the swimming pool, turn the gymnasium into a continuous pink tea reception and use up all the club stationery for curl papers. . . . A few men suggested that instructing women in the expert use of Indian clubs and dumbbells could be a menace to society. Most of the new members' husbands seemed to take the whole idea as a good joke, and even the kindest of them liked to call Mrs. Armour aside and whisper that she should expect the club to last no longer than six months at the outside.

THANK YOU, MRS. MCKINLEY

However, the snickering had stopped cold by the club's first anniversary. In a shrewd public relations coup, the WAC named Mrs. Ida McKinley, wife of the president, as its first honorary member. Club members pulled every string possible to get the first lady and her husband to the club during an 1899 visit to Chicago, instantaneously making the gathering the hottest society ticket in town. Mrs. McKinley received a thank-you gift of a five-foot-tall floral bouquet made entirely of spun sugar.

It made perfect sense. The first lady's sweet gesture put the WAC firmly on the map of American society, where it remains to this day. The WAC rushed to add other honorary members to its list, Susan B. Anthony and Julia Ward Howe among them. The best benefit of the WAC's rising social value? The husbands stopped grousing— their wives' WAC memberships had become a status symbol for them as well.

FROM PERSPIRATION—TO REAL SWEAT

The WAC was a must-have membership among society matrons, but getting members to actually *exercise* at the club? That was radical. It wasn't so much a question of laziness as the reality that the male concept of athletic exertion was still extremely foreign to women. Could a physically fit woman still be a lady? That's where the WAC was something truly out of the ordinary. Hilliard writes:

> Maybe a handful of the ladies at the opening reception played golf on a regular basis, rode bicycles or swam at the seashore during summer holidays. Even most of these were utterly baffled by the rope ladders, pulleys, and boxing gloves they saw in the gymnasium, and it is safe to say that few of them had ever held a bowling ball or a fencing foil before.

Still, for those who dared, the WAC provided a great place to recover from their labors:

> After a swim the members would typically snatch up a towel, slip into sandals and go dripping to the Turkish baths, where they sat first in a tiled hot room to induce heavy perspiration. This was followed by a shower and a massage to soothe over-strained muscles. After this, they could nap in one of the cozy blue and white soundproofed resting rooms where a large "Silence!" warning was posted on the wall. Sometimes they went directly to the hairdressing department, where they would be shampooed at a marble basin "by a coiffeuse," as one of them remembered years later "who only used her fingertips and never got so much as a soap bubble on her white cuffs."

FAREWELL, CZARINA LYON

Proper governance was apparently the last thing on the minds of members of the wildly successful new club. Paulina Lyon, who cofounded the club with Belle Armour, was named club manager and also a member of the board, eliminating more than a few key checks and balances. She had a male secretary and did "all the hiring, firing, choosing and deciding. . . . Written complaints went directly to her, and verbal complaints were not allowed." She believed that someday there would be a chain of Woman's Athletic Clubs where members could have reciprocal privileges at every sister institution.

In 1901 Lyon asked the Chicago architectural firm of Pond & Pond to draw plans for a six-story freestanding clubhouse. She suggested that its new swimming pool might be built into a grotto and fed from a central fountain. "A sort of jeweled rendezvous patterned after the baths of ancient Rome," Hilliard comments. Raising the money was slow, so she thought of another great public relations scheme. Lyon insured her life for $300,000 on the condition that 60 members would annually contribute a dollar a day (nearly $22,000 a year) toward the erection of this new palace. She also created a class of corporate membership with a bond issue, and 200 of the members bought in.

But questions eventually arose about the seemingly endless parade of money-raising programs implemented by Lyon. It became clear that the board was rubber-stamping her requests while spending was out of control. By 1907 an investigation showed that the WAC was teetering on bankruptcy, with rent six months overdue. Quietly, Lyon quit after 11 years, got married, and moved to New York. Mrs. Lyman A. Walton was declared president—for some reason, a vote wasn't held—and the dining room supervisor, Mrs. Ida Cronk, was given the management post, although without "the far-reaching authority Mrs. Lyon has exercised." Within a year revenues were headed above expenses.

In 1908 events forced the WAC's hand on the clubhouse issue. Management received word that the clubhouse had been sold to Peoples Gas and the utility wanted to tear it down. Financially, the club still wasn't ready to build its own space, so it settled on rented space in the Harvester Building (the former International Harvester Co.'s headquarters) at Michigan and Harrison. The WAC got someone to remove every fixture from the original space and move it to the new place. Every tile of the swimming tank was removed and reinstalled piece by piece.

The new rooms in the Harvester Building were much more open and designed with an eye to simplicity and comfort. A large living

The old International Harvester building on Michigan Avenue, now part of Columbia College. It was the WAC's second clubhouse. (Photo by Lisa Holton.)

room 50 feet square was furnished with wicker chairs and settees; rose-colored draperies framed the broad windows overlooking the park. Mrs. Darius Miller brought in two live canaries in a brass cage. The new quarters officially opened on January 16, 1909.

During the next 14 years the club was a hub of activity, though again athletics weren't the top focus. The club became a center for the arts, top social events, and sought-after lecturers. There was even a midday tango class for members and their husbands that the men agreed to attend as long as no one spoke of it. Apparently, the men did not want to be caught in the public act of learning. Monologist Ruth Draper appeared at the WAC before she became famous, and younger members of the club put on annual shows that were both hits and great fund-raisers.

During World War I (as it did again during World War II) the club hosted soldiers headed off to war. In November 1917 the club was thrown open every Saturday evening for soldiers and sailors, with more than 2,000 servicemen being entertained. According to the club's history, a few of the mothers (and some of the daughters, too) were apparently cautious about all this social mixing.

A story from those days tells of a young lady who declined to dance with a good looking private, explaining to her next partner that she never danced with any man under the rank of second lieutenant. He informed her that she had missed a turn with one of the finest men in the world. "I ought to know," he told her. "I was his chauffeur for three years."

The Roaring Twenties introduced a battle royal between the flappers and the dowagers. As younger club members went for bobbed hair, shorter skirts, and cigarettes, there were heated debates over whether such radicalism would be tolerated in the club. "Progress" won, however, and by 1924 a woman who could bob hair was hired for the salon, and the same year, the smoking ban went, too.

Class and generational warfare aside, the best news of all was that the wac's financial position continued to improve under Mrs. Walton and the club's next president, Helen Hall Upham. Upham bolstered the wac's balance sheet by raising annual dues to $60 and was able to convince many of the original bondholders to turn their bonds over to the club, essentially converting their investments into contributions. These strategies couldn't have come at a better time, because in 1923 the wac was facing one of its biggest challenges.

MOVING TO THE MAGNIFICENT MILE

The emergence of a younger, more aggressive generation also signaled upstart competition to the stately wac. The new Casino club on Delaware, then in its shocking pink first building, had captured a strong segment of the well-heeled ladies' luncheon and party business and was hosting outrageous parties in the evening (which upset their dowager membership, as mentioned earlier). The Arts Club, then in small quarters at 610 S. Michigan Avenue, was shocking the arts community with avant-garde exhibitions; performances with actors, musicians, and playwrights; and tea with luminaries like Igor Stravinsky and Robert Frost.

The Fortnightly announced plans to move its tapestries, furniture, and historic artifacts into the old Lathrop House on Bellevue

Loyola University's Lewis Towers, at 820 N. Michigan Avenue, was the original home of the Illinois Women's Athletic Club. (Courtesy of Loyola University.)

Place. Even the Chicago Woman's Club, with its long-standing reform-minded membership, had retained architects to design glamorous new headquarters farther south on Michigan Avenue at 11th Street. And the new Racquet Club, on Dearborn Street, hired Rue Winterbotham Carpenter to decorate quarters specifically for women guests.

The club's lease in the Harvester Building was up in 1926. It was time to resuscitate Paulina Lyon's dream of a freestanding club.

The most direct threat to the WAC's standing came from a new organization that dared call itself the Chicago Women's Athletic Club. The name was later changed, under pressure from the WAC's lawyers, to the Illinois Women's Athletic Club.

The IWAC had a considerably more activist membership than the WAC. Mrs. Waller Borden and Mrs. Robert McCormick, both active in the women's suffrage movement, launched the club in 1918 from land purchased from the Prentice estate. The skyscraper clubhouse at 820 N. Michigan Avenue had a pool with an award-winning women's swim team, tennis courts, billiards, a ballroom, and, unlike the WAC, a full-size running track and lodging space. IWAC member Jane Fauntz competed in the 1928 Olympics in the breaststroke and in the 1932 Olympics in springboard diving. (At one point, the IWAC's membership stood at 1,700—well above the WAC's—but it failed during the Great Depression. Today the IWAC's building is known as the Lewis Towers, part of Loyola University's downtown campus.)

Yet amid all this aggressive development—the last Chicago would see for several decades after the stock market crash—the WAC couldn't make a deal work despite a healthy quarter-million dollars in the bank. It ended up signing another short-term lease at the Harvester Building.

NORTH MICHIGAN AVENUE IN THE 1920S

Before the bubble popped and the Great Depression began, construction in downtown Chicago was everywhere. The Loop's prime spaces were being filled in, but the real story was happening near the lake just north of the Chicago River. The city had begun construction of the double-decker Wacker Drive along the river that would connect to a redeveloped Pine Street—to be renamed North Michigan Avenue and known colloquially as the Magnificent Mile.

Many old and beautiful homes and gardens were sacrificed along Pine to make way for a Parisian-style boulevard lined with smart shops, hotels, and offices—obviously an inspiration for the new WAC building. Enterprises like auto showrooms, poolrooms, laundries, garages, and bars were banned. The Drake Hotel anchored the north end of the street and the Wrigley Building the south, with the Tribune Tower following a short time later. The Allerton Hotel and the Lake Shore Trust and Savings Bank appeared in between.

For a while it looked like the developers of the 333 N. Michigan Avenue building—the longtime home of the Tavern Club—would win the WAC. The club had actually signed a deal for the fourth and fifth floors of the building and part of the sixth.

It was then that an opportunity suddenly emerged from one of Chicago's earliest merchants and landowners, John V. Farwell. Farwell owned the northwest corner of Michigan and Ontario and didn't want to pay taxes on an outright sale. So he offered the WAC a 99-year ground lease with an agreement to bring in $40,000 a

CLUB NOTES

⨳ ONLY THE BEST FOR THE WAC ⨳

It was the end of the Roaring Twenties, and money was being spent like water, particularly by the ladies at the WAC. The club's history shows that Philip Maher— the club's architect and designer of the Farwell Building (later the Terra Museum), the Blackstone Shop, the old Jacques Building (demolished, now 900 N. Michigan), and the now demolished Decorative Arts Building— received a whopping $45,000 and a commission on the lighting fixtures and kitchen equipment. Meanwhile, the club's interior designer earned $150,000 plus a $20,000 commission.

The club's history points out that the wildly expensive $1.02 million building that would open in May 1929 fell under considerable member scrutiny during the coming days of the Great Depression. At the time, many men involved in the project, including Farwell and Philip Maher, the architect, were involved in many interrelated business deals. Many wondered whether the ladies were hoodwinked.

To close the gap the WAC needed to raise the price of a resident membership to a staggering $1,000 and a life membership to $5,000. Yet in those happy months before the bottom fell out, nobody blinked an eye. The club opened the doors to its new clubhouse on April 25, 1929— the exact month that the nation began its slide into the Great Depression.

Like their male counterparts, the WAC would eventually struggle to keep its doors open.

At the same time, The Casino was taking a big bite out of the WAC's meeting business. The Children's Memorial Hospital board moved their meetings to The Casino because they could get the space for free. The WAC's leaders had to get creative. According to Hilliard, senior members "were quietly knocking on doors" to get members to stay. They played around with membership categories, cut initiation fees for new resident members, and they even carried resigned members free for three months. Junior memberships were created with annual dues of $50 and no initiation fees. By the mid-1930s, the WAC lost 25 percent of its membership, but the club held on.

year in retail income from ground floor rental space that could significantly reduce its overhead.

The dealmakers also included an equally attractive carrot that would allow the club to retain its fixtures for 99 years, and at the last minute Farwell threw in a $375,000 loan to help the club complete the construction. The deal had become too good to refuse. According to its history, "Gingerly, [the club] pulled out of the agreement at 333, explaining simply, 'The trend is uptown.'"

While the 333 site came back with a better offer, the decision was made to go with the Farwell lot and finally construct the independent site the club had long hoped for.

Thus the WAC became one of the first major settlers of what legendary developer Arthur Rubloff would later dub the Magnificent Mile.

THE GROWTH OF THE SUBURBS

The WAC, like all women's organizations, repeated their support of the war effort during the 1940s and cut back their traditional social schedules. But when the boys came home, it had a profound effect on the WAC.

Until the 1970s, the WAC's membership didn't contain many working women. Most were homemakers, albeit wealthy ones. And while the second and even third generation still lived relatively close to the club, their daughters had other ideas. The postwar expansion of the Chicago suburbs carried even the wealthiest

CLUB NOTES

THE THORNE ROOMS AND THE WAC

The Thorne Rooms, a collection of 68 miniature rooms now on display at the Art Institute of Chicago, were first viewed in the 1930s and 40s at the WAC. Mrs. James Ward Thorne, a WAC member, stored "half a dozen" enameled wood chests on the club's 5th floor. Hilliard writes, "They were filled with intriguing bits and pieces she used to make new Thorne Rooms every year for the Presbyterian–St. Luke's Hospital Christmas sale."

young women—all WAC targets—farther from the club. Writes
Hilliard: "Ladies came into town less and less. They lunched at the
country club."

And the WAC would soon get new neighbors. Between 1957 and
1963, Hilliard writes, over $500 million was committed to new con-
struction along Michigan Avenue. Down went the last of the old
homes of Pine Street still owned by the wealthy. Up went the high-
rises with the John Hancock building planned for the north end of
the boulevard and the Equitable building to the South:

> "The last of the townhouses, those enchantingly remodeled
> remnants of old Pine Street, were disappearing. The Italian
> Court across the street, that little web of shops and studios
> where so many Chicagoans had been introduced to French
> cooking at Le Petite Gourmet, where Irene Castle [a WAC
> member] had once taken a pied-a-terre upstairs, was demol-
> ished. A tall concrete office building went up in its place. The
> . . . neighborhood was changing rapidly."

By the time the 1960s arrived, the WAC's younger targets were
shocking the old guard in ways the flappers never dreamed of,
Hilliard writes. In short, the flower children of the 1960s had little
use for Mother's club.

According to Hilliard, "The social upheaval of the 1960s left
their bewildering mark on the WAC. . . . Daughters, always the
promise and future of the WAC, were now inclined not to follow in
Mother's footsteps. They were not flocking to join a club the newspapers now referred to as 'Sleepy Hollow.'" Local society colum-
nists, really in their last great heyday, didn't do the WAC any
favors during this period; Hilliard quotes one who offered this
description of the WAC — "The casual visitor sees a most unathlet-
ic scene. Elderly women sip sherry in high-ceilinged quiet
lounges." To which Hilliard quipped, "With friends like this, who
needed enemies?"

Through the 1970s and 1980s, Hilliard's history outlines a WAC
filled with distinguished presenters and guests—Indira Gandhi,
Claire Booth Luce, pioneering female broadcaster Nancy Dickerson

(winner of one of its Distinguished Woman Awards), and Suzy, the gossip columnist, among them.

But because the club did not participate in this book—and several members contacted declined to comment—there's unfortunately not much of a sense of who today's WAC member is. It's a shame for such a vibrant center of Chicago women's history. By all reports the WAC, which sits on some of the most valuable real estate in Chicago, continues to operate profitably and with exclusivity except for one point. Since the 1987 City Council ordinance was passed banning sex discrimination at private clubs, the club now admits men—though we could not determine if any have joined.

A member of the WAC believes the club has stayed relevant as women have gone into the workforce and as they've risen to powerful positions in organizations. "I think our membership reflects the many roles of women today. We have career women, stay-at-home mothers and women who do creative work, and the club has offerings to fit all those schedules," she said. "I think what we do today reflects the forward thinking of the women who founded the club."

Sources:

Anonymous club members. Interviews by author. February 2006.

Hilliard, Celia. *The Woman's Athletic Club of Chicago, 1898–1998: A History.* Chicago: The Woman's Athletic Club, 1998.

SPOTLIGHT

THE RISE OF THE EAST BANK CLUB

In the mid- to late 1970s, the area now known as River North was an assortment of rundown industrial addresses and peep shows that nobody quite saw as a future boomtown. But it was on the verge of something that not only would change the downtown commercial and residential real estate landscape but also delivered a broadside to the private clubs as well.

Residential developer McHugh Levin Associates was planning the city's largest private recreational complex, the East Bank Club, on Wolf Point near the Apparel Center. It promised more than 400,000 square feet of finished space, to include ten indoor tennis courts, two jogging tracks, exercise rooms, a golf green with a sand trap, private dining rooms, two cocktail bars, a pro shop, a nursery, and rooms for sauna, steam, massage, and sun.

The development, which opened in 1980 at 500 N. Kingsbury Street, was different not only for its sheer size but for the membership it targeted. In a 1979 *Chicago Tribune* piece, the developer was targeting "moderately affluent" members for the East Bank Club. Levin was quoted as saying that most of the members were expected to be in the $35,000 to $75,000 annual income range, adding, "I'll be surprised if we have anyone who joins making under $20,000.

It was the age of the yuppie, when any young professional, regardless of class, race, or bloodline, could at least play at status as long as they could pay for it— or charge it. The East Bank didn't care about bloodlines—membership was open to anyone willing to pay the then-steep $500 charter membership fee with annual dues of $250. This particular invention put the cramped-by-comparison gyms, courts, pools, and exercise facilities within the city's landlocked traditional clubs at a disadvantage. And they're still trying to catch up today.

THE
ARTS CLUBS

XXV

THE
ARTS CLUB
OF
CHICAGO

The Arts Club of Chicago
Founded: 1916
Address: 201 E. Ontario Street, Chicago, IL 60611
Architect: Current clubhouse by John Vinci and Philip Hamp;
interior of previous clubhouse (at 109 E. Ontario)
designed by Ludwig Mies van der Rohe.

Author's Note: The Arts Club of Chicago declined to be
interviewed for this book. Therefore, much of the information
you see here comes from the club's 75th anniversary book,
published in 1991, and various news clippings since. There
is no listing for this organization in Appendix A.

As it approached the Roaring Twenties, Chicago was ready for something new. The old-line art community that produced the Art Institute of Chicago and the city's world art reputation had also produced some 30 or more galleries that sold . . . more of the same.

There was no real home for avant-garde art in Chicago until the creation of the Arts Club of Chicago. The controversial New York Armory Show, which had been staged at the Art Institute in 1913, whetted everyone's appetite, but it was up to a group of Chicago's top society women to turn the tide. The club has served as a gallery and a gathering and performance space for cutting-edge artists and performers for nearly a century.

The current Arts Club of Chicago opened at 201 E. Ontario in 1997.
(Photo by Lisa Holton.)

Among those who received their first U.S. or Midwestern solo exhibitions at the Arts Club were Constantin Brancusi (installed by Marcel Duchamp), Georges Braque, Alexander Calder, Marc Chagall, Salvador Dalí, Jean Dubuffet, Arshile Gorky, Marsden Hartley, Fernand Léger, Robert Motherwell, Isamu Noguchi, Pablo Picasso, Jackson Pollock, Auguste Rodin, Georges Seurat, and Henri de Toulouse-Lautrec. Many of these artists either donated or sold works to the club's permanent collection.

On the performance side, the club has hosted artists as varied as John Cage, John Updike, Ann Beattie, Leonard Bernstein, W.H. Auden, and Robert Altman.

During its regular fall–spring season, the club hosts three or four public exhibitions annually.

RICH & RENEGADE

There was a certain division of Chicago society that had money, breeding, and a wild streak. These were the women who would found The Casino as well as the Arts Club. Rue Winterbotham Carpenter, wife of the modern composer John Alden Carpenter, was one of the new club's first supporters. She was also the designer of its first spaces, at 610 S. Michigan Avenue and later in the Wrigley Building, where it moved in 1924.

There were other leaders on that first board, too. Among them were Alice Roullier, Katherine Dudley, Arthur Heun, George Higginson, Eames MacVeagh, Arthur Aldis, Frederick Clay Bartlett (designer of the landmark stained-glass windows and ornamentation at the University Club), Robert Allerton, John Alden Carpenter, Mrs. Arthur Ryerson, and Alice Greenberg.

Like so many other clubs formed during the late teens and early 1920s, the Arts Club was born into a city that was becoming a world center for all the arts. At the time, each of the city's ten newspapers had multiple reporters assigned to covering the arts alone. There was an arts infrastructure in Chicago at that time that didn't exist before.

THE MOVE TO ONTARIO

After several moves within the Wrigley Building to increasingly larger spaces, the club lost its lease there in 1947 and led a fairly nomadic existence with stops at The Fortnightly for performances and readings while its multimillion-dollar permanent collection went into storage. In 1951 the club was able to rent new space at 109 E. Ontario Street between Michigan Avenue and Rush Street in Philip B. Maher's Erskine-Danforth Building. The striking street-level clubhouse, gallery space, dining room, and office were designed by Ludwig Mies van der Rohe, with a glass front that featured the memorable suspended steel staircase that was its modernist trademark. The Arts Club was the only example of an interior Mies design in a building he did not design as well.

How the Arts Club got to its current quarters at 201 E. Ontario is a sad moment in Chicago preservation history. In the early 1990s, the Arts Club had to vacate its space because developer John Buck won the right to build a $100 million retail and entertainment complex that now fills the canyon of tourist attractions and residential towers just west of North Michigan Avenue. The Arts Club and the Landmark Preservation Council of Illinois fought to save the Maher building, but were unsuccessful.

Yet a short time after it evacuated, the club announced that local architect John Vinci beat out 40 other architects to build the Arts Club current home at 201 E. Ontario. At an estimated cost of $6 million — financed, sources said, mainly by the sale of a few pieces from its art collection — the Arts Club would finally own the building and land for its home with no chance of eviction. At 19,000 square feet, it is twice the size of its predecessor and Vinci preserved many details of the original Mies design, including the glass front and suspended staircase from the original Ontario clubhouse. The clubhouse includes a 1,600-square-foot garden along St. Clair Street. It replicates the lounge and performance space of the old club and is full of Mies designs — including the leather and metal Barcelona, Brno, and Tugendhat chairs — partnered with an eclectic mix of other furnishings.

Sources:

The Arts Club of Chicago. *The Arts Club of Chicago Seventy-Fifth Anniversary Exhibition*, 1916–1991. Chicago: The Arts Club of Chicago, 1992.

XXVI

THE
CAXTON
CLUB

―――――◆―――――

The Caxton Club
Founded: 1895
Address: No clubhouse; meetings held
through 2007 *at the Mid-Day Club.*

Anyone who has visited South Dearborn Street might already
have a small taste of what Chicago's book community was like in
the late 1800s. Indeed, the immediate South Side was a printing
headquarters not only for Chicago's artisan book community but
also for the world, with companies like R.R. Donnelley cornering
the market on catalogs and phone books, and with and the Sears
and Montgomery Ward catalogs changing retailing throughout the
country.

Chicago not only had close to ten newspapers at the turn of the
last century, but it also supported the biggest names in the encyclopedia business (World Book and Encyclopedia Britannica have
been based in Chicago for decades). Moody Bible Institute established its own press. And even Marquis's *Who's Who* got its start in
Chicago.

Though it's shrunk considerably, publishing was once one of Chicago's largest industries. And that environment formed the Caxton Club.

The Caxton Club is a tribute to anyone who makes a book: writers, artists, designers, printers, and binders. Named in honor of the first British printer, William Caxton, the organization was founded by 15 Chicago bibliophiles who wanted to support the publication of fine books "in the spirit of the Arts and Crafts movement."

Today the club has 300 members, and it still publishes high-quality, limited edition books on subjects of interest to its members. Its most recent title, published in 2002, was *Inland Printers: The Fine Press Movement in Chicago, 1920–45.*

THE BEGINNING

The club's 2002 history by Wendy Cowles Husser points out that Chicago in the 1870s was truly a city of readers, with 68 bookstores in operation by 1871. That doesn't sound like much until you consider the fact that it worked out to one bookstore for every 4,000 readers. (With as many Barnes & Noble's and Border's stores dotting today's landscape, it might seem a similar situation, but in reality it's nowhere close.)

The Caxton Club was a book club founded by Eugene Field, a writer for the *Chicago Daily News* who promoted books in his columns. Field died before the club launched, but others took over, including George Armour, James W. Ellsworth, George M. Higginson Jr., Charles L. Hutchinson, George S. Payson, and J.H. Wrenn. These organizers met for the first time at the University Club and used New York's Grolier Club as their model for the Caxton.

Ellsworth, an industrialist, a book collector, and one of the organizers of the World's Columbian Exposition, was the first president of the Caxton Club. The club would move to the Fine Arts Building in 1899 and into the Wrigley Building in 1923. Unlike The Arts Club, also a resident of the Wrigley Building beginning in 1924, the Caxton almost closed during the Great Depression. In the ensuing years the Caxton moved around quite a bit—to the Tavern Club, the Saddle & Cycle Club near Edgewater, the Cliff Dwellers, and finally the Mid-Day Club, where it met through 2007.

SPOTLIGHT

~ THE FINE ARTS BUILDING ~
& ITS ROLE IN CLUB LIFE

The Fine Arts Building
(Photo by Lisa Holton.)

Some buildings just give birth to creative ideas and camaraderie. The Fine Arts Building at 410 S. Michigan Avenue was a starter clubhouse for a number of the city's best-known clubs.

Originally known as the Studebaker Building (1885–98), the Fine Arts Building was first a carriage assembly and showroom that was renovated in 1898 into what would become a landmark for the Arts and Crafts movement. According to the Commission on Chicago Landmarks, the renovation added three floors and created an interior that would reflect the interests of the new tenants.

The interior public spaces, including murals on the tenth floor, remain virtually untouched from the 1898 remodeling.

The building's motto, "All passes—Art alone endures," greets visitors as they enter.

Sculptors, painters, bookbinders, printers, musicians, music teachers, and various craftspeople have moved into the studio and office spaces in the building throughout its history. Many in those roles remain there today.

Several prominent literary publications launched during that time were in that building as well, specifically *The Dial* and *Poetry* magazine, the latter of which still survives but has moved to 444 N. Michigan Avenue.

The Fine Arts Building was also an early home to several of the city's most historic clubs, including the Cliff Dwellers, Chicago Woman's Club, Little Room, and Caxton Club. The Fine Arts was also home to the Illinois Equal Suffrage Association.

THE CHICAGO ARCHITECTURAL CLUB

As Chicago became a world-renowned center of architecture in the aftermath of the Great Chicago Fire, draftsmen poured into the city with plenty of ambition but not much training. The year was 1885.

The Chicago Architectural Sketch Club provided the first real architectural training most of these individuals would have. More than 1,600 members would pass through the club during its initial 50-year history, providing the lifeblood for the most important era in Chicago architecture.

In Wilbert R. Hasbrouck's 2006 book, *The Chicago Architectural Club: Prelude to the Modern*, he describes the role that James H. Carpenter had on the city's skyline. Carpenter, an English-born draftsman in his 40s, realized that there were too few men who could finalize designs and produce working drawings for the overwhelming demands of Chicago's building industry. Hasbrouck writes about Carpenter:

> It was he who brought eighteen "draughtsman" colleagues together to form The Chicago Architectural Sketch Club in the spring of 1885. This organization, later renamed The Chicago Architectural Club, was responsible for the evolution and development of the Chicago School of Architecture more than any other individual, firm, or professional society.

The club died out in the late 1930s, but a group of architects led by Stanley Tigerman brought it back in the 1970s. In 1976 Chicago's Museum of Contemporary Art launched One Hundred Years of Architecture in Chicago, a major retrospective that once again drew attention to the city's accomplishments. Tigerman helped organize a group of seven other architects: Ben Weese, Stuart Cohen, Laurence Booth, James Nagle, Thomas Beeby, and James Ingo Freed. Together they decided to relaunch the Chicago Architectural Club in 1979.

Today the club is based at the I-Space gallery at the University of Illinois at Chicago. Because most architects are now taught at universities, its primary function is discussion about and display of current work. Also in 1979, the club launched the prestigious

Burnham Prize, named for Daniel Burnham, which gives Midwestern architects a three-month fellowship at the American Academy in Rome. The competition is held every two years.

Sources:

Hasbrouck, Wilbert R. *The Chicago Architectural Club: Prelude to the Modern*. Chicago: Monacelli Press, 2005.

Piehl, Frank J. *The Caxton Club*, 1895–1995: *Celebrating a Century of the Book in Chicago*. Chicago: The Caxton Club, 1995.

XXVII

THE
CHICAGO LITERARY
CLUB

———————

The Chicago Literary Club
Founded: 1874
Address: *No clubhouse; meetings are*
held at the Cliff Dwellers.

As Easterners began to flood into Chicago to seek their fortune during the 1800s, you might say they had a collective inferiority complex about their dirty, bustling new home. Literary clubs were formed by the dozen in both the white and African-American communities to raise Chicago's reputation out of the muck and grime with a very aggressive and public dedication to the arts.

The city's early literary clubs were a big part of that, and one of the best still remains—the Chicago Literary Club. In 1874 the all-male club devoted itself to writing, presenting, and publishing papers on politics, the labor movement, and Civil War topics.

Keep in mind that the Chicago Literary Club is in a completely different league from your sister-in-law's neighborhood book club.

The organization was dedicated to the presentation of the literary essay, a dead art for many of today's college graduates but in its heyday a litmus test for the intellectual depth of an individual. Frank Lackner, the club's historian, notes:

> An essay is the summary of an idea or a thought. We present papers of about 45 minutes in length just for the joy of doing so, and it may be on virtually any topic as long as the rigor is there. Playing with the Internet doesn't teach you the quality of thought such a piece should have. It's a nineteenth-century relic, but it's an art. You can present a great paper poorly, or the other way around.

Since 1995 the organization has been coed, though it's met for years every Monday evening at the Cliff Dwellers from October through May. One essay is delivered each evening, and each meeting features friendly drinks and conversation. The club has met in the Art Institute and the Sherman House hotel (a center for many clubs in Chicago's early days), as well as the Fine Arts Building.

Most of its members are not professional writers. They come from a host of occupations, but they are "expected to express themselves competently in English, and to present their essays in typewritten or printed form to the secretary for inclusion in the club archives."

It all sounds terribly formal, but according to Lackner—whose father and uncle were also members—it's a rare joy that doesn't really exist many places in today's society. He says that it gives people the opportunity to write about and research topics they truly love and also the chance to share their writing with an appreciative audience, which is a rare experience in today's world—one that more people would appreciate if they had the setting to do so.

When the Chicago Literary Club started, it had plenty of company, including such names as the Chicago Polemical Society (founded 1833), Chicago Lyceum (1834), and Young Men's Association (1841). On the women's side, the leading literary club among white women (African-American women had literary clubs as well) was The Fortnightly, which was founded in the 1870s and exists today.

Sources:

Lackner, Frank. Interview by author. July 2005.

Shilton, Earle A. *A Twenty-Minute History of the Chicago Literary Club.* The Chicago Literary Club Online Archives. 28 November 1960.

http://www.chilit.org/Histories/Shilton%20History.PDF.

XXVIII

THE
CLIFF DWELLERS

The Cliff Dwellers
Founded: 1907
Address: 200 S. Michigan Avenue, Chicago, IL 60604
Architect: *First clubhouse space (in Orchestra Hall,*
220 S. Michigan Avenue) designed by Howard Van Doren Shaw;
current clubhouse space (at the Borg Warner Building)
designed by Larry Booth.

The bottle of wine sits opened with the loosened cork jammed inside as the regulars start trailing in for lunch around 11:30. At two special wooden tables — the Members' Tables — near the wrap-around windows of the Borg Warner Building penthouse, the first to arrive is Glen N. Wiche, an antiquarian bookseller. He reaches his hand out to welcome a female newcomer. By rote one of the waiters walks up with Wiche's familiar bowl of mixed nuts, and he digs in before considering the day's lunch menu.

It's a Friday in July, and the lunch crowd is sparse. Wiche leans in and says, "Doesn't matter. Nobody has to sit alone here."

Indeed, within an hour the table is filled by two architects, an attorney, Wiche, and a guest, all talking — and sometimes arguing—about the history of an organization the members have known and loved since their early adulthood—the Cliff Dwellers, one of Chicago's oldest private clubs devoted solely to the arts. Its charter reads as follows: "A congenial place for artists and writers, a rallying place for the Midland arts."

The Cliff Dwellers has withstood a fire in its current clubhouse, a forced eviction from its longtime first home at the top of Orchestra Hall, and a changing world where fewer people gather after busy workdays just to talk casually about art, writing, architecture, and sculpture.

Today when many ambitious young people gather to support the arts, they network at fundraising activities that almost act as extensions of their busy workplaces and schedules. Connections are made, business cards are exchanged, then they head home or on to the next scheduled activity.

That's never been the case at the Cliff Dwellers. As Wiche observes, "There's an old British expression: 'No paper across the bar,' which means, there's really no need to conduct business here." While the club has long offered a well-attended forum for speakers on all the arts (it also provides a home to the Chicago Literary Club and the Society of Midland Authors), it takes pride in the

A club sketch of the reconstructed Sullivan Room, located just off the main dining area. When the Cliff Dwellers were at Orchestra Hall, the original version of this room was where member and renowned architect Louis Sullivan wrote his autobiography. (Courtesy of the Cliff Dwellers.)

notion that the arts should be a more worthy topic of conversation than business or politics.

The Cliff Dwellers was Louis Sullivan's last clubhouse. In his last years, defeated by dwindling commissions and his own rough temperament, the architect's meager earnings came mainly from sporadic commissions, mostly small community banks throughout the Midwest. The Cliff let Sullivan remain a member for free. He wrote his autobiography at a desk in a small library preserved and named for him.

Today's Cliff Dwellers clubhouse, located in the gleaming, modern Borg Warner Building at 200 S. Michigan Avenue, seems a bit of an anachronism for a club formed during the high days of the Arts and Crafts movement. But in the early 1990s Orchestra Hall management decided it wanted to develop its own club space and gave the Cliff Dwellers their walking papers. So in 1996 moving trucks loaded up virtually every stick of furniture, paneling, and even the fireplace, and one door north, the members reassembled their Howard Van Doren Shaw kiva in the building's window-lined penthouse. Though it's a bit shoehorned in, it's all there—even the buffalo head donated by former mayor Carter Harrison II.

FROM WEBSTER'S REVISED UNABRIDGED DICTIONARY (1913)

Kiva \Ki"'va n. [Hopi name, sacred chamber.] A large chamber built under, or in, the houses of a Pueblo village, used as an assembly room in religious rites or as a men's dormitory. It is commonly lighted and entered from an opening in the roof.

The clubhouse is essentially one open meeting and dining room with alcoves off to the side—one for the Sullivan library, the other for the reading area, holding walls of books and magazines and several leather and Eames chairs brought from the old club. When visitors arrive they'll take a brief left into a dark, paneled corridor that winds into the clubhouse. Then it's a blast of light from all three window-lined walls overlooking Michigan Avenue as a familiar sight (for moviegoers, at least) stands front and center— *The*

As you enter the club, you see The Bird Girl, *a copy of the original sculpture by Sylvia Shaw Judson. This copy actually had its close-up in the movie* Midnight in the Garden of Good and Evil. *(Photo by Lisa Holton.)*

Bird Girl, a sculpture that made a notable appearance in the book and film *Midnight in the Garden of Good and Evil*.

FROM THE LITTLE ROOM TO THE CLIFF

The Cliff Dwellers, like so many arts-focused clubs of the time, owes its genesis to the 1893 World's Columbian Exposition, which helped transform Chicago from a muddy prairie town into a diverse metropolis with a significant dedication to culture and publishing. The Cliff Dwellers' own history points to several lures for new writers that occurred right around the time of the fair—the *Dial* and the *Chap-Book*, notable Chicago literary journals, got their start around the 1880s as a dedicated publishing community for Midwestern writers started to form. Hamlin Garland, who eventually won the Pulitzer Prize for his novel *A Daughter of the Middle Border*, was one writer who decided to make his fortunes in Chicago around this time.

Like every group of newcomers to the city, these early writers and artists began to form their own recreational clubs—chief among them was the Little Room, a rare coed arts club whose name was taken from a short story by Madeleine Yale Wynne. The story, which appeared in *Harper's Monthly* in the 1890s, was about a

Hamlin Garland, founder of the Cliff Dwellers. (Courtesy of the Cliff Dwellers.)

mysterious room where strangers with the right attitude would find friends and contentment.

At the turn of the century Garland, a native of Lacrosse, Wisconsin, told his brother-in-law, sculptor Lorado Taft, about an idea he had to expand the reach of the literary club into one that embraced all the arts. Garland told Taft, "The time has come . . . when a successful literary and artistic club can be established and maintained." Garland discussed the idea with other members of the Little Room and decided to start gathering members for a male-only club.

As with most new club efforts that attempted to pull members from older groups, not everyone was happy with Garland's efforts. In particular, fellow Little Room member Henry Blake Fuller—who, though he never joined, had a particular connection to the Cliff Dwellers that will become clear in the next few paragraphs—thought Garland's idea was misguided. Garland wrote later that Fuller told him that Chicago "was a pestilential slough in which he . . . was inextricably mired, and though he was not quite so definite with me, he said to others, 'Garland's idea is sure to fail.'"

Yet Garland reached a critical point of interest and invited key members—including Charles L. Hutchinson, one of the founders of the Art Institute of Chicago—to discuss a startup plan at the

City Club on June 12, 1907. There he read a letter defining the club's mission:

> Broadly speaking, this club will bring together men of artistic and literary tastes who are now widely scattered among the various social and business organizations of Chicago and unite them with artists, writers, architects and musicians of the city in a club whose purposes are distinctly and primarily aesthetic, taking hints from the Players, The National Arts and the Century Association of New York.
>
> The membership is to be composed of, first—men concerned with some form of creative art—that is, to say, painters, sculptors, novelists, poets, musicians, architects, historians, illustrators, and those who make handicraft and art. Second—distinguished men in other professions who are patrons of art, or sympathetic with the fundamental purpose of the club.

The letter was approved, and the formal organization of the club—initially called the Attic Club—was completed on November 6, 1907, at the Fine Arts Building, 410 S. Michigan. (The Attic Club actually reconstituted in 1923 and finally closed in the mid-1990s—for more information, turn to Chapter 7, "The Lost Clubs.")

The club's own histories show some disagreement over how the Cliff Dwellers got its name. Henry Fuller's novel *The Cliff-Dwellers* seems to provide a rather obvious answer to the question, and one might reasonably think that Garland adopted the name as a tongue-in-cheek response to Fuller's disregard for Garland's fledgling club. But in 1947 *Chicago Tribune* journalist and Cliff Dwellers member Charles Collins called the Fuller namesake theory "a standard legend of Michigan Avenue—a persistent distortion of the facts in the case." He adds:

> The Club's name was intended to point a finger toward the ancient cliff-dwelling Indians of the Southwest, who perched their communal homes on ledges and precipices. They were picturesque Americans of the remote past whose peaceful

ways of life found expression in artwork. For Indians, their cultural level was high. Therefore, the name by which they are commonly known was chosen as appropriate for a social group of art-minded, modern Chicagoans, also addicted to perching on high ledges during their working hours in art studios, music conservatories, etc.

After its birth in the Fine Arts Building— a first home for many Chicago arts and literary clubs— the Cliff Dwellers made its first permanent kiva in 1908 in an eighth-floor space in Orchestra Hall. The building was designed by Daniel Burnham, but the interior of the club was tackled in true Arts and Crafts style by Howard Van Doren Shaw. That first clubhouse required a steep walk up 31 steps from the eighth-floor lobby to the penthouse area, which became the bane of purveyors and more than a few club members. (Courtesy of the Cliff Dwellers.)

THE 31 STEPS

At its first anniversary, the Cliff Dwellers was still without a permanent home. Garland and his members had considered space at the Harvester Building at 600 S. Michigan Avenue (currently part of Columbia College and at one time home to the Woman's Athletic Club), but that was really their third choice. Garland's second choice was to stay in the Fine Arts Building, where the club was born and where so many members already worked and gathered after hours. But Garland's real hope was space on the roof of the four-year-old Orchestra Hall.

Like so many clubs that formed after Chicago gave birth to the skyscraper, the Cliff Dwellers wanted architectural significance for its clubhouse space. It also wanted an address that fit the creative passions of its club members. Daniel Burnham's D.H. Burnham Co. completed the eight-story Orchestra Hall in 1904, and as a member, Burnham himself agreed to take responsibility for the façade of the penthouse, which would contain the club's open dining, reading, and meeting facilities. The landmark Arts and Crafts architect and Chicago native Howard Van Doren Shaw tackled the interior.

That first clubhouse was an open space of 70 by 28 feet entered from the west—all the better to see Michigan Avenue from a full wall of ornate windows pointing east as visitors entered the room. (It should be noted that the current Cliff Dwellers clubhouse duplicates this effect at its current home.) The west wall included a large fireplace toward its south end with a portrait of Hamlin Garland above it, painted by Garland's friend and club cofounder Ralph Clarkson. (At that time the area held a much-used grand piano that couldn't make the trip to the club's more compact quarters in 1996. More on that to follow.)

A door on the south wall, provided with hardware designed by Louis Sullivan, also an early member, led to an anteroom for private functions that also contained a library. It was this room that was later dedicated to Sullivan and picked up, paneling, furniture, and all, and reinstalled at the club's current space. The remaining walls, which were wainscoted in oak, afforded space for art exhibits that continue to be a feature of the club. The Cliff Dwellers held its inauguration of its first kiva on January 6, 1909.

It included poetry and songs composed for the occasion, a pageant symbolizing the position of the club in Mid-America, and at the end, the lighting of a small, ceremonial fire. The ritual continues today.

NOT EXACTLY PARTY CENTRAL

Garland wanted the Cliff Dwellers to be a world-class destination for artistic and literary thought, where luminaries from all over the globe could come and share their interests with members. But Garland governed the club with an iron fist and a stern set of rules. Chief among them — no booze. As member Henry Regnery's history points out, "Hamlin Garland didn't drink and apparently saw no reason why anyone else should." But Regnery adds that with or without alcohol, the Cliff Dwellers was definitely a men's club. In fact, he points out that 1912 board minutes reflect "'some misunderstanding regarding the use of the club for ladies' afternoon teas.' In response to this threatening development, the minutes go on to say, 'The House Committee desires to notify the members that ladies are not invited to the club until 6 p.m.'"

Women would not be accepted as full members of the Cliff Dwellers until 1984. Unusually, nonwhite males have been accepted throughout the group's history.

By 1915 it appeared that club members had had enough of Garland. They elected Art Institute of Chicago founder Charles Hutchinson as the club's second president. With Hutchinson's election, so went a change in the articles of incorporation that didn't allow any president to serve more than two terms in succession. There's no precise record of the date when alcohol was first poured in the club, but club lore holds that when Garland returned to the club, there was a bar installed in the club with a sign above it stating "This place is under new management." Regnery notes that the story might be apocryphal, but as in many clubs, that hasn't stopped anyone from telling it.

When Garland returned to the club after moving to New York, which happened shortly after he left as president of the Cliff Dwellers, members presented him with a rather ironic gift — a loving cup.

THE LAST YEARS OF LOUIS SULLIVAN

The famed architect Louis Sullivan, like so many other Chicago luminaries, was a member of most of the leading private clubs particularly at his height of wealth and fame. But after 1900 Sullivan fell on hard times, and his history with the Cliff Dwellers becomes all the more touching because of that.

Sullivan was not an easy man to know or work for—notably, he fired fellow Cliff Dweller Frank Lloyd Wright for moonlighting—but it was the 1893 World's Columbian Exposition that was a fateful turning point for Sullivan's architectural philosophy and his business. The planners of the fair rejected the Chicago School of architecture in favor of a neoclassical style, and Sullivan famously predicted that the exposition "would set architecture back 50 years"—a statement that would help set back his career permanently. He went so far as to design the fair's Transportation Building in the Chicago style and eventually dissolved his legendary partnership with Dankmar Adler in 1895.

He came to the Cliff Dwellers not long after it opened. His memberships at the other clubs had long since lapsed because he couldn't afford their fees. While he created a series of notable small Midwestern banks and commercial buildings during his last years, he was essentially without any major commissions after 1900.

Two architect members of the Cliff Dwellers, Max Dunning and George Nimmons, reached out to Sullivan. They were considerably younger than Sullivan, but according to Sullivan biographer Willard Connely, "the Transportation Building clung to their memory like an unchanging sunset." They realized not only that Sullivan needed money but that he needed something to keep his brilliant mind working.

In 1922 the men suggested two projects for Sullivan. First was an assignment to design a set of 20 plates to illustrate his philosophy of architectural ornament, and the second was an autobiography. For the first project they got the Burnham Library of the Art Institute to make a grant of $500, and other architect members matched it. Because Sullivan no longer could afford an office, Regnery writes that the American Terracotta Co., where many of his designs had been modeled, provided him with a desk and drafting table in their offices at 1701 Prairie Avenue. When finished, he named the plate series *A System of Architectural Ornament According with a Philosophy of Man's Powers.*

For the autobiography, Dunning and Nimmons arranged for initial publication in the *Journal of the American Institute of Architects* in at least 12 monthly installments for $100 each. These were windfalls for Sullivan, who at the time was having trouble pulling together the $9 a week for his room at the Warner Hotel. According to Connely, Sullivan worked on his plates during the day, and after dinner at the Cliff Dwellers (his membership and expenses paid in full by architect members of the club) he'd retreat to the desk and chair the club provided him and write. That desk and chair remain in the anteroom of the Cliff Dwellers clubhouse named for Sullivan.

Sullivan died alone in his hotel room in April 1924, just three months after publishing the book he wrote at the Cliff Dwellers entitled *The Autobiography of an Idea.* According to the club's own history, one of the last people to see him alive was his old employee, Frank Lloyd Wright. It's written that they patched things up before Sullivan died.

SURVIVING PROHIBITION & THE GREAT DEPRESSION

A tongue-in-cheek letter submitted to the board in June 1917 from the "Women's Committee for National Defense" (the club at that time neither admitted women nor supported any kind of political agenda), seeking information concerning "the sale of liquors to the members of the club," was answered with equal wit by the board: "The Cliff Dwellers maintains no bar and never sells liquor to its members." This artifice was a game at the club, which had been managing its own private stash since Garland stepped down as president in 1915 and left Chicago soon afterward.

At the Cliff Dwellers' January 1919 annual meeting—in the year Prohibition was ratified—a motion was passed authorizing the appointment of a committee to redouble their efforts to secure and store an adequate supply of "alcoholic beverages to provide for as many years as may be against the arid season which faces us."

Club life wasn't all about the booze in the late teens and 1920s, but looking back in today's health-conscious times, it certainly was close. "Czar Garland's" reign had prohibited any alcohol in the club, so after 1915—no precise day is recorded when the Cliff Dwellers let the wine flow—alcohol was as much a sign of independence as conviviality. That's why when Prohibition finally hit, it inspired some genuinely comical behavior to hide the Cliff Dwellers' attachment to demon rum.

In January 1922 then-president Ralph Clarkson gave instructions that all the glassware used for "drinking" be removed to the basement and replaced by "fudge sundae" glasses. Soon afterward a petition came, signed by 53 members, "that the glasses, serving table and other utensils, recently removed from the clubs rooms be restored to their original places or others convenient."

Yet the Cliff Dwellers needn't have worried so much. Former Chicago mayor Carter Harrison II was an active member. A letter kept by the club from President William A. Nitze documents a conversation he had with Harrison about shutting down booze entirely. The former mayor reportedly responded, "The police will never interfere because of a little liquor that raises our spirits."

The bigger challenge turned out to be the Depression, which grew into a membership crisis for most Chicago clubs by the early 1930s. For so many clubs it wasn't about the money—it was about losing the membership that made the club what it was.

Obviously, the Cliff Dwellers survived the Depression and continued through the decades as a center for lively conversation and debate about the arts so central to the life of Chicago. For nearly as long as the club has been in existence, it has operated a nonprofit foundation to provide funds to various individuals and groups chosen from nominations made by the membership.

Most recently, the Cliff Dwellers Arts Foundation recently made grants to the Mostly Music Series at Northeastern University, Dance Chicago, The American Guild of Organists, Merit School of Music, William Ferris Chorale, Chicago Youth Symphony, and the Chicago Artists' Coalition. All grants were funded via yearly donations by Cliff Dwellers members.

In 2000, the club initiated its Artists-in-Residence program as a way to bring local younger artists and performers together for a free one-year membership at the club. "The one-year memberships are free to the designated artists who are given a site for meetings and presentation of their abilities to a compatible audience of club members." The artists-in-residents have the option to apply for full club membership at the end of the year. The program has allowed anywhere from five to 20 participants between 24 and 38 years of age to be recruited from various arts organizations and schools throughout the city.

This convivial atmosphere continued in the weathered space at Orchestra Hall for decades—but that was to end in the 1990s.

The reconstructed Cliff Dwellers library in the club's current home. (Photo by Lisa Holton.)

The view of Millennium Park from the Cliff Dwellers' terrace. (Photo by Lisa Holton.)

Members Roger Ebert and Andrew Patner at a black-tie Cliff Dwellers function. (Courtesy of the Cliff Dwellers.)

THE MOVE FROM ORCHESTRA HALL

When the Chicago Symphony announced its plan for a renovation of the world-renowned concert space, it was the news the Cliff Dwellers hadn't exactly been hoping for. The longtime club space, a landmark of the Arts and Crafts movement, would be replaced by a private club for the Orchestral Association. The Cliff Dwellers were informed in the early 1990s that their top-floor meeting rooms overlooking Grant Park would be scuttled after 86 years.

There ensued a fairly public battle of words between the club and the Orchestral Association, which briefly demurred and offered the club the use of a new dining room on non-Symphony dates. The Cliff Dwellers refused and threatened legal action, but eventually the symphony supporters won out and the club moved out in 1996.

The Cliff Dwellers now enjoys the same view of Grant Park, only 13 stories higher.

In January 2001 the club suffered a kitchen fire that closed the club until November of that year while insurance companies haggled out the settlement.

WHY THE CLUB IS IMPORTANT TODAY

Asked to explain why the Cliff Dwellers remains relevant, Jack Zimmerman, a former president of the club, begins by paraphrasing the motto on the lobby floor of the Fine Arts Building:

> There's a saying over the door that "all else perishes but art endures," and I find a certain truth in that. For a century, we've offered our members a place to meet and to discuss art. We have a wonderful young artists program. We bring art to a very accessible place for a lot of people. For people who belong to clubs, it's a third place. It's a place to go that's not home, and it's not your job. It's another place where you can interact with people differently than you do at these other two places—and that enriches your life.

Sources:

Regnery, Henry. *The Cliff Dwellers: The History of a Chicago Cultural Institution*. Chicago: Chicago Historical Bookworks, 1990.

Zimmerman, Jack. Interview by author. 28 June 2005.

THE
TAVERN CLUB

The Tavern Club
Founded: 1927
Address: 333 N. Michigan Avenue, Chicago, IL 60601
Architect: Building by Holabird & Root (1928);
clubhouse by Winold Reis

All these guys wanted was a drink, legal or not, and a place to let their hair down. Way down.

The Tavern Club, perched on a 25th-floor aerie with a still-unobstructed view of North Michigan Avenue, was formed by writers, painters, actors, and other artistic men who broke with their teetotalling brethren at the Cliff Dwellers—even in the midst of Prohibition. That number grew to include admen, CEOs, and more than a few local celebrities.

In the twenty-first century, the Tavern Club's membership consisted of many sons and daughters—and more than a few grand-children—of that original connected, hard-partying crowd, which included such names as Frank Lloyd Wright, Ludwig Mies van der

Rohe, Carl Sandburg, Enrico Fermi, and even the first Mayor Daley, who stopped by a few times.

In 2007, the Tavern Club became mostly a quiet place to have a meal, a wedding, or an occasional drink after work. No longer was it a temple to the three-martini lunch or the lengthy after-work cocktail hour followed by the semicomatose ride home on the train with the wife waiting at the station. Of course, that's pretty much over everywhere now. The culprits? Some sourpusses blame the women who integrated all of Chicago's male-only clubs in the 1980s. It changed things, somehow. Others blame the workaholic yuppie generation who fled to neighborhood sports bars for loud relaxation and wouldn't touch Daddy's club with a ten-foot pole. Then there's the state of today's workplace, which is nothing like it was even 20 years ago, much less 80. Today's working men and women are expected to finish up a ten-hour workday with quality time for the kids.

In the end it was probably all of those things. But the personality of the Tavern Club left it exposed to other cultural forces — the creeping consolidation of newspapers, magazine, and book publishers, and the advertising and PR community. While the Cliff Dwellers' members were artists, serious writers, architects, and musicians, the Tavern Club's members were the creatives linked more closely to commerce — journalists, admen, publicists, publishers, and booksellers. Chicago is, after all, the city that gave the world Tony the Tiger, Playboy Enterprises, Kroch's and Brentano's, the Sears Catalog, Who's Who, and — at its peak — ten daily newspapers. Jonathan Dedmon, the Tavern Club's current president and son of one of its more famous members puts it succinctly:

> It was a different time. There were six decent places to eat downtown, and now, there are probably more than 200. Now, you have a culture where people are grabbing a sandwich at their desk and calling London and Tokyo. Before, people in Chicago did business with people in Chicago, and it was all about seeing people and being seen, and it was important to do that in a place like the Tavern Club.

Carl Kroch was known as "The Baron of Books" in his role as chairman of Chicago independent bookstore legend Kroch's & Brentano's. He was a daily attendee at the club until his death in 1999. Club Historian Bruce Felknor tells the story of Kroch and his wife, Jet, whom he met while she was a dancer at the Chez Paree nightclub. They ate in the club every day. (Courtesy of The Tavern Club.)

But it was also about something else, Dedmon explains. The world that created the Tavern Club—and most clubs in general—was a much more literate society, or at least a society that judged itself more on its appreciation of the written word, ideas, and art and a person's facility at simple camaraderie. That's what the Tavern Club was—an extremely lighthearted and sophisticated place that allowed for some very hard partying, yet each member had a certain substance underneath.

These men weren't just their jobs. Of course, nobody expected them to be.

FLOREAT TABERNA CHICAGINIENSIS

Right up until the yuppified 1980s started taking the last of the fun out of the workday, the Tavern Club was to gray eminences like the Chicago and Union League clubs what the fictional Animal House was to Omega—only classier. While the University Club held lectures with literary giants, the Tavern Club sponsored sketch nights with nude female models. Naked women tended to be something of a theme at the Tavern Club, and it all started on the walls.

The artist most closely identified with the club is Edgar Miller. In 1933 he created the club's mural, *Love Through the Ages*, which represented some of the famous love affairs of history. After the mural's completion the club threw a party called "A Night of Ancient and Deathless Rapture." Jonathan Dedmon's father, Emmett Dedmon, describes the night of the party in the club's 50th anniversary history:

> The dedication began about 11 P.M. with a flourish of trumpets, followed by a Hymn to Apollo, composed for the occasion by Rudolph Ganz. President Karleton Hackett then appeared on the outdoor terrace dais, on which stood the stat-

Another dull night at the Tavern Club: Member Al Shaw chases Aphrodite in a later reenactment of The "Night of Ancient and Deathless Rapture" from the 1930s. (Courtesy of The Tavern Club.)

ue of a completely veiled goddess. He was dressed as poet Homer in flowing grey robes banded in gold. Beneath this classic costume appeared some very practical long underwear, which ended just above his sandaled bare feet. He carried a full-sized golden lyre and read with elocutionary effect "Aphrodite Renata," an ode to the goddess of love. As Hackett finished, the windblown crowd burst into applause and the veils dropped from the "goddess" who appeared completely nude in the chill night wind.

Indeed, while the elite members of most of the city's leading clubs held dignified, efficient meetings that were a model of governance, no Tavern Club annual meeting was considered a success unless a sizable majority of attendees were nursing serious hangovers the next day. In fact, one memorable annual meeting ended with all attendees filing out to throw an irksome bathroom door into the Chicago River.

The Tavern Club, like the Cliff Dwellers, tended toward more open membership policies from the start. While most of the city's clubs went through cycles of barring Jews and other male minorities, the Tavern Club and the Cliff Dwellers say they held no such restrictions. In Bruce Felknor's 2005 history, *Of Clubbable Nature: Chicago's Tavern Club at 75*, he reported that the club created a women's membership as far back as 1934, controversial for the time, yet still very restrictive. Women could pay full membership fees, but they were not allowed in the club until after 4 p.m. and they had no voting privileges. That membership drew only nine women and terminated a few years later — full voting membership would have to wait until 1987.

In Chicago the Tavern Club was truly the premier boy's club for men.

CHICAGO'S CREATIVE COMMUNITY
IN THE 1920S AND 1930S

The Chicago that begat the Tavern Club was an exciting place. Far from its ramshackle early days, Chicago of the mid-1920s was an improbable cultural mecca that had found its way onto the world stage.

Mrs. O'Leary's cow had produced a city of brazenly bold architecture, and the city's newspapers attracted creative types from all over, not the least of whom included Carl Sandburg, the great poet who once worked as a cub reporter for the great *Chicago Daily News*. By the Roaring Twenties, Chicago was home to not only Al Capone but the nation's advertising industry, long before the words Madison Avenue became common shorthand for New York's agency dominance.

Admen and copywriters flocked to Chicago to support its legendary mail-order catalog companies (Sears, Roebuck and Co., Montgomery Ward, Spiegel) and a diverse bounty of manufacturers of consumer and industrial goods. Long before the days of globalization, Chicago literally fed, clothed, and promoted the people and businesses of the nation. Quentin J. Schultze, writing for the *Encyclopedia of Chicago*, points out that Chicago's first legendary ad agency, Lord & Thomas, got Americans to try orange juice (everyone thought oranges were only for eating). It also dubbed Schlitz the "Beer That Made Milwaukee Famous" and wrote the old "Shot from Guns!" campaign for Quaker Oats' Puffed Rice Cereal. When three employees bought the agency and renamed it Fairfax Cone (predecessor to Foot, Cone & Belding), they created some of the most memorable radio and TV brands of all time, including the Hallmark Hall of Fame and Clairol's "Does She or Doesn't She?" In the thick of the Great Depression, Leo Burnett would start his eponymous agency and later create Tony the Tiger, The Jolly Green Giant, the Pillsbury Doughboy, and the Marlboro Man.

These agencies were in close walking distance of the Tavern Club.

Besides having an almost unbelievable glut of daily city newspapers (in 1900 the number stood at ten and has been dwindling ever since), Chicago also was the nation's largest publishing center for commercial printing, maps, books, encyclopedias, and magazines. The Sears and Montgomery Ward catalogs rolled off the presses at R.R. Donnelley; mapmaker Rand McNally gave the world directions to the most remote places on the globe; World Book and Encyclopedia Britannica competed for the groaning bookshelves of American homes; Time Inc. was a major employer here. And in the

1950s, Hugh Hefner's little magazine and eventual television and retail empire would put Chicago on the map for a new kind of cool and sophistication.

Chicago was a city that drew witty wordsmiths and paid them well. And those wordsmiths filled the clubs—particularly the Tavern Club.

MOVING UP MICHIGAN AVENUE

Maybe it's a bit of an oversimplification to say that the split with the Cliff Dwellers downtown was all about booze, but life had apparently gotten way too serious under its prohibitionist founder Hamlin Garland, who by then had picked up the nickname Czar Hamlin. There might have been other reasons, too, as writer and Tavern Club member Emmett Dedmon explains in the 50th anniversary history of the Tavern Club:

> In the late summer of 1925, a brash idea was born. It proposed the organization in Chicago of a club whose members would include "readers as well as writers"—men who enjoy art, music or theater as well as those who produce same. Artists, musicians, actors, to say nothing of architects, dramatists and newspapermen would be welcome. So would business magnates who had strong cultural interests.
>
> Founding members have always stated that the organization of the tavern had nothing to do with a split off from the Cliff Dwellers. The Cliff Dwellers' interest ran markedly to music, possibly because their location made it so handy [at the time, their clubhouse was at Orchestra Hall], and to writing and art. The Tavern claimed it roamed wider fields. Both groups are friendly.

ENTER THE PENTHOUSE CLUBHOUSE

Athletic clubs like the Illinois Woman's Athletic Club and the Medinah had built freestanding, majestic buildings as a monument to themselves, but the Tavern Club was truly a first in Chicago— the first true destination clubhouse in a twentieth-century modern

The Tavern Club's two-level dining room with its signature spiral staircase. (Courtesy of The Tavern Club.)

The club's drawing room, where sketch nights were regularly held in the old days. (Courtesy of The Tavern Club.)

From an earlier history of the Tavern Club, reproduction of its legendary "Love Among The Ages" mural designed by member Edgar Miller, which was partially sold off after a renovation in 1959. (Courtesy of The Tavern Club.)

office skyscraper. Many other top-story clubhouses would follow, but the Tavern Club was truly the first.

The landmark 333 N. Michigan Avenue building was close to completion as the Tavern Club organized, and its architects, Holabird & Root, took full advantage of the polished granite structure's unique site. Due to the jog of Michigan Avenue by the bridge, which had recently been completed, the 333 building still appears to be located in the center of Michigan Avenue as an observer looks southward. It was a natural for any club wanting a premier address, and the developers wanted the Tavern Club. In fact, 333 almost had two clubs: the Tavern and the Woman's Athletic Club, which elected to build its own clubhouse in the then-undeveloped stretch of what would become North Michigan Avenue.

While the Tavern Club originated on the 25th floor, it eventually expanded to the 26th with the creation of a winding staircase that led to more meeting space and the club's signature Sky Terrace, where gatherings were held in the summer.

GOING FORWARD

As 2007 drew to a close, the Tavern Club was literally planning for its last big bash in the 333 building. As mentioned, the club had lost its lease and was considering various alternatives to assure its continued existence, including a merger with the Cliff Dwellers.

Back in 2005, worries were already circling that the end was coming for the Tavern Club. Dedmon responded this way:

> Well, we have Trump Tower going up across the street, and we're in an older building. I like to think that we're part of the city's history and there will always be a place for us. But if it appears that we can't continue as we are, I'd love to throw one huge Artist & Models party, let everyone get crazy and then shut off the lights. Go out the right way.

And that's exactly what happened.

Sources:

Dedmon, Jonathan. Interview by author. August 2005.

Dedmon, Emmett. *Our 50th Year View from the Top of the Tavern Club*. Chicago: the Tavern Club, 1978.

Felknor, Bruce. *Of Clubbable Nature: Chicago's Tavern Club at 75*. Chicago: the Tavern Club, 2006.

PART III

THE FUTURE

I

THE
FUTURE
OF
PRIVATE CLUBS

———————

It happens to be a matter of record
that I was first in print with the discovery
that the tastelessness of the food offered
in American clubs varies in direct proportion
to the exclusiveness of the club.
— *Calvin Trillin*, Third Helpings

In a bygone day the most successful private clubs in Chicago depended on the right people, an opulent address, great food and drink, athletic facilities, and guest rooms that provided a home away from home. Today there are plenty of great restaurants, fancy hotels, and sprawling athletic clubs throughout the city that aim not just for the wealthy but for everyone. So what's left to attract members to the historic private clubs?

The most successful clubs, at least in today's world, continue for two reasons: the people, and the club's ability to adapt to the changing needs of its members.

Throughout this book I've mentioned the de-evolution of social class from a business perspective. Today's most elite clubs are not as likely to pay attention to *The Social Register* as they might have only 20 years ago. Today accomplishment, talent, money, personality, and power are almost as strong a lure as bloodline.

Yet there is an even stronger engine behind the growing irrelevancy of elite groups, and that's the marketplace. In May 2005 the *New York Times* published a series entitled "Class Matters" that pointed to the new mass availability of so-called luxury goods at all income levels. It said:

> Social class, once so easily assessed by the car in the driveway or the purse on the arm, has become harder to see in the things Americans buy. Rising incomes, flattening prices and easily available credit have given so many Americans access to such a wide array of high-end goods that traditional markers of status have lost much of their meaning.
>
> A family squarely in the middle class may own a flat-screen television, drive a BMW and indulge a taste for expensive chocolate.
>
> A wealthy family may only further blur the picture by shopping for wine at Costco and bath towels at Target, which for years has stocked its shelves with high-quality goods.
>
> Everyone, meanwhile, appears to be blending into a classless crowd, shedding the showiest kinds of high-status clothes in favor of a jeans-and-sweatsuit informality. When Vice President Dick Cheney, a wealthy man in his own right, attended a January ceremony in Poland to commemorate the liberation of Nazi death camps, he wore a parka.

Traditional clubs have to work much harder to distinguish themselves in a world where luxury and exclusivity can be bought instead of bestowed. Clubs also need to deal with changing demands on people's time. For instance, Saturday mornings at the club are much more likely to include the kids—that's right, kids. Twenty-five years ago members' kids might be allowed into the club for a Christmas or Easter brunch. At many of the city's full-service clubs, they're regular users of facilities with their parents—particularly dads who never had to shoulder child-care burdens on the weekend.

The clubs that survive through the end of the decade and beyond will need to monitor what people under the age of 50 require. In so many of Chicago's private clubs, 50 now represents the younger end of the age spectrum. But with costs heading up and so many entertainment and networking alternatives for Generations x and y, tradition alone won't sustain the clubs.

If Chicago's private clubs want to survive, they will have to innovate. They'll also need to make their history part of their sales pitch, and in the fast-paced global city Chicago has become, that may not be an easy task.

APPENDIX A

THE
CLUB GUIDE

———◆———

The following clubs, listed in alphabetical order, participated in a survey of their services, fees, and features. Not all of the clubs discussed in this book participated in the survey.

General points of clarification:

* Initiation fees and monthly dues generally do not cover meals, gym usage, or other individual charges.
* Guest rooms are fully featured hotel space for club members and guests. They cannot be rented by the general public without sponsorship by a member of the club.

All of this information is accurate as of January 15, 2008, unless otherwise marked.

THE ADVENTURERS CLUB

ADDRESS: 714 S. Dearborn Street, Unit #6, Chicago, IL 60605
PHONE: 312/291-0810
WEB SITE: www.advclub.org
FOUNDED: 1911
FAMOUS MEMBERS: Marlin Perkins (president of the club in 1955),
  Roald Amundsen, Thor Heyerdahl, Ernest Shackleton, Sir
  Edmund Hillary, Steve Fossett.
MISSION STATEMENT/MOTTO: "To provide a hearth and home for
  those who have left the beaten path and made for adventure."
MEMBERS: 70 resident members, 50 nonresident members.
DOMINANT PROFESSIONS OF CLUB MEMBERS: No dominant pro-
  fession; members are entrepreneurs, industrialists, profession-
  als, and physicians.
TO JOIN: Prospective members must fill out an application that
  details the adventures they've taken, be sponsored by two
  members, and be at least 21 years of age.
INITIATION FEE: $250 for resident and nonresident members.
DUES: Junior members: 21-25 years old: $100; 26-30 years-old:
  $200. Full-resident annual dues are $1,000 (or $300 quarter-
  ly). In addition to dues, resident members are assessed a
  $50.00 monthly minimum charge toward meals and programs.
  Nonresident dues are $200 annually.
COLLECTION HIGHLIGHTS: Wild game trophies, weapons, shrunk-
  en heads, and adventure memorabilia from prehistoric times
  through present day. Over 200 Adventurers Club expedition
  flags have been carried around the world by members and
  hang from the clubhouse ceiling.
MEETING FACILITIES: The Printers Row clubhouse consists of an
  open dining room and exhibit space. The Walgreen Room is
  available for board meetings and can be reserved for private
  dining.
ATHLETIC FACILITIES: N/A.
GUEST FACILITIES: N/A.
CLUB ACTIVITIES: Monthly lecture programs on topics of interest
  to the membership, annual outdoor activities, and fishing tournaments.

SPECIAL SERVICES: Club is available for private parties during evenings and weekends as long as a member reserves the space. Full catering service is also available.

PARENT/CHILDREN'S SERVICES: N/A.

RECENT RENOVATIONS: Upgraded sound and television system; Knudsen Library and Study for Expedition Planning.

YEAR WOMEN MEMBERS ADMITTED: 1989.

WOMEN AS PERCENTAGE OF TOTAL MEMBERSHIP: Four women members as of June 2006.

YEAR NONWHITE MEMBERS ADMITTED: Never a prohibition against nonwhite members.

NONWHITES AS PERCENTAGE OF TOTAL MEMBERSHIP: As of June 2005 no nonwhites are members of the club.

AVERAGE AGE OF MEMBERSHIP: 35 to 50.

MAJOR ANNUAL EVENTS: Wild game dinner and other themed events; muskie tournament at Chippewa Flowage near Hayward, Wisconsin; and educational tours of local zoos.

THE CHICAGO CLUB

ADDRESS: 81 E. Van Buren Street, Chicago, IL 60605

PHONE: 312/427-1825

WEB SITE: www.thechicagoclub.org

FOUNDED: March 25, 1869

FAMOUS MEMBERS: Robert Todd Lincoln, Marshall Field, Potter Palmer, and many old Chicago families; also most major CEOs in the city.

MISSION STATEMENT/MOTTO: "The Chicago Club is and shall continue to be the premier club in the city, serving the business, civic, educational, and philanthropic leaders and their families, by providing a private club organization with outstanding dining, service, and clubhouse facilities."

CIVIC ACTIVITIES/SOCIAL MISSION: The club does not support any particular civic organization; rather, club members chair and/or serve on many civic and charitable boards outside the club.

MEMBERS: 1,175.

DOMINANT PROFESSIONS OF CLUB MEMBERS: Top executives of major Chicago corporations and institutions.

TO JOIN: Strictly by invitation; prospective members must have one sponsor and two seconds, plus three supporting letters and must know two members of the Board of Directors.

INITIATION FEE: $8,500 (none for those under age 40 until they reach 40, then 50 percent of the then-current initiation fee.)

DUES: $4,350 annually, ($2,175 annually for members under age 40).

ART COLLECTION HIGHLIGHTS: N/A.

MEETING FACILITIES: 12 meeting rooms, one with ballroom seating 250. The Inner Clubs (clubs within a club) were vibrant from the 1920s through the 1970s but are now primarily specialized meeting space that members reserve. Today there are five Inner Clubs, some meeting weekly and others only for special programs. The Inner Clubs are Room 100 (founded in 1920), Room 19 (1923), Room 800–803 (created from the merger of Rooms 800 [1926] and 803 [1927] in 1996), and Room 1871 (which was founded for younger members in 1976). In 2006 a group of associate members (under 40) formed a new inner club using the name of Room 503 (Room 503 was originally founded in 1925 and the few remaining members were absorbed by Room 19 in 1990).

ATHLETIC FACILITIES: One squash court, a modest fitness center, and a billiard room.

GUEST FACILITIES: 36 overnight guest rooms, including two suites.

CLUB ACTIVITIES: Variety of cultural and social programs for members and their guests and the activities of the five Inner Clubs.

SPECIAL SERVICES: Private business offices for members outfitted with computer, printer, fax, and high-speed Internet access.

PARENT/CHILDREN'S SERVICES: N/A.

RECENT RENOVATIONS: The club's former Main Dining Room has been restored as a ballroom with seating capacity of 250 and renamed the Daniel Burnham Room.

YEAR WOMEN MEMBERS ADMITTED: 1982.

WOMEN AS PERCENTAGE OF TOTAL MEMBERSHIP: N/A.

YEAR NONWHITE MEMBERS ADMITTED: N/A (club does not track).

NONWHITES AS PERCENTAGE OF TOTAL MEMBERSHIP: N/A.

AVERAGE AGE OF MEMBERSHIP: 60.

MAJOR ANNUAL EVENTS: Members' New Year luncheon, a tradition since the club's founding in 1869 (it used to be held on New Year's Day; it is now held on the first Friday after New Year's Day); July 3 Independence Day Family Celebration and City of Chicago fireworks; and December Holiday Family Celebration.

THE CHICAGO LITERARY CLUB

ADDRESS: P.O. Box 350, Kenilworth, IL 60043 (office only—no clubhouse; meetings are presently held at The Cliff Dwellers)

PHONE: 847/251-1400

WEB SITE: www.chilit.org

FOUNDED: 1874

FAMOUS MEMBERS: Orville T. Bailey, Elmer Gertz, William Le Baron Jenney, Paul Howard Douglas, William Rainey Harper, David Swing, Thomas Elliott Donnelly.

MISSION STATEMENT/MOTTO: The object of the club is literary culture.

CIVIC ACTIVITIES/SOCIAL MISSION: Development of literary and presentation skills through writing and reading of original essays; support of poetry and other literary enterprises.

MEMBERS: 167.

DOMINANT PROFESSIONS OF CLUB MEMBERS: Professionals in the fields of medicine, law, and business.

TO JOIN: Prospective members must fill out a simple form and have letters from a proposer and two seconders.

INITIATION FEE: None.

DUES: $165 per year.

MEETING FACILITIES: The Cliff Dwellers clubhouse.

CLUB ACTIVITIES: Members present essays at club meetings.

YEAR WOMEN MEMBERS ADMITTED: 1995.

WOMEN AS PERCENTAGE OF TOTAL MEMBERSHIP: Roughly 15 percent.

YEAR NONWHITE MEMBERS ADMITTED: N/A.

NONWHITES AS PERCENTAGE OF TOTAL MEMBERSHIP: Roughly 15 percent.

AVERAGE AGE OF MEMBERSHIP: 65.

MAJOR ANNUAL EVENTS: Reunion Dinner, Closing Meeting, and Arthur Baer Fellowship Address.

THE CITY CLUB OF CHICAGO

ADDRESS: 360 N. Michigan Avenue, Suite 903, Chicago, IL 60601 (office only—no clubhouse; public policy breakfasts and luncheons are held at various downtown locations)
PHONE: 312/565-6500
WEB SITE: www.cityclub-chicago.com
FOUNDED: 1903
FAMOUS MEMBERS: Mayor Richard M. Daley, Governor Rod Blagojevich, Barack Obama.
MISSION STATEMENT/MOTTO: "Since its inception in 1903, the City Club of Chicago has served as a venue for nonpartisan forums and debates on public issues that pertain to Chicago metropolitan–area residents. The City Club of Chicago proudly attracts the expertise of city officials, prominent state leaders, and people of national acclaim. These persons use the forums as a conduit to share their viewpoints on timely and important policy issues."
MEMBERS: Approximately 1,050.
DOMINANT PROFESSIONS OF CLUB MEMBERS: Varied.
TO JOIN: Membership is open to the general public.
ANNUAL FEE: Per year: Student—$25; Individual—$50; Business—$250; Corporate—$500; President's Club—$1,000.
DUES: None.
YEAR WOMEN MEMBERS ADMITTED: 1962.
YEAR NONWHITE MEMBERS ADMITTED: 1912.
AVERAGE AGE OF MEMBERSHIP: N/A.
MAJOR ANNUAL EVENTS: Annual Civic Salute and Awards Dinner.

THE CLIFF DWELLERS

ADDRESS: Borg Warner Building, 200 S. Michigan Avenue, Chicago, IL 60604
PHONE: 312/922-8080
WEB SITE: www.cliff-chicago.org

FOUNDED: 1907

FAMOUS MEMBERS: Louis Sullivan, Daniel Burnham, Hamlin Garland, Frank Lloyd Wright, Roger Ebert.

MISSION STATEMENT/MOTTO: To establish a place where people seriously interested in the arts, both professionally and, so to speak, as committed observers, could come together in a congenial and friendly way.

CIVIC ACTIVITIES/SOCIAL MISSION: N/A.

MEMBERS: 400.

DOMINANT PROFESSIONS OF CLUB MEMBERS: Architects, writers, and attorneys.

TO JOIN: Prospective members must be at least 25 years of age and have two letters of recommendation.

INITIATION FEE: $300. The Artists-in-Residence Program allows certain new members between the ages of 24 and 38 dues-free guest privileges in the club. They must work in one of the following areas to be considered: architecture, cinematic arts, criticism, curating, dance, graphic arts, literature, music, painting, photography, poetry, theater, or sculpture. Students are not eligible to apply.

DUES: $115 to $135 a month.

ART COLLECTION HIGHLIGHTS: Various paintings by members and others and a copy of *The Bird Girl*, the sculpture made famous in the film *Midnight in the Garden of Good and Evil*. The sculpture was designed by Sylvia Shaw Judson, mother of Alice Ryerson Hayes, a Cliff Dwellers member. Hayes allowed filmmaker Clint Eastwood's team to use a fiberglass-epoxy copy of the sculpture, and once it was returned, Hayes donated it to the club.

MEETING FACILITIES: The club's main dining room holds 120.

ATHLETIC FACILITIES: N/A.

GUEST FACILITIES: N/A.

CLUB ACTIVITIES: Regular series of lectures and parties from fall to spring.

RECENT RENOVATIONS: The club underwent a complete renovation after a kitchen fire in 2001.

YEAR WOMEN MEMBERS ADMITTED: 1984.

WOMEN AS PERCENTAGE OF TOTAL MEMBERSHIP: 25 percent.

YEAR NONWHITE MEMBERS ADMITTED: No restrictions on non-white males from 1907 to 1984; no restrictions on nonwhite males or females after 1984.
NONWHITES AS PERCENTAGE OF TOTAL MEMBERSHIP: N/A.
AVERAGE AGE OF MEMBERSHIP: 55.
MAJOR ANNUAL EVENTS: Annual parties on the City of Chicago's Venetian Night and for the July 3 lakefront fireworks display. The annual James Joyce Bloomsday Celebration (around June 16) has become a Chicago institution.

THE COMMERCIAL CLUB OF CHICAGO

ADDRESS: 21 S. Clark Street, Suite 3120, Chicago, IL 60603 (office only—no clubhouse; meetings are by invitation only and held in various venues around Chicago)
PHONE: 312/853-3693
WEB SITE: www.commercialclubchicago.org
FOUNDED: 1877
FAMOUS MEMBERS: Prominent business leaders of Chicago.
MISSION STATEMENT/MOTTO: "To promote the social and economic vitality of the metropolitan area of Chicago."
CIVIC ACTIVITIES/SOCIAL MISSION: The Commercial Club of Chicago is a nonprofit membership organization of the leading men and women of Chicago's business, professional, cultural, and educational communities. Its main accomplishments are as follows:
* Underwriting the first *Plan of Chicago*, which was coauthored by Daniel Burnham and Edward H. Bennett in 1909.
* Creation of the Civic Committee to undertake projects to bolster core industries and pursue new economic opportunities for the region in 1983.
* Release in 1996 of *Chicago Metropolis 2020: Preparing Metropolitan Chicago for the 21st Century* and the creation of a new organization, Chicago Metropolis 2020, to implement the report's recommendations.

In addition to these efforts, the Commercial Club and its Civic Committee have created and supported several affiliated organizations to develop and conduct specific initiatives to improve the City of Chicago and its surrounding region: Civic

272

Consulting Alliance, Leadership for Quality Education,
Chicago Metropolis 2020, and the Renaissance Schools Fund.

MEMBERS: 309 active members; 500 total members including life
and nonresident members.

DOMINANT PROFESSIONS OF CLUB MEMBERS: Senior business,
professional, educational, and cultural leaders of Chicago.

TO JOIN: To be considered for membership, candidates must be
nominated in writing by a Commercial Club member and sec-
onded by at least six other members. Election to membership is
limited to residents of the Chicago metropolitan area who shall
be deemed qualified by reason of their reputation, position in
their business or profession, and service in the public interest
and who shall have demonstrated a strong and continuing personal commitment to the club's goals of promoting the social
and economic vitality of the metropolitan area of Chicago.

INITIATION FEE: None.

DUES: N/A.

ART COLLECTION HIGHLIGHTS: N/A.

CLUB ACTIVITIES: Monthly (September through June) lunches
for members featuring speakers who address a broad range of
business, economic, and political issues—including matters of
importance both nationally and locally.

YEAR WOMEN MEMBERS ADMITTED: N/A.

WOMEN AS PERCENTAGE OF TOTAL MEMBERSHIP: N/A.

YEAR NONWHITE MEMBERS ADMITTED: N/A.

NONWHITES AS PERCENTAGE OF TOTAL MEMBERSHIP: N/A.

AVERAGE AGE OF MEMBERSHIP: N/A.

MAJOR ANNUAL EVENTS: Holiday family dinner.

THE ECONOMIC CLUB OF CHICAGO

ADDRESS: 177 N. State Street, Suite 404, Chicago, IL 60601
(office only—no clubhouse; meetings and events are held at
various locations around Chicago)

PHONE: 312/726-1628

WEB SITE: www.econclubchi.org

FOUNDED: 1927

FAMOUS MEMBERS: Mayor Richard M. Daley; Chicago-area CEOs.

MISSION STATEMENT/MOTTO: The Economic Club of Chicago
was organized in 1927 "to aid in the creation and expression of
an enlightened public opinion on the important economic and
social questions of the day." The club also works to identify
upcoming young leaders and to insure a continuum of knowledge and traditions within Chicago's civic and business
community.

CIVIC ACTIVITIES/SOCIAL MISSION: N/A.

MEMBERS: 1,500 active members.

DOMINANT PROFESSIONS/INDUSTRIES OF MEMBERS: Varied.

TO JOIN: New members must be sponsored by two current members of the club and approved by a committee of their peers.

INITIATION FEE: N/A.

ANNUAL DUES: $850.00.

ART COLLECTION/ARCHIVE: Chicago Historical Society.

YEAR WOMEN MEMBERS ADMITTED: 1972.

WOMEN AS PERCENTAGE OF TOTAL MEMBERSHIP: N/A.

YEAR NONWHITE MEMBERS ADMITTED: N/A.

NONWHITES AS PERCENTAGE OF TOTAL MEMBERSHIP: N/A.

AVERAGE AGE OF MEMBERSHIP: N/A.

MAJOR ANNUAL EVENTS: The Club traditionally holds four black-
tie Dinner Meetings, three Forum Luncheons, and a Fifth Night
social event each year.

THE EXECUTIVES' CLUB OF CHICAGO

ADDRESS: 8 S. Michigan Avenue, Suite 320, Chicago, IL 60603
(office only/no clubhouse; meetings and events are held at various locations around Chicago)

PHONE: 312/263-3500

WEB SITE: www.executivesclub.org

FOUNDED: 1911

FAMOUS MEMBERS: Most current and past chairmen and CEOs of
leading global corporations.

MISSION STATEMENT/MOTTO: Founded in 1911, The Executives'
Club of Chicago is a business forum for thought leadership,
education and best business practices. The Club provides the
Chicago business community with the information and

resources needed to establish effective global partnerships, enhance intellectual exchange, develop future diverse business leaders, and promote Chicago as a world class business center.

CIVIC ACTIVITIES/SOCIAL MISSION: N/A.

MEMBERS: 2,100. The club's membership includes 1,155 corporate and 945 individual members. Broken down by category, membership comes from 25 major industry sectors: 55 percent from multinational corporations; 17 percent from medium-size companies; 22 percent from small companies; and 6 percent from not-for-profits, academia, and the diplomatic corps.

DOMINANT PROFESSIONS OF CLUB MEMBERS: Senior business executives, upcoming middle management, and professionals.

TO JOIN: Membership is by invitation only. Prospective members can be nominated by current members or other leaders of the Chicago civic and business communities. Applications may be submitted via mail, email, or in person.

INITIATION FEE: Individuals, $50; corporations, $100.

DUES: Depends upon the type of membership.

ART COLLECTION HIGHLIGHTS: N/A.

MEETING FACILITIES: None. Meetings are held at leading downtown hotels or private clubs.

ATHLETIC FACILITIES: N/A.

GUEST FACILITIES: N/A.

THE METROPOLITAN CLUB

ADDRESS: Sears Tower, 233 S. Wacker Drive, 67th Floor, Chicago, IL 60606

PHONE NUMBER: 312/876.3200

WEB SITE: www.metclubchicago.com

FOUNDED: 1974

FAMOUS MEMBERS: Stedman Graham, Frank Clark, Judy Baar Topinka, and John Challenger.

MISSION STATEMENT/MOTTO: "We build relationships and enrich lives."

CIVIC ACTIVITIES/SOCIAL MISSION: Various.

MEMBERS: 3,027.

DOMINANT PROFESSIONS OF CLUB MEMBERS: Area professionals.

TO JOIN: Membership is by invitation only. Prospective members must be nominated by current members in good standing, must be 21 years of age or older, and are subject to review by the Membership Committee/Board of Governors.

INITIATION FEE: Between $250 and $700.

DUES: Between $92 and $240 per month.

ART COLLECTION HIGHLIGHTS: Various styles and artists represented.

MEETING FACILITIES: 17 private dining rooms are available for parties of 2 to 1,000. Meal facilities include: The Globe Dining Room and Wine Bar (à la carte breakfast, lunch, and dinner menu); the Met Grille (all-day menu); The East Room (luncheon buffet).

ATHLETIC FACILITIES: State-of-the-art athletic club featuring a spin studio, group exercise classes, a Pilates studio, massage therapy, a Club Cafe, and cardio and resistance equipment.

CLUB ACTIVITIES: Board of Governors, Ambassadors' Council, Young Executive Board, Metropolitan Club Connections, Kid's Club Committee, Business Alliance, Culinary Committee, Social Committee, Uncorked Members, Wine Committee, Wellness Committee, Charity Advisory.

SPECIAL SERVICES: Wireless access throughout the club and four private offices for use during business hours. Video-conferencing available.

PARENT/CHILDREN'S SERVICES: Kid's Club committee hosts special evenings for adults where parents can drop kids off in a separate room for crafts, games, and entertainment. Children's etiquette course is offered for ages 7-13.

RECENT RENOVATIONS: A $6.3 million renovation of the main dining room, West Lounge, and East Room Buffet. The club also added a wine bar that offers more than 200 wines by the glass.

YEAR WOMEN MEMBERS ADMITTED: From inception - 1974.

WOMEN AS PERCENTAGE OF TOTAL MEMBERSHIP: 25 percent.

YEAR NONWHITE MEMBERS ADMITTED: From inception - 1974.

NONWHITES AS PERCENTAGE OF TOTAL MEMBERSHIP: N/A (information not tracked).

AVERAGE AGE OF MEMBERSHIP: 45.

MAJOR ANNUAL EVENTS: Wine Extravaganza, Gingerbread Workshop, Annual Grand Gala, Go Vertical Charity Event, and holiday brunches.

THE MID-AMERICA CLUB

ADDRESS: Aon Center, 200 E. Randolph Drive, 80th Floor, Chicago, IL 60601

PHONE: 312/861-1100

WEB SITE: www.midamclub.com

FOUNDED: 1958

FAMOUS MEMBERS: Mayor Richard M. Daley; William M. Daley, chairman of the Midwest for J.P. Morgan Chase & Co.; John Bryan, former chairman of Sara Lee Corp.; John E. Swearingen, former chairman of the board at Standard Oil Co.

MISSION STATEMENT/MOTTO: The Mid-America Club is a distinctive, private club with world-class ambience serving the needs of the business, professional, civic, and philanthropic leaders of Chicago by providing the finest services, culinary program, and facilities at its premier location atop the Aon Center.

CIVIC ACTIVITIES/SOCIAL MISSION: N/A.

MEMBERS: Approximately 1,800.

DOMINANT PROFESSIONS OF CLUB MEMBERS: Corporate executives and lawyers.

TO JOIN: Membership is by invitation only and is extended by the Board of Governors upon recommendation by the Membership Committee. There are five categories of membership: resident membership, age 36 or older; young executive ages 21 to 35; nonresident; Signature Gold Society; Chicago Society.

INITIATION FEE: Resident membership—$400; Young Executive membership—$250; nonresident membership—$200; Chicago Society—$700; Signature Gold Society—$700.

DUES: Per month: resident membership—$130; Young Executive membership—$87; nonresident membership—$85; Chicago Society—$180; Signature Gold Society—$230.

ART COLLECTION HIGHLIGHTS: Paintings by such contemporary American artists as Roland Ginzel, James Brooks, Kenneth Noland, Roger Brown, Sam Francis, Frank Stella, and Michael Goldberg, as well as French artist Bernard Buffet.

MEETING FACILITIES: Full-service dining in the main dining room and grill rooms and an 8,500-square-foot ballroom and smaller private dining and conference rooms. The library also can be used for events.

ATHLETIC FACILITIES: None on site, but the club has reciprocal relationships with several clubs through the Chicago Society membership.

GUEST FACILITIES: Guests get a special discounted rate at the Hard Rock Hotel Chicago and the Club Quarters Hotel.

CLUB ACTIVITIES: Fine arts series, cooking classes, regular speakers series, and various club committees, including Women's Business Leader Committee, Associate Member Committee, and Social Committee.

SPECIAL SERVICES: Wireless high-speed Internet access, library, and full audiovisual services.

PARENT/CHILDREN'S SERVICES: N/A.

RECENT RENOVATIONS: N/A.

YEAR WOMEN MEMBERS ADMITTED: From inception.

WOMEN AS PERCENTAGE OF TOTAL MEMBERSHIP: Approximately 20 percent.

YEAR NONWHITE MEMBERS ADMITTED: From inception.

NONWHITES AS PERCENTAGE OF TOTAL MEMBERSHIP: The club does not discriminate or maintain records of ethnic background.

AVERAGE AGE OF MEMBERSHIP: 56.

MAJOR ANNUAL EVENTS: Christmas brunch, Mother's Day brunch, Fourth of July fireworks, Taste of Chicago Food Festival, Easter brunch, and Clam and Lobster bake.

THE STANDARD CLUB

ADDRESS: 320 S. Plymouth Court, Chicago, IL 60604

PHONE NUMBER: 312.427.9100

WEB SITE: www.stclub.org

FOUNDED: 1869

FAMOUS MEMBERS: Julius Rosenwald, Dankmar Adler, Simon Florsheim, Bernhard Kuppenheimer.

MEMBERS: Approximately 2,000.

DOMINANT PROFESSIONS OF CLUB MEMBERS: Lawyers, bankers, financial services, real estate developers.

TO JOIN: Membership is by invitation only.

INITIATION FEE: $300 to $1,500.

DUES: $20 to $345 per month.

ART COLLECTION HIGHLIGHTS:

✤ A series of glass panels and murals created by noted WPA artist Edgar Miller, including:

    1. Twelve glass carved panels in various doors leading into the club's Cocktail Lounge and Grill Room.

    2. Four carved linoleum murals in the club's Cocktail Lounge: *The Chicago Fire Outbreak, The Chicago Fire with the Mrs. O'Leary's Barn, Historical Transportation in Chicago,* and *The Rebuilding of Chicago and Columbian Exposition.*

✤ Two pieces by Pablo Picasso: the lithograph *La Pose Habillée* and the colored linocut *Picador et Torero.*

✤ Jasper Johns's colored lithograph *False Start I.*

✤ Sol Lewitt's floor-to-ceiling wall mural in the main dining room entitled *Complex Forms of Color with Ink Washes Superimposed.*

✤ Egon Weiner's six glass window panel etchings of Nuclear Research, Transportation, Industry, Art and Music, City Planning, and Science and Industry.

MEETING FACILITIES: Twenty-five meeting rooms that can be configured to fit many different sized groups from 2 to 500.

ATHLETIC FACILITIES: Indoor swimming pool, indoor track, basketball and paddleball courts, strength-training and cardio equipment, and free weights. Men's and women's locker rooms have lounges and massage, steam, sauna, and resting rooms.

GUEST FACILITIES: 60 guest rooms.

CLUB ACTIVITIES: Author and book signings, cocktail parties, singles events, wine tastings, cooking classes, networking opportunities, mentor nights, a book and movie clubs, card playing, trips, theatre outings, museum tours, concerts, and sporting events.

SPECIAL SERVICES: Fourth Floor Business Center, Reading Room, and wireless Internet access throughout the club.

PARENT/CHILDREN'S SERVICES: Several events throughout the year for families and children, and babysitting services provided at all major holiday events so parents can enjoy a relaxing day or evening in the Main Dining Room.

RECENT RENOVATIONS: Guest rooms and locker rooms have been recently renovated and more updates are planned for the near future.

YEAR WOMEN MEMBERS ADMITTED: 1974.

WOMEN AS PERCENTAGE OF TOTAL MEMBERSHIP: 30 percent.

YEAR NONWHITE MEMBERS ADMITTED: N/A.

NONWHITES AS PERCENTAGE OF TOTAL MEMBERSHIP: N/A.

AVERAGE AGE OF MEMBERSHIP: 53.

MAJOR ANNUAL EVENTS: Annual Member Holiday Celebration, Annual Children's Holiday Party, Boxing Nights, Thanksgiving, Major Jewish Holidays, and the Dankmar Adler Society Dinner to honor member sponsors.

THE TAVERN CLUB

ADDRESS: As of early 2008, the club was without a permanent home. It lost its historic space in the 333 N. Michigan Avenue building in Chicago in late 2007, and was weighing other downtown locations.

PHONE: N/A.

WEB SITE: www.thetavernclub.com

FOUNDED: 1927

FAMOUS MEMBERS: Mortimer Adler, Saul Bellow, Irving Berlin, Joseph Cardinal Bernardin, Reverend Preston Bradley, Jack Brickhouse, Katherine Cornell, Mayor Richard J. Daley, Richard Dent, Enrico Fermi, Francis Cardinal George, Chester Gould, Helen Hayes, William Holabird and John Root of Holabird & Root (architects), Robert Maynard Hutchins, Don McNeill, A.A. Michelson, Ludwig Mies van der Rohe, Fritz Reiner, Carl Sandburg, Justice John Paul Stevens, Frederick Stock, Frank Lloyd Wright, William Wrigley, and several governors: Dwight Green, Otto Kerner, Richard Ogilvie, William Stratton, and James R. Thompson.

MISSION STATEMENT/MOTTO: "Floreat Taberna" (Let the Tavern Club Flourish).

CIVIC ACTIVITIES/SOCIAL MISSION: "Anyone who has ever done anything or thought anything and is of clubbable nature will be at home at The Tavern Club, whether engaged in the arts or sciences, in the world of romance or adventure, in 'practical' affairs,' or in thoughtful contemplation."

MEMBERS: Approximately 400.

DOMINANT PROFESSIONS OF CLUB MEMBERS: Broad mix of business and professionals; no dominant profession.

TO JOIN: Prospective members must be sponsored by one current member. After that the application must be approved by the board. Members under the age of 38 are considered junior members; those older than 38 are regular members.

INITIATION FEE: N/A.

DUES: $155 per quarter for juniors, $175 monthly for regulars. Includes a credit of $50 a month for food.

ART COLLECTION HIGHLIGHTS: Mural by Edgar Miller, *Love Through the Ages*, and sketches and framed fragments of an earlier mural of the same name (the complete mural was removed when air conditioning was installed decades ago). John Norton's murals in the bar area known variously as *Elysian Fields*, *Pagan Paradise*, *Paradise*, and *Garden of Eden*. Norton, a renowned muralist, said simply that the murals were "just a nice place to be." (Since the closing of the Tavern Club's clubhouse at 333 N. Michigan Avenue, most of the club's entire art collection was placed in storage. However, because the Edgar Miller murals could not be removed without significant expense, they were sold to Rick Strilky Fine Arts Restoration, Inc. who removed the murals and is looking for a public space and funding to remount them.)

MEETING FACILITIES: Three main meeting areas: the North Lounge and Bar, the main dining room, and the Sky Pavilion and Deck, for a total 22,000 square feet of space.

ATHLETIC FACILITIES: N/A.

GUEST FACILITIES: N/A.

CLUB ACTIVITIES: Juniors Group with its own club room including a flat-screen TV; a monthly sketch class (nude model, charcoal on newsprint); occasional book-and-author evenings; occasional post-dinner trips to museums (with docent), opera, or theater; and boat trips.

SPECIAL SERVICES: N/A.

PARENT/CHILDREN'S SERVICES: N/A.

YEAR WOMEN MEMBERS ADMITTED: Women were admitted as members to the club in 1987 but were briefly admitted as members in the 1930s.
YEAR NONWHITE MEMBERS ADMITTED: N/A.
AVERAGE AGE OF MEMBERSHIP: N/A.
MAJOR ANNUAL EVENTS: Easter Sunday brunch, Mother's Day brunch, Cape Cod Night, Artists and Models Party (live sketching), Festival of Lights, Wassail Bowl (Christmas party).

THE UNION LEAGUE CLUB OF CHICAGO

ADDRESS: 65 W. Jackson Boulevard, Chicago, IL 60604
PHONE: 312/427-7800
WEB SITE: www.ulcc.org
FOUNDED: 1879
FAMOUS MEMBERS: Charles H. Wacker, chairman of the Chicago Plan Commission from 1909 to 1926; Ferdinand Wythe Peck, who brought opera to Chicago 1885; Charles Gates Dawes, vice president of the United States; "Long John" Wentworth and Carter Harrison II, both Chicago mayors; Louis Sullivan; Dankmar Adler; Daniel Burnham; Philip Armour; Robert Hall McCormick; Julius Rosenwald.
MISSION STATEMENT/MOTTO: Commitment to Community and Country.
CIVIC ACTIVITIES/SOCIAL MISSION:
+ Public Affairs Committee: Since its inception, the ULCC has worked to achieve honesty and efficiency in governmental affairs through this committee. From initiating efforts to combat election fraud in the 1890s, to forming the Chicago Crime Commission in 1919, to trimming patronage and waste in the Metropolitan Sanitary District in the 1960s, establishing the Armed Forces Council of Chicago in the 1970s, to protecting Chicago's Personnel Code in the 1980s, the club has been a partner in the development and growth of the city. More recently, the club had a major voice in the debate over the expansion of O'Hare International Airport, in calling for a moratorium on executions in the state of Illinois, and

passage of strong ethics legislation. The Public Affairs Committee has forged partnerships with leading Chicago organizations to address significant public policy issues and conduct forums on topics of key concern.

+ Military Affairs Committee: This committee was organized for the purpose of providing administrative services to the Armed Forces Council of Chicago, which it continues to do. The ULCC founded and continues to provide administrative assistance to the 721 Club, a support group for the nuclear submarine the USS *Chicago* 721. The ULCC founded the Chicago 502, a support group for the soldiers (and their families) of the U.S. Army's elite volunteer 502 Infantry Regiment, 101st Airborne Division.

+ Union League Boys & Girls Clubs (founded in 1918): The ULCC established and continues to support four inner-city clubs and a summer camp in Salem, Wisconsin. Today more than 7,000 of the city's youngsters are enrolled annually. The clubs provide a safe place for these young people to grow, socialize, and develop a strong character. Programs offer opportunities to enhance self-expression, leadership skills, and creativity and to develop academic, athletic, and artistic skills.

+ Civic & Arts Foundation (founded in 1945): This foundation provides scholarships and grants to individuals and organizations to promote creative efforts in art, music, writing, performance, and civic and academic affairs.

+ Chicago Engineers' Foundation: This foundation provides incentive grants to college-bound engineering students and continued support throughout their college careers as long as they continue to excel.

MEMBERS: Total resident and nonresident members—3,761; total veteran members—741.

DOMINANT PROFESSIONS OF CLUB MEMBERS: Attorneys, traders, bankers, and financial services professionals.

TO JOIN: Candidates must be U.S. citizens, 21 years of age, and sponsored by two members.

INITIATION FEE: $1,250 (less for those under age 35).

DUES: $227 per month (less for those under age 35).

ART COLLECTION HIGHLIGHTS: After decades of acquisitions, the club has amassed one of the nation's largest privately held art collections—more than 750 works of art are catalogued, including a Monet purchased for $500 in the early days of the club. Most works are paintings, but the club also has sculpture, ceramics, and antique furnishings. There is an art acquisition fund, which enables the Art Committee to purchase art on an ongoing basis. Some of the artists represented in the current collection include Ivan Albright, George Bellows, George Healy, Victor Higgins, and Pauline Palmer, as well as contemporary artists such as Ruth Duckworth, Roger Brown, Richard Hunt, Ed Paschke, and Vera Klement.

MEETING FACILITIES: Three dining rooms including the historic Wigwam, two ballrooms, two bars, and 20 private dining/meeting rooms.

ATHLETIC FACILITIES: The spa area features four private massage rooms, including manicure and pedicure services and shoeshine; a 20-yard swimming pool; a gymnasium for basketball and volleyball; racquetball, handball, and squash courts; and a weight room and cardiovascular fitness center. The fitness studio offers cycling, Pilates, yoga, tai chi, boxing, aerobics, and free weights. The facility also includes a golf driving range as well as steam rooms, saunas, whirlpools, and tanning beds. Lessons and clinics are available in racquet sports, swimming, and scuba diving. The Family Athletic Program consists of programs designed for youngsters from two to 12 years of age.

GUEST FACILITIES: Nearly 200 guest rooms and suites for overnight guests.

SPECIAL SERVICES: A collection of books, reference materials, books on tape, periodicals, and audiotapes, videos, and DVDs in the library; Internet access; five private offices and five carrels equipped with phones, computers, and plug-in access for laptops in the Business Information Center; fax and photocopy machines. Rooms are available for two hours a day; if no one is waiting, time may be extended.

PARENT/CHILDREN'S SERVICES: Club-sponsored petting zoo at Easter and a Halloween event complete with a haunted house and trick-or-treating throughout the clubhouse. There is also an annual Father-Daughter Dance, a Mother-Daughter Tea, and a Youngsters Golf Outing. Other periodic events include an Indoor Campout in the gym, a pajama party in the Crystal Room, outings to children's theater events, and the Family Athletic Program already mentioned.

RECENT RENOVATIONS: The club's meeting rooms, conference rooms, reception and public spaces on the first, second, seventh and eighth floors.

YEAR WOMEN MEMBERS ADMITTED: 1987.

YEAR NONWHITE MEMBERS ADMITTED: 1969.

AVERAGE AGE OF MEMBERSHIP: N/A.

MAJOR ANNUAL EVENTS: George Washington's birthday celebration (this patriotic event has been held since the 1890s. Keynote speakers have included U.S. presidents and other national leaders); homecoming (a club-wide extravaganza, where theme rooms throughout the clubhouse feature food, beverages, and entertainment focusing on a particular theme; some 1,000 individuals attend each year).

THE UNIVERSITY CLUB OF CHICAGO

ADDRESS: 76 E. Monroe Street, Chicago, IL 60603

FOUNDED: 1887

FAMOUS MEMBERS: Architects Irving K. Pond, Martin Roche, and William Holabird; Frederick Clay Bartlett and Ed Paschke; a lengthy list of high-powered members in the business community; and dozens of authors. (The club's library houses an entire bookshelf of member-authored books, including works by Paul Shorey, Karl Menninger, James Henry Breasted, Charles Merriam, Edgar Goodspeed, and Hobart Chatfield-Taylor.)

MISSION STATEMENT/MOTTO: From the Articles of Incorporation: "The object for which it is formed is the promotion of literature and art, by establishing and maintaining a library, reading-room and gallery of art, and by such other means as shall be expedient and proper for such purposes." More casually from the club's brochure: "A place where members, their guests and all future members can draw upon the sustaining values of a common education experience."

CIVIC ACTIVITIES/SOCIAL MISSION: The club doesn't have a formal social mission, though many of its members are involved in cultural institutions and civic activities in and around Chicago. It grants members the opportunity to share that knowledge and passion with other members through its Civic Affairs society.

MEMBERS: 3,088, including 2,100 resident members.

DOMINANT PROFESSIONS OF CLUB MEMBERS: Most professions are represented in the club with heavy emphasis on law and finance.

TO JOIN: "Our one unwavering requirement is that prospective members must have a university or college degree from an accredited four-year institution. In addition, candidates must complete a nomination form which is obtained from a current member, supply three letters of recommendation from current club members, interview with the Committee on Admissions and finally have their name posted in the lobby for a two-week period of time before they are granted membership."

INITIATION FEE: $1,500.

DUES: $224 per month.

ART COLLECTION HIGHLIGHTS: Works of art have been a permanent part of the University Club of Chicago from the opening of the present building in 1909. There are the stained-glass windows and decorations by the artist who created the club's seal, Frederic Clay Bartlett. Literature and Art committee members have over the years acquired prints, paintings, sculptures, and ceramics to further enhance the architectural beauty of the clubhouse. In addition, the University Club of Chicago is the only institution in the city that has focused its collection on the works of post–World War II Chicago Artists, including members of the Monster Roster, the Hairy Who, the Allusive Abstractionists, and other noted Imagists.

MEETING FACILITIES: The University Club houses 14 private meeting rooms and is able to accommodate groups from 3 to 300. Members use the facilities for both business and social needs, and there is a catering staff of five on hand to make certain every detail is taken care of to exact specifications.

ATHLETIC FACILITIES: Athletic facilities are separated into three areas: the Fitness Center, the Bath Department (pool), and the Squash Department.

* The Fitness Center is located on the top floor of the clubhouse and features exercise equipment, free weights, personal training, and fitness classes.
* The Bath Department includes a five-lane pool, a sauna, a steam room, a whirlpool, a tanning bed, and additional exercise equipment. Massage is also available from professional massage therapists.
* The Squash Department boasts one of the finest squash facilities in the country, with more than 200 active squash players, four international courts, and one doubles court. The club also hosts local, national, and major international tournaments, including the largest club tournament in the world.

GUEST FACILITIES: In the midst of a complete renovation, the club has 60 sleeping rooms including some with flat-screen TVs, stereos, and new upscale baths.

CLUB ACTIVITIES: Wine, Golf, Wing & Clay, Cigar, Business Networking, Civic Affairs, Garden, Younger Members', and Investment societies, as well as dinner-theater, Fight Night, ballroom dance lessons, cabaret nights, book signings, drawing classes, Learn at Lunch lectures, cooking classes, riverboat cruises, and foreign language classes.

SPECIAL SERVICES: A private library with just under 13,000 volumes; Wi-Fi access on seven floors; a business center with private cubicles containing computers with Internet access, copiers, laser printers, and fax machines; a barber shop; massage therapy; and manicure and pedicure services.

PARENT/CHILDREN'S SERVICES: Yoga and squash classes for children as young as three; numerous special events including a father-daughter dance, Halloween party, and a holiday party in December; and family-fun weekends.

RECENT RENOVATIONS: The Front Grill was completely renovated in 2003, the club's guestrooms have been completely renovated in the last three years, a private dining room underwent over $100,000 of renovations in 2004, the Bath Department (pool) was updated in 2005 as well as renovations in the 12th Floor Gallery. The Men's locker room on the 10th and 11th floors will complete renovation in 2006.

YEAR WOMEN MEMBERS ADMITTED: 1976.

WOMEN AS PERCENTAGE OF TOTAL MEMBERSHIP: 23 percent of
members are women—this does not include spouses of members, who have full privileges in the facilities.

YEAR NONWHITE MEMBERS ADMITTED: There has never been a
restriction.

NONWHITES AS PERCENTAGE OF TOTAL MEMBERSHIP: "As race is
not a restriction or requirement for membership, we do not
track race."

AVERAGE AGE OF MEMBERSHIP: Resident members, 48; nonresident, 55; senior or retired, 76; other, 71. Average age of membership as a whole is 55.

MAJOR ANNUAL EVENTS: Butterfly Ball, Fight Night, Pre–St. Pat's
party, children's holiday party, children's Halloween party,
Valentine's dinner, candlelight holiday buffets, New Year's Day
party, smelt fry, 3rd of July celebration, Mother's Day buffet,
Easter buffet, Thanksgiving buffet, and Venetian Night
fireworks buffet.

THE
ABCs
OF
CLUB MEMBERSHIP

A GLOSSARY

———

Bath Department: A club's swimming facilities.

Dual-Spouse Membership: Membership for a member's spouse whereby the club allows the spouse full privileges just shy of voting or ownership rights.

Dues: A nonrefundable fee paid usually monthly, quarterly, or annually to support the club's operations. In nearly all cases, this fee will not cover the cost of food, drink, or other special services offered by the club.

Initiation Fee: A nonrefundable, one-time fee paid at the time of entry into a club.

Legacy: Special consideration given to family members of current members in their approval for membership.

Nomination Forms: Part of a package of information that must be completed by prospective members and their nominators for any private club membership. Membership to most private clubs is by invitation only, and prospective members may require multiple nomination letters and forms.

Nonresident Membership: Membership whereby the member lives at least 40 or 50 miles away from the club. This type of membership typically offers lower fees but less-than-full privileges.

Privileged: Refers to a person who in some way qualifies for use of the club due to some special work-related position he or she holds. In many communities heads of universities have special privileges at local clubs.

Reciprocal Clubs: Clubs that offer a member, with the price of membership, the chance to freely visit clubs in other cities where they have a relationship. When weighing a club membership, potential members should consider travel plans to see if reciprocal clubs add more to the value of their membership.

Retired: Refers to a member over a certain age with a certain number of years of membership who qualifies for lower or elimination of dues.

INDEX

ACKNOWLEDGMENTS

I have many people to thank in connection with this project, not the least of which are the past and present members of the city's storied clubs you see here in this book.

In particular, I'd like to thank Jonathan Dedmon of the Tavern Club, Hanna Gray of the University of Chicago, John Spidalette of the University Club, Jane Kenamore and Jonathan McCabe of the Union League Club, Roland Burris and Dr. Everett White of the Boule, Frank Stover of the Chicago Club, Peter Borzak of the Standard Club, Howard Rosen of the Adventurers Club, and Donald Santelli, Bob Thiebout, and the denizens of the Members' Tables at the Cliff Dwellers. These individuals were not only helpful in sharing their own club experiences; they helped me tell the history of this culture.

Tim Samuelson, cultural historian for the City of Chicago, and Michael Flug at the Chicago Public Library's Vivian G. Harsh Research Collection of Afro-American History and Literature were invaluable in my research on the city's African-American clubs. Terry Tatum, Supervising Historian and Director of Research for the Chicago Department of Planning and Development/Landmarks Division, graciously allowed permission to use many of the pictures you see in this book. Preservation Chicago and the J.P. Morgan Chase Archives also contributed key images to this book, as did the clubs themselves.

Researchers at the Chicago Historical Society, the Newberry Library, and the Chicago Jewish Archives were extraordinarily helpful in this project. The Winnetka Public Library and their enthusiastic staff provided a most unexpected treasure trove of resources on club life, Chicago society, and the city's business history.

I owe special thanks to James D. Nowlan, author of *Glory, Darkness, Light: A History of the Union League Club of Chicago*, for his gracious help and perspective on club life in Chicago.

Lastly, I owe thanks to three key groups—my publisher, my friends, and my family. Lake Claremont Press championed this book, emphasizing that Chicago's often-overlooked business history is an important part of our city's legacy.

My friends Dean and Nora Francis, and Bill Linden and Karen Randolph proved that when you're on a long road to publication, it's great to have friends who will pour you a glass of wine and just listen.

Most of all, I want to thank Lea Holton, the best support system any sister could have.

ABOUT
THE AUTHOR

———◆———

Lisa Holton began her career as a business writer at the *Chicago Sun-Times* and today writes about business history and other topics at her own firm, The Lisa Company (www.TheLisaCompany.com). A prolific corporate writer, ghost-writer, and author, *For Members Only* is her eleventh book.

Holton has written for a variety of national magazines and newspapers including *Corporate Board Member* magazine, the *American Bar Association Journal*, *Parents*, *American Demographics*, *Latina*, *Working Mother*, *the Boston Globe*, and the *Chicago Tribune*. She also writes for associations and universities worldwide.

A graduate of Northwestern University's Medill School of Journalism and a former national board member of the Society of American Business Editors and Writers (SABEW), Holton is a member of the Authors Guild, the International Association of Business Communicators, and the Society of Midland Authors.

In her spare time, Holton writes short stories and screenplays. Her feature screenplay *The Plant* was a quarterfinalist for the 2002 Nicholl Fellowships in Screenwriting offered by the Academy of Motion Picture Arts and Sciences. She has attended the film program at Chicago's Columbia College and completed film production courses at Chicago Filmmakers Workshop.

A native of Moline, Illinois, Holton grew up in Louisville, Kentucky, and now considers the Windy City her home. She lives in suburban Evanston.

Publisher's Credits

Cover design by Timothy Kocher. Interior design and layout by Charisse Antonopoulos. Editing by Laura R. Gabler. Proofreading by Diana Solomon and Sharon Woodhouse. Index by June Sawyers.

Note

LAKE CLAREMONT PRESS

Founded in 1994, Lake Claremont Press specializes in books on the Chicago area and its history, focusing on preserving the city's past, exploring its present environment, and cultivating a strong sense of place for the future. Visit us on the Web at www.lakeclaremont.com.

Selected Booklist

Rule 53: Capturing Hippies, Spies, Politicians, and Murderers in an American Courtroom

I Am a Teamster: A Short, Fiery Story of Regina V. Polk, Her Hats, Her Pets, Sweet Love, and the Modern-Day Labor Movement

The Chicago River Architecture Tour

From Lumber Hookers to the Hooligan Fleet: A Treasury of Chicago Maritime History

Finding Your Chicago Irish

On the Job: Behind the Stars of the Chicago Police Department

Great Chicago Fires: Historic Blazes That Shaped a City

Graveyards of Chicago: The People, History, Art, and Lore of Cook County Cemeteries

Oldest Chicago

Food, Lodging, Liquor: Signs You're In Chicago

The SportsTraveler's Fanbook to Chicago

Wrigley Field's Last World Series: The Wartime Chicago Cubs and the Pennant of 1945

Today's Chicago Blues

Chicago TV Horror Movie Shows: From Shock Theatre to Svengoolie

The Golden Age of Chicago Children's Television

A Native's Guide to Chicago

Award-winners

The Chicago River: A Natural and Unnatural History

The Politics of Place: A History of Zoning in Chicago

Near West Side Stories: Struggles for Community in Chicago's Maxwell Street Neighborhood

Finding Your Chicago Ancestors: A Beginner's Guide to Family History in the City and Cook County

The Streets & San Man's Guide to Chicago Eats

A Cook's Guide to Chicago

A Chicago Tavern: A Goat, a Curse, and the American Dream